De-mystifying Translation

This textbook provides an accessible introduction to the field of translation for students of other disciplines and readers who are not translators. It provides students outside the translation profession with a greater awareness of, and appreciation for, what goes into translation. Providing readers with tools for their own personal translation-related needs, this book encourages an ethical approach to translation and offers an insight into translation as a possible career.

This textbook covers foundational concepts; key figures, groups, and events; tools and resources for non-professional translation tasks; and the types of translation that non-translators are liable to encounter. Each chapter includes practical activities, annotated further reading, and summaries of key points suitable for use in classrooms, online teaching, or self-study. There is also a glossary of key terms.

De-mystifying Translation: Introducing Translation to Non-translators is the ideal text for any non-specialist taking a course on translation and for anyone interested in learning more about the field of translation and translation studies.

Lynne Bowker is Full Professor at the School of Translation and Interpretation, University of Ottawa, Canada, and a certified translator with the Association of Translators and Interpreters of Ontario. She is the author of *Computer-Aided Translation Technology* (2002), *Working with Specialized Language* (2002), and *Machine Translation and Global Research* (2019).

De-mystifying Translation
Introducing Translation to Non-translators

Lynne Bowker

Routledge
Taylor & Francis Group
LONDON AND NEW YORK

Designed cover image: Getty Images | happyphoton

First published 2023
by Routledge
4 Park Square, Milton Park, Abingdon, Oxon OX14 4RN

and by Routledge
605 Third Avenue, New York, NY 10158

Routledge is an imprint of the Taylor & Francis Group, an informa business

© 2023 Lynne Bowker

The right of Lynne Bowker to be identified as author of this work has been asserted in accordance with sections 77 and 78 of the Copyright, Designs and Patents Act 1988.

The Open Access version of this book, available at www.taylorfrancis.com, has been made available under a Creative Commons Attribution-Non Commercial-No Derivatives 4.0 license.

Trademark notice: Product or corporate names may be trademarks or registered trademarks, and are used only for identification and explanation without intent to infringe.

British Library Cataloguing-in-Publication Data
A catalogue record for this book is available from the British Library

ISBN: 978-1-032-10922-0 (hbk)
ISBN: 978-1-032-10924-4 (pbk)
ISBN: 978-1-003-21771-8 (ebk)

DOI: 10.4324/9781003217718

Typeset in Sabon
by Newgen Publishing UK

Contents

Acknowledgements x

Introduction 1
Why this book? 1
Who is this book for? 3
What's in this book? 4
Key points in this chapter 6
Topics for discussion 7
Find out more 7

1 Basic concepts and terms in translation 9
What is translation? 9
What is meant by source, target, *and* equivalence? *10*
What gets translated? 12
Where do a translator's loyalties lie? 14
What is involved in the translation process? 15
Is it true that...? 17
  Is it true that all translators speak many languages? 17
  Is it true that all bilingual (or multilingual) people make good translators? 18
  Is it true that translating and interpreting are the same? 18
  Is it true that translation is just about substituting words in one language for words in another language? 18
  Is it true that a good translator can translate a text on any subject? 19
  Is it true that there is one true or perfect translation for every text? 19
  Is it true that translation is actually impossible? 20
  Is it true that computers are going to replace translators before too much longer? 20
Concluding remarks 21
Key points in this chapter 21
Topics for discussion 23
Exercises 23
Find out more 24

2 Brief history of translation — 25

Tower of Babel 25
Septuagint (3rd century BCE) 26
Rosetta Stone (196 BCE) 26
St. Jerome (c. 342–420) 27
Xuanzang (602–664) 27
House of Wisdom (9th–13th century) 28
School of Toledo (12th and 13th centuries) 29
Gutenberg press (c. 1440) 29
William Tyndale (c. 1494–c. 1536) 29
La Malinche (c. 1501–c. 1550) 30
Anne Sullivan (1866–1936) 31
Navajo code talkers (1942–1945) 31
United Nations (1945) 31
Nuremberg trials (1945–1946) 32
Weaver's memorandum (1949) 33
International Federation of Translators (1953) 33
Internet and World Wide Web (1980s to present) 34
Concluding remarks 35
Key points in this chapter 35
Topics for discussion 37
Exercise 37
Find out more 38

3 The translation profession today — 39

What does it mean to be a professional? 40
What is the translation industry? 40
How do translators work? 43
What about pay and job satisfaction? 48
What are professional associations? 51
What kind of training do professional translators need? 53
Concluding remarks 54
Key points in this chapter 54
Topics for discussion 56
Exercises 56
Find out more 57

4 Words, terms, and lexical resources — 59

What is the difference between language for general purposes and language for special purposes? 61
What's in a dictionary? 64
What's in a term bank? 67
How are lexical resources useful for translation? 70

*What other contributions do lexicographers and
  terminologists make? 71*
Concluding remarks 72
Key points in this chapter 72
Topics for discussion 74
Exercises 74
Find out more 75

5 Other tools and resources   77
  How can I tell if a tool or resource will be useful? 77
  What kinds of resources are useful for translators? 80
  How can I find linguistic resources for translation? 81
  What are online bilingual concordancers? 82
  What are translation communities and discussion forums? 86
  What tools can support revision? 87
  Concluding remarks 88
  Key points in this chapter 88
  Topic for discussion 89
  Exercises 90
  Find out more 91

6 Machine translation   92
  What is machine translation's origin story? 93
     Early efforts: Rule-based MT 93
     A bump in the road: The ALPAC report 94
     A new way of thinking: Data-driven MT 95
     Where are we today? Neural MT and an emerging need for MT literacy 96
  What is machine translation literacy? 97
     What are some implications of data-driven approaches? 97
     Why is transparency important? 101
     What's involved in risk assessment? 103
     How can we interact with MT? 104
  Concluding remarks 105
  Key points in this chapter 106
  Topics for discussion 107
  Exercises 107
  Find out more 109

7 Localization   111
  What is GILT? 111
  Why does localization matter? 115
  What gets localized? 115
  How do languages vary from one region to the next? 116
  What non-linguistic elements differ in language varieties? 118
  What tools and resources can help with localization? 120

Concluding remarks 123
Key points in this chapter 123
Topics for discussion 124
Exercises 125
Find out more 126

8 Adaptation and transcreation 127

How does transcreation differ from localization and translation? 128
What does a transcreation look like? 129
Why is transcreation important? 132
How do transcreators work? 133
Concluding remarks 135
Key points in this chapter 136
Topics for discussion 136
Exercises 137
Find out more 138

9 Summarization and cross-modal communication 139

What is a summary? 140
How can summarization help to build translation skills? 141
How can you write an effective summary? 142
   Step 1: Understand 143
   Step 2: Analyze 144
   Step 3: Select 144
   Step 4: Compress 144
   Step 5: Draft 145
   Step 6: Revise 145
What is cross-modal communication? 146
How can summarization and cross-modal communication come together in a translation context? 147
Concluding remarks 148
Key points in this chapter 148
Topics for discussion 149
Exercises 150
Find out more 150

10 Audiovisual translation 152

Is audiovisual translation a recent development? 153
What are some of the general challenges in audiovisual translation? 154
What is involved in subtitling? 155
What is involved in dubbing? 157
What is involved in voiceover? 158
What affects the choice of audiovisual translation method? 158

Who carries out audiovisual translation? 159
How are these techniques used beyond translation? 162
Concluding remarks 163
Key points in this chapter 164
Topics for discussion 165
Exercises 165
Find out more 167

11 Interpreting   168
What are the different types of interpreting? 168
What are some different settings for interpreting? 173
What else can affect interpreting? 174
What about sign language interpreting? 175
What about non-professional interpreting? 176
What key skills does an interpreter need to develop? 177
Concluding remarks 180
Key points in this chapter 180
Topics for discussion 181
Exercises 182
Find out more 183

Conclusion   185
What have you learned? 185
Where can you go from here? 188
Topics for discussion 191
Exercises 191
Find out more 191

Glossary   193
References   197
Index   202

Acknowledgements

This book has taken shape through interactions with students of all disciplines and varied linguistic and cultural backgrounds who expressed an interest in learning more about translation, and particularly those who participated in the *TRA1301: Introduction to Translation* course at the University of Ottawa between 2018 and 2022. Developing and teaching this course has been extremely rewarding, and I thank all the students for sharing their diverse perspectives on and experiences with translation and for their engagement with and feedback on the course material.

The Social Sciences and Humanities Research Council of Canada awarded me a grant to learn more about how everyday people interact with translation, particularly in a digital environment. I am also grateful for the two grants I received in 2019 from the University of Ottawa's Teaching and Learning Support Service as part of their Blended Learning Initiative. These grants enabled me to hire Dara O'Connor and Julián Zapata Rojas – both very talented graduates of the School of Translation and Interpretation – who worked with me to develop some of the content for early versions of the online modules for TRA1301. Additional funding was provided by the Faculty of Arts during the Covid-19 pandemic to employ graduate student assistants Hailey De Jong, Marie-Hélène He, Rania Jarrar, and Katherine Walker, whose support facilitating the online discussion forums was greatly appreciated.

I am grateful to my colleagues at the School of Translation and Interpretation, particularly Elizabeth Marshman and Salah Basalamah, for their support when I proposed to re-orient the nature of the TRA1301 course and for working with the faculty administration to have it offered in multiple sessions each academic year, where it continues to attract registrations from students across the university.

Thanks to Sergey Tyulenev, editor of the *Routledge Introductions to Translation and Interpreting* series, for planting the seed that this subject matter could make a valuable course book. Although this book did not end up becoming part of that series, Sergey's encouragement and support were invaluable in helping to get it off the ground. Likewise, Christopher

D. Mellinger, a reviewer of the initial proposal, provided numerous very constructive suggestions that helped to strengthen the work.

Finally, thanks are also owed to my family. My sister Lisa, nephews Jasper and Oscar, and parents Keith and Joyce all took brave decisions to make major life changes in the wake of the Covid-19 pandemic, inspiring me to believe that it can be valuable to break the mould. My university-bound teenagers Nicolas and Esmée – neither of whom have any intention of becoming translators and so made perfect test subjects – not only allowed me to monopolize many dinner table conversations with "book talk" but also chimed in with their own perspectives and suggestions for topics and activities. My husband Peter continued his long service of providing free IT support while also taking on extra duties around the house during the utterly overwhelming period of flipping multiple courses into an online format during the pandemic, followed by the period of actually writing this book. It wouldn't have happened without you all!

Introduction

Why this book?

Have you ever read a manga comic in English or watched a dubbed or subtitled movie on Netflix? Or maybe you've even tried subtitling one of your favourite anime or K-drama programs yourself? Perhaps you've helped a friend or family member who speaks another language to fill out a form, decipher an email, or communicate with someone else? Or used a tool such as Google Translate to converse with a restaurant server or taxi driver while on holiday? If so, you've encountered the world of translation! You might not have given it much thought at the time, but there's a broad field of study and practice known as translation, and this book aims to de-mystify translation by giving you a sneak peek into this fascinating world.

When practised professionally, translation is a highly specialized discipline that requires very specific training. As such, translation is typically taught at universities as part of a translation-specific program. For example, in Europe, the European Master's in Translation (EMT) is a network of more than 80 translator training programs offered across Europe. Likewise, Africa, Asia, Oceania, and the Americas also offer specialized degree programs to train translators. However, you don't need to be planning a career as a professional translator to have an interest in translation. Indeed, having a bit of knowledge about translation can help you to appreciate some of the challenges involved, which can in turn empower you to make more informed decisions about whether or not to trust certain information, or encourage you to be more tolerant in situations where you or others must engage with multilingual information, or enable you to help pave the way for successful translation by others.

Many members of the general public construct their basic understanding of translation using sources such as science fiction or the popular media. For example, in shows such as *Star Trek* and *Doctor Who*, technologies such as the "universal translator" or the "TARDIS translation circuit" make translation seem almost magical. Meanwhile, news articles about translation technologies can be polarizing. On the one hand, the media sometimes overhype these tools by claiming that they will soon put translators out of

DOI: 10.4324/9781003217718-1

business. On the other hand, they often mock the tools for doing a poor job of translating certain kinds of texts, such as poetry or song lyrics. There is even a popular YouTube channel called "Twisted Translations", created by Malinda Kathleen Reese, that includes a series called "Google Translate Sings" and another called "Google Translate DESTROYS Movie Quotes". Here, Reese takes song lyrics or well-known lines from movies and runs them through automatic machine translation tools until the texts are mangled beyond recognition, and often quite hilarious! Of course, Reese's goal is to provide entertainment, and in this she is very successful. However, this particular approach to using automatic machine translation is not representative of other ways in which it can be used. Nevertheless, people whose only knowledge of machine translation comes from *Star Trek*, "Google Translate Sings", or other popular media sources will most likely have a distorted view of the capabilities of this technology.

And technology is not the only area of translation where the general public can get the wrong impression. There's a widespread notion that a good translation is more or less imperceptible. In other words, if a translation is done well, then the reader will not even know that what they are reading is a translation and not the original text. In contrast, if a text has been poorly translated, then it might contain meaning errors, awkward constructions, or peculiar expressions, which could frustrate the reader and signal that the text is a translation and not a piece of original writing. As a result, people may end up developing mainly negative associations with translation rather than appreciating translations that are well done.

In yet another scenario, a person may be watching an important event where there is simultaneous interpretation. A simultaneous interpreter is a language professional who listens to a speaker and then, in real-time, conveys that speaker's message in another spoken or signed language. Simultaneous interpreters are extremely specialized and highly trained professionals, so they make the job look deceptively easy. If someone's only experience of interpretation is watching one of these skilled professionals, then they can be forgiven for thinking that interpreting is a straightforward task, when in reality it is very challenging.

Understandably, many people who have never taken a translation course do not have a deep or nuanced view of translation, just as many people who drive a car may not understand how an engine works. It's true that you don't need to understand everything about how an engine works to drive a car, but having some basic knowledge could help you to operate it more efficiently or to determine if something is wrong before the consequences become too serious. In the case of translation, members of the general public may not realize that there is a difference between translation (which deals with written language) and interpretation (which deals with spoken or signed language). What's more, they are often led to believe that translation is either virtually impossible or ridiculously easy, while the truth lies somewhere in between these two extremes. In addition, many people use free online machine translation tools, such as Google Translate or similar tools embedded into browsers or social media platforms, in a very uncritical way, and they remain unaware of some really helpful free tools that could potentially be more useful to them. Finally, people may actually interact with translators or interpreters without knowing how they could facilitate the work of these professionals and thus improve the experience and results for everyone involved.

Although it's understandable that average people don't have a deep understanding of translation, there are some benefits to be gained by learning even a little bit about this field. Therefore, the overall goal of this book is to help people with no prior training in translation to learn more about what translation involves and how they can become more informed users of translation services, translated products, and translation tools. Clearly, you will not be able to work as a professional translator after reading this book, but that is not the objective here. Instead, the goals are to raise your awareness about what is involved in translation; to give you a greater appreciation for translators and for translated products that you might encounter; to allow you to be a more informed user of tools such as free online machine translation systems or other translation resources; to help you to recognize your own limits and to determine when turning to a professional translator or interpreter may be preferable or even necessary, rather than trying to do the job yourself; and to encourage you to interact with language professionals in a way that helps to set them up for success for your mutual benefit. And if after learning all this you feel inspired to find out even more about translation, you'll be ready to take the next step and investigate courses intended to train translation professionals. Hurrah! But we're not quite at that stage yet.

Who is this book for?

As the title indicates, this book is intended to introduce the topic of translation to people who are non-translators. By non-translator, we mean someone who has not received any formal training in translation and who does not practise translation professionally (i.e., as a job for which they are paid). As noted above, many people do engage in translation in a more informal way, such as by using Google Translate or similar tools, or by mediating a conversation between a family member and a teacher, doctor, or other person who speaks a different language (a type of activity often referred to as language brokering). Because most people are likely to encounter or even participate in some kind of informal translation, it may be helpful for them to develop a deeper appreciation for this field. If you are someone who wants to learn more about translation for any reason, then this book is for you! For example, perhaps you are:

- Studying another language as part of your degree program.
- Studying a subject (architecture, business, law, science, medicine, or anything else) through another language.

4   *Introduction*

- Participating in an exchange program where you are spending a semester or a year abroad.
- Planning to incorporate an international element into your career, such as working with newcomers to your country, engaging in international diplomacy or business, or practicing your discipline abroad as a digital nomad or an employee of a multinational organization.
- Living in a community that has more than one official language or is home to one or more Indigenous languages or heritage languages.
- Living as part of a family that has emigrated from another country and speaks a heritage language.
- Spending some of your leisure time travelling, reading novels from other countries, or watching foreign-language films or series.
- Working in a job that brings you into contact with translators or other language professionals.
- Considering a career in the language professions and just beginning to explore this possibility.
- Feeding your curiosity about translation!

In other words, you don't need to be embarking on a career in translation to be interested in this subject or to benefit from knowing a little more about it. Most of us encounter some form of translation in our daily lives, even if it's just checking out the list of ingredients on food packaging. If you are ready to take a behind-the-scenes look at translation, then this book is for you!

Meanwhile, if you are an instructor looking to teach a course on translation to non-translators or novice translators, then this book will provide you with a structure and content that can be used to support the delivery of a typical one-semester course. Each chapter corresponds to one weekly unit and includes not only subject content but also ideas for discussion topics, practical exercises, and further reading.

What's in this book?

It's a book *about* translation rather than a book about how to *do* translation. It offers a broad overview of this diverse field, with a view to raising your awareness of how the field of translation developed, what contributions it makes, and has made, to society, who works in this area, when you might encounter it, why it can be so challenging, and where you can learn more about it.

Translation always involves at least two languages, and some of the specific challenges encountered or techniques used to overcome them may depend on which two languages are being used. In other words, the issues facing a translator who works with two languages that are closely related (e.g., French and Spanish) may be quite different from those facing a translator who works with unrelated languages (e.g., Russian and Arabic). To make this book accessible to as many people as possible, we have written it in English – currently the most widely used language in higher education – and presented it in a way that does not assume knowledge of any specific language pair. In other words, while all readers will need to have some knowledge of English to read this book, it doesn't matter what other language(s) you know. We have tried to incorporate examples from a variety of languages to help explain different concepts, and when it comes to the exercises and discussion topics, you are encouraged to use whatever languages you are familiar with to conduct your own investigations or to share your own experiences.

Are you ready to learn more? Come along as we de-mystify translation by exploring ways in which it intersects with our everyday lives. We explain translation using accessible examples, stories, and humour and demonstrate how translation can be interesting, exciting, relevant, and even necessary to life as we know it.

Chapter 1 introduces you to some fundamental concepts and terms in the field of translation while also dispelling some commonly held misperceptions about translators and translation.

Chapter 2 takes you on a journey through the history of translation, where you will learn about key figures, important products, and memorable events that changed the course of our multilingual society.

Chapter 3 tells you a bit about the contemporary translation industry and gives you some insight into what it's like to work as a professional translator.

Chapter 4 delves into the world of words and terms, exploring the difference between everyday language and the more specialized language that is used to discuss concepts in various fields of research, professions, and even hobbies. It also introduces dictionaries and term banks, two types of lexical resource that are useful for translation.

Chapter 5 moves beyond lexical resources to explore a variety of other free online resources and tools that you can use to support different types of translation activities. These include tools such as multilingual metasearch engines and bilingual concordancers, as well as discussion forums and revision tools.

Chapter 6 takes a closer look at a category of tool that has become particularly prominent: automatic machine translation (e.g., Google Translate). These automatic translators are both easy to use and easily available, but this doesn't mean that you should use them without thinking. In this chapter, you'll learn how to improve your machine translation literacy to become a savvy user.

Chapter 7 investigates the notion of language varieties and presents a subfield of translation known as localization, which is concerned with translating digital products (e.g., websites, videogames, software, and apps) for different regions.

Chapter 8 gives you a chance to explore your creative side by immersing you in the world of adaptation and transcreation, which blends the activities of translation and copywriting to produce marketing or advertising texts that really speak to audiences with different linguistic and cultural backgrounds.

Chapter 9 tackles summarization and cross-modal communication, which are required for some types of translation. For example, creating subtitles for a film or series requires a translator both to condense the content and to transfer it from a spoken to a written mode. Sight translation is another form of cross-modal communication, while most types of interpreting require the interpreter to summarize the main points of the speaker's message.

Chapter 10 builds on the ideas of summarization and cross-modal communication by taking a deeper look at audiovisual translation. If you've ever watched a foreign-language series on Netflix or a similar streaming service, then you have no doubt been exposed to audiovisual translation, which includes subtitling, dubbing, and voiceover.

Chapter 11 presents a more in-depth exploration of interpreting, which deals with the transfer of messages between spoken or signed languages. Interpreters are pretty amazing multitaskers who can do things such as listening to a speaker while transferring their message into another language at the same time. In addition, this chapter also introduces the concept of non-professional interpreting (also known as language brokering), such as a family member interpreting for others in a setting like a school or hospital.

The **Conclusion** wraps up the essential ideas provided in this introductory text and also provides suggestions for areas that were not addressed or were discussed only briefly but would be excellent topics to explore further for those readers who want to continue learning more about the fascinating world of translation.

The volume also includes a quick-reference **Glossary** of key terms and accompanying explanations.

Key points in this chapter

- Translation is a professional sphere of activity, but also something that is regularly carried out by everyday people in one form or another.
- Common ways that people encounter translation in their daily lives include using automatic machine translation tools (e.g., Google Translate), reading translated literature, watching subtitled or dubbed films or series, or acting as a language broker to help a friend or family member converse with someone else.
- Professional translation is a highly specialized activity that requires specific training.
- Having a deeper appreciation for translation can still benefit people who are not professional translators by empowering them to make more informed decisions about translated content, encouraging increased tolerance in multilingual contexts, and helping them to pave the way for a smoother translation experience.

- Many people learn about translation through science fiction or the popular media, which often present the task as being very easy or virtually impossible rather than giving a more nuanced and realistic presentation.
- This book aims to help people with no prior training in translation to learn more about this process and field, but it will not prepare you to work as a professional translator.
- This book is suitable for students studying languages or any other subject (whether in their own country or abroad), people planning to incorporate an international component into their career, people living in a community or family with multiple languages, people whose leisure activities (e.g., reading, watching films, travelling) include contact with other languages or cultures, people who need to work with translators as part of their job, people who are considering a career in the language professions, or people who are simply curious to learn more about translation.
- This book is also suitable for instructors who want to deliver a course on translation to non-translators or novice translators.
- This book is *about* translation, not how to *do* translation.
- This book assumes knowledge of English, but readers are encouraged to use their own additional languages when learning and applying the translation-related concepts that are presented.
- The content of this book covers key concepts and terms, a brief history of the field, an overview of the contemporary translation industry, words and terms, resources and tools, machine translation literacy, language varieties and localization, adaptation and transcreation, summarization and cross-modal communication, audiovisual translation, and interpreting.

Topics for discussion

As part of a class discussion, or as a prompt for an online discussion forum, consider the following:

- What are some of the ways that you have come into contact with translation in your life?
- What are some of your reasons for reading this book or taking an introductory course on translation?

Find out more

Halley, Mark, and Lynne Bowker. 2021. "Translation by TARDIS: Exploring the Science Behind Multilingual Communication in *Doctor Who*". In *Doctor Who and Science: Essays on Ideas, Identities and Ideologies in the*

Series, edited by Marcus K. Harmes and Lindy A. Orthia, 62–77. Jefferson, NC: McFarland & Co.

- For those interested in representations of translation in science fiction and how these compare with reality, this article draws parallels and distinctions between how automatic machine translation tools actually work and the way that translation appears to be facilitated by the TARDIS in the *Doctor Who* series.

Vieira, Lucas Nunes. 2020. "Machine Translation in the News: A Framing Analysis of the Written Press". *Translation Spaces* 9, no. 1: 98–122.

- This article explores how translation technologies, and in particular machine translation tools such as Google Translate, have been represented in the popular media. A key finding is that news reporting on this subject often lacks nuance and that, overall, journalists tend either to overstate this technology's capabilities or to position it as being highly problematic, whereas the truth falls somewhere between these extremes. The article concludes that the frequent overly positive presentation of machine translation tools may prompt users to underestimate the complexities of translation while overestimating the capabilities of the technology, which in turn could lead to its misuse.

Zetzsche, Jost, and Nataly Kelly. 2012. *Found in Translation: How Language Shapes our Lives and Transforms the World*. New York: Penguin Books Ltd.

- This accessible and entertaining introduction to the world of translation provides a wealth of stories and examples from around the globe of the many ways that translation affects the lives of everyday people, from saving lives to keeping the peace, from doing business to spreading the gospel, and from entertaining us to protecting our rights. In the words of the authors from the book's opening line: "Translation. It's everywhere you look, but seldom seen. This book will help you find it".

1 Basic concepts and terms in translation

Have you ever noticed how people who share a common interest, hobby, or profession also seem to use a sort of special language to discuss it with one another? People who enjoy baking might talk about *Swiss buttercream*, *proofing drawers*, or the *rub-in method*. Meanwhile, lawyers might be overheard chatting about *affidavits*, *holograph wills*, or *real property*. If you don't belong to these groups, you might not fully understand what they are talking about. You've picked up this book because you are interested in learning more about translation. Like baking and law, translation has its own concepts and terms, so as an essential first step in learning more about translation it's important to get a handle on some of the fundamental concepts and terms in this field. This opening chapter will help you to do exactly that! We'll introduce a range of basic concepts and terms, and, along the way, we'll also bust some common myths or misperceptions about translation to help you gain a better understanding of what's really involved. Let's get started!

What is translation?

In English, the word "translation" comes from Latin. In Latin, "trans" means "across", and there are many examples of it being used with this meaning as part of our everyday language. For instance, if you take a trans-Atlantic flight, it means that you will be flying across the Atlantic Ocean from one side to the other, such as flying from New York to London. If you are driving in Canada, you might find yourself on the Trans-Canada Highway, which is a road that stretches all the way across the country. So in the first part of the word "translation", "trans" means "across". The other part of the word – "lation" – comes from the Latin verb that means "to carry". So if we put the two elements together, we can see that "translation" essentially means "to carry across". In this case, we are concerned with carrying across a message from one language to another. In other words, we start with a message in one language, and, through the act of translation, we end up with that same message in another language.

DOI: 10.4324/9781003217718-2

10 Basic concepts and terms in translation

In general language, the term translation is sometimes used as a sort of umbrella term to describe in a broad way any activity where a message is transferred from one language to another. However, within the language professions, translation has a more restricted meaning. We can have different modes of communication, including a written mode, a spoken mode, and a signed mode. In its narrower sense, translation means the transfer of a written message from one language to another. If we are talking about transferring a spoken or signed message, then the term used to describe this is interpretation. This means that translators only work with written texts, while interpreters – whom you might have seen on television or the Internet – are the ones who convert a spoken or signed message to another language. The majority of this book will focus on the translation of written texts, but, in Chapter 9, we'll introduce the idea of cross-modal translation (e.g., starting with a written text and ending with a spoken text, or vice-versa), and, in Chapter 10, we'll explore audiovisual translation, which can include multi-modal translation (e.g., subtitling films). Finally, in Chapter 11, we'll investigate interpreting in detail, although you will notice that concepts related to interpreting do get introduced in other chapters, too, since translation and interpreting are activities that take place in the same general sphere.

What is meant by *source, target,* and *equivalence?*

The notion of **equivalence** is a central concept in translation. At its simplest, equivalence is usually understood to be the relationship between the original text and its translation. Whenever we translate a text, we always start with a message in one language and end with a message in another language. In other words, we are dealing with a pair of languages, and, indeed, we use the term **language pair** to refer to the two languages in question. Let's say that, in this case, we are dealing with the language pair English and Arabic. But it is not enough to know only the language pair. It is also important to specify the **direction** in which the translation is happening (i.e., translation *from* and *into*). If we are working with the language pair English and Arabic, then, in some cases, we might be starting with a message in English and ending with a message in Arabic, but, in other cases, we might be doing the opposite by starting with a message in Arabic and ending with a message in English. In the first case, the translation direction is *from* English *into* Arabic, and, in the second case, the translation direction is *from* Arabic *into* English. By convention, the language of the starting message is written first, followed by the language of the ending message. So English-Arabic or English>Arabic translation means translation *from* English *into* Arabic, while Arabic-English or Arabic>English translation means translation *from* Arabic *into* English. A translator or translation company that offers translation services in both directions might indicate this in the following way: Arabic< >English.

Source (the starting point)	Target (the end point)
Source text: The text that will be translated.	**Target text:** The translated text.
Source language: The language that you are translating *from* (i.e., the language in which the source text is written).	**Target language:** The language that you are translating *into*.
Source audience (source readers): The intended audience or readers of the source text.	**Target audience (target readers):** The intended audience or readers of the translated text.
Source culture: The cultural context in which the source audience is immersed and on which they will draw to understand the source text.	**Target culture:** The cultural context in which the target audience is immersed and on which they will draw to understand the translated text.

Figure 1.1 The notions of source and target in translation.

Two key terms are used to describe things related to the starting situation and the end situation in translation: **source** and **target**. As summarized in Figure 1.1, *source* is used to describe the various elements associated with the starting point of the translation, while *target* is used to refer to those things associated with the end point.

The concepts of *source* and *target* are relative to one another. As noted above, sometimes the translation direction is from English into Arabic, which means that the source language is English, the source text is written in English, and the intended readers of the text are English speakers. Meanwhile, the target text will be in Arabic and intended for an Arabic-speaking audience. In other cases, the translation might be from Arabic into English, meaning that all the source-related concepts are Arabic, while English takes on the role of target (text, language, audience, and culture). When the translation is complete, the source text and target text are assumed to be equivalent, although you will see in an upcoming section why the notion of equivalence is not always straightforward.

Directionality is important for another reason, too. Translators may be very comfortable working in one direction (e.g., from English into Arabic) but less confident working in the opposite direction (e.g., from Arabic into English). The reason for this is that most of us have a dominant language. This may be the first language that you learned (sometimes called a native language or a mother tongue), or it could be the language that you use most often. While there may be a few exceptionally bilingual people, most of us tend to have one dominant language, and we are most comfortable and competent working into that language. It could mean that we have a broader vocabulary in that language, that we have a more complete mastery of the grammar, that words come to us more easily, or that we can be more nuanced or even funny in our dominant language. In contrast, even if we are reasonably good speakers of a second language, we may find that it takes us a bit longer to find the right words, that it's more challenging to say exactly what we mean, or that engaging in wordplay or humour is very difficult. This is completely normal! And it's normal for translators, too. Even though translators may be advanced speakers of more than one language, they are still likely to have one dominant language in which they can work more easily and accurately. This means that a translator might choose to work out of several languages (i.e., they will work with several source languages) but into only one language (i.e., they work with a single target language). When searching for a translator, it is therefore important to take note of not only the working languages but also the preferred language direction(s) of that translator since not all translators work in multiple language directions. For example, a translator who advertises as French/Spanish>German works out of both French and Spanish (i.e., two source languages) into German (i.e., one target language). In contrast, a translator who advertises German< >Spanish is comfortable working in both directions in these two languages.

Although interpreting will be the topic of a more in-depth investigation in Chapter 11, it is worth noting here that interpreters *do* need to be comfortable working in both directions because sometimes they are the only link between two people who need to communicate but who do not share a common language.

What gets translated?

It would be easy to think that translators are primarily concerned with translating words, but this is not exactly how translation works. For the most part, translators focus on translating the message or the ideas that are contained in the source text. Words are important too, of course, because they are the means through which the ideas are expressed. But if a translator is too focused on translating each individual word rather than trying to extract and then repackage the message, the result can sound stilted and be difficult to understand. This is why the notion of equivalence is not as straightforward as it might first appear. The equivalence is not likely to be at the word level, since word-for-word translation is not possible or desirable in many cases. Therefore, equivalence is typically understood to be at the level of meaning. A source and target text are usually accepted as being equivalent if they have the same meaning, even though they do not necessarily match up precisely at the word level.

Words are used to represent concepts, but the list of words available in each language is not exactly the same. Language is closely tied to culture, and speakers of a given language may reside in a given geographical region.

Words are developed to refer to the concepts that are relevant to a given culture or region. Of course, there are many concepts that are common to people all around the world, but there are differences too, such as the climate in different regions, the types of food commonly produced and consumed, the religions, the leisure activities, and more. As a result of these differences, there are words that exist in some languages but not in others. For instance, you have probably heard the frequently used example that the Inuit people who live in the far north of Canada have many words for different types of snow. Since snow is an important feature of their reality, it is not really surprising that their vocabulary is rich in ways to describe different types of weather conditions involving snow. In contrast, in regions of the world that do not have a snowy climate, there is less need to discuss snow in such a nuanced way, so the Indigenous languages in Australia and Africa have a far more limited vocabulary on this topic, although they may have more words pertaining to a desert or rainforest climate that do not feature in the Inuit language.

In addition to having differences in vocabulary, languages also have different rules and conventions for the order in which words can be combined to form longer units, such as phrases or sentences. In other words, each language has its own grammar. In related languages, such as the group of Romance languages that includes French, Spanish, Portuguese, and Italian, the grammar may share some features. However, in languages that belong to different families (e.g., English and Chinese), the grammar can be very different. Grammar is essentially concerned with how different words can be organized, so let's look at a few simple examples that reveal some grammatical differences.

In this first example, we can see that, in English, the normal position for an adjective (e.g., yellow) is before the noun (e.g., car). In contrast, in Spanish, it is more typical for the noun to come first, followed by the adjective.

English: the yellow car (article, adjective, noun)
Spanish: el coche amarillo (article, noun, adjective)

If we were to translate the Spanish phrase *el coche amarillo* into English in a very literal or word-for-word way, we would end up with the phrase *the car yellow*. It is possible to discern the overall meaning of this phrase, but it does not sound natural and does not follow the conventions of English.

In the next example, we can see the different ways in which English, French, and German organize the sentence that people normally use to introduce themselves. In the parentheses after the French and German sentences, you can see a literal translation into English. Again, it is possible to understand the intended meaning, but it's not the most typical way that English speakers would introduce themselves. Here, a translator's job is not to analyze and reproduce each individual word but to understand that the essence of the source-text message is about introducing yourself, so the best translation is the phrase that corresponds to the typical way of introducing yourself in the target language.

English: My name is Alex.
French: Je m'appelle Alex. (I call myself Alex.)
German: Ich heiße Alex. (I am called Alex.)

As the sentences get longer and more complex, it becomes more and more difficult to produce meaningful literal or word-for-word translations. What you often end up with is a text that uses target-language words that are organized according to source-language grammar. For anyone who is a fan of the *Star Wars* film series, you will probably have noticed that the character Yoda speaks in this way: he uses English words, but he combines them in an order that does not correspond to English grammar but which probably corresponds to the grammar of his own dominant language. For instance, Yoda says, "Powerful you have become", "Ready are you?", and "Size matters not", whereas according to the typical conventions of English, we would normally expect these sentences to read, "You have become powerful", "Are you ready?", and "Size doesn't matter".

Yoda's pattern of speaking presents a fun, quirky trait in a movie where the character has relatively few lines, but would you like to watch an entire film where everyone speaks like this? How about reading a whole text? Even if it is possible for a reader to work out the intended meaning of a sentence that has been translated in a literal or word-for-word way, you can imagine that it would quickly become tiresome or frustrating to have to wade through an entire text that has been translated in this fashion.

Where do a translator's loyalties lie?

So we can see that translators need to take into account two main things. On the one hand, they are concerned with transferring the message or meaning of a source text, and, on the other hand, they need to be sure that they are expressing this message using words and grammatical constructions that sound natural in the target language. It is not always easy to accomplish both at the same time, which can create a sort of tension. This tension can be attributed to the fact that translators must navigate being faithful to the source-text author's intended message and chosen form of expression and being faithful to the expectations and needs of the intended target-text readers. For instance, to ensure that the target audience can understand the text, the translator may need to adjust the form and even some parts of the message of the source text. Translation is therefore usually presented as a spectrum, as shown in Figure 1.2. At one end of the spectrum, we have **literal translation**, while, at the other end, we have **free translation**.

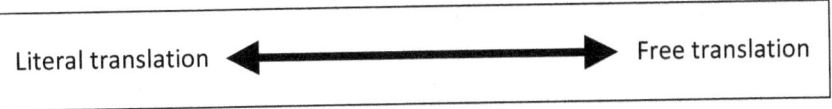

Figure 1.2 The two ends of the translation spectrum.

In a literal translation, a translator aims to keep as much of the grammatical or structural form of the source text as possible while also conveying the meaning. Literal translations often take a largely word-for-word approach or use a word order that is based on the underlying source text. In contrast, a free translation is one that aims to convey the meaning of the source text but does so in a way that is far less constrained by the form found in the source text. Between these two extremes, a translation can lean more towards being a literal translation or more towards being a free one.

For many types of texts, especially those that are mainly intended to be informative or pragmatic (e.g., textbooks, user manuals, administrative texts, policy documents), it is possible to strike a balance between being faithful to the source-text author's message and being faithful to the target audience's expectations with regard to the language conventions. However, in other types of texts where there is more regional or culture-specific content (e.g., a website targeted at consumers in a particular country), or where the form of the text is particularly creative and may involve wordplay or humour (e.g., advertising texts, poetry), it may be necessary for translators to adopt an approach that is further towards the free translation end of the spectrum and to deviate more from both the content and form of the source text. We will look at some of these special cases in more detail in Chapter 7, where we discuss website localization, and Chapter 8, where we explore the transcreation of marketing texts, but, for the moment, we can observe that in these cases the translator may decide to strive for achieving equivalence not at the level of the word or even of the meaning but rather at the level of *effect*. In other words, in the case of an advertising text, a translator may try to ensure that the target-language text has the same type of emotional *effect* on the target audience that the source text has on the source audience, even though the two texts may not share the same literal meaning or even use the same stylistic techniques. As you can see, the notion of equivalence is more complicated than it might first appear, since there are different ways in which equivalence can be viewed (e.g., at the level of word, meaning, or effect).

What is involved in the translation process?

Translation is a complex activity, and Chapter 3 will go into more detail about what's involved in working as a professional translator. In the section below, we'll take a more high-level look at the two main stages in the translation process – comprehension and production – for which we can identify two corresponding categories of challenges.

First, translators need to be able to understand the source text, which means that this stage is about decoding and comprehending the source-text author's original message. Remember that translators are not really translating words. Instead, they are translating the underlying ideas that are being expressed by the words. So in order to be able to translate a text, translators must understand the content of that text. Some texts contain relatively general knowledge that is familiar to many people (e.g., newspapers) or are written for non-specialist audiences (e.g., user guides). However, other types of text deal with very specialized subjects, such as law or medicine. Even within these very specialized areas, there may be subfields that are not familiar to everyone working in that field. For instance, a doctor that specializes in family medicine may not be familiar with all the procedures used in emergency medicine. Similarly, a lawyer who specializes in preparing wills may not know all the concepts that pertain to immigration law. Because texts are written on every subject you can imagine, and because no one person can know everything, many professional translators specialize in a relatively small number of fields rather than trying to tackle texts on any topic. By developing a specialization, translators can really get to know that field in detail and be confident that they have properly understood the content of the source text and are familiar with the associated terminology used to discuss it. Translators also need to be prepared to do research about the subject matter of the text they are translating. In fact, research is one of the main activities that translators undertake, and Chapters 4 and 5 explore some resources and tools that translators can use to comprehend the subject matter of the source text.

Following the comprehension stage, translators next enter the production stage, where the focus shifts to encoding a message or producing a target text for the target audience. It is at this stage that translators must act as wordsmiths, crafting a text that will meet the needs and expectations of its intended readers. This is trickier than it sounds because language offers many choices, meaning that a translator needs to become a master decision-maker. For example, all languages contain synonymy, which is when two or more words can have a very similar meaning. Think about the weather, for example. If you need to describe a day when the temperature is moderately low, what word would you use? Cool? Chilly? Brisk? Perhaps invigorating? To help them make such choices, translators can once again turn to various resources and tools, a selection of which will be covered in Chapters 4 and 5. But translators also need to rely on their knowledge of the text type, the target-language culture, and the specific target audience in order to make the best possible choices. For instance, if the text in question is on a medical subject but is an information leaflet aimed at patients rather than at healthcare professionals, a translator must know to use a term such as *heart attack* rather than the more technical term *myocardial infarction*, which would be more appropriate for a scientific research article. Similarly, a translator may make different term choices when translating for adult patients (e.g., *intestinal discomfort*) and when translating for children (e.g., *tummy ache*). And as mentioned previously, translators need to be very familiar with the grammatical rules and conventions for combining words so that, rather than sounding like it was written by Yoda, the text meets the expectations of the target audience. Cultural knowledge also comes into play, such as in the case of dealing with idiomatic expressions. These expressions are often culture bound and cannot be translated literally or they will be meaningless to a target audience. For instance, a word-for-word translation of the Spanish-language expression "tomar el pelo" would be "to grab the hair", but a more appropriate way to translate this idiom into English would be to substitute the equivalent expression "to pull someone's leg" because both of these expressions refer to the same idea, which is about teasing someone or playing a little trick on them. Slang is another area of language that can be very culture-specific and where a literal translation may not be adequate. For example, in Spain, a slang word that can be used to refer to "money" is *pasta*, but if your audience consists of English speakers, then *dough* would be a better choice. So translators need to consider the range of options available to them for expressing a given concept, then make the choice that they feel will best convey that idea to the target audience, taking into account the likely knowledge, needs, and expectations of this audience. It's a tall order, which is why becoming a professional translator requires a specialized education and lots of practice.

Is it true that…?

It's completely normal for people outside the field of translation to have a limited understanding of how this process works. Few of us are experts in things that we haven't studied or practised. Just because we have seen or encountered something in our lives doesn't mean that we know all there is to know about it. For instance, seeing a piano or hearing someone play one doesn't make you a musician or a music expert. Translation is no different. You might have encountered translation in some way, but this brief contact may have left you with some unanswered questions or even led you to make some assumptions that might not be entirely correct. No problem! That's what this book is for – to help you de-mystify translation! Learning the foundational concepts and terms has been a great first step in understanding what translation is all about, but to end this introductory chapter, let's look at translation from another perspective by dispelling some commonly held myths and misperceptions about this field.

Is it true that all translators speak many languages?

Not necessarily. Translation involves working with written texts, and writing and speaking are different skills. A translator may be perfectly comfortable reading a source text in another language but less comfortable chatting away in that language. In addition, many translators work mainly into their dominant language, meaning that they need to have an active mastery of that language, but their knowledge of the source language could be more passive. Although many translators do work from more than one source language (and some work into more than one target language), there are other translators who have built a fruitful career translating from just one source language into their dominant language. There is no single linguistic profile for a translator! In contrast, interpreters do need to have an excellent command of at least two spoken (or signed) languages, and they must be able to work in both directions. Many (though not all) interpreters also have a third (or even fourth) working language, which broadens their job opportunities.

Is it true that all bilingual (or multilingual) people make good translators?

Even though we have only scratched the surface of what's involved in translation in this introductory chapter, it's already clear that translation involves much more than simply knowing two (or more) languages. Translators need cultural knowledge, subject matter knowledge, knowledge about tools and resources, strong research and writing skills, and much more. We could say that being bilingual is a pre-requisite for being a good translator, but this alone is not sufficient to set a translator up for success.

Is it true that translating and interpreting are the same?

Not exactly. Although both translating and interpreting are concerned with transferring a message from one language to another, translation deals with written texts and interpreting deals with spoken or signed texts. While there are some commonalities in the skillsets required, there are also some significant differences in the way that translators and interpreters work. For instance, translators often work iteratively by producing a first draft and then revising that draft to arrive at a polished final version. In contrast, interpreters work more or less in the moment and only have one shot at transferring the message before they have to move on to the next sentence. In addition, there are some activities that cross from one mode to another (e.g., subtitling or sight translation). More details will be provided about interpreting in Chapter 11.

Is it true that translation is just about substituting words in one language for words in another language?

Nope. If it were that simple, then anyone with a good dictionary could do it. As we've seen, translators need to choose between words that have very similar meanings. Translators also need to change the order of words so that they follow the grammatical conventions of the target language. What's more, not all words have a direct equivalent, so translators focus on translating a message rather than a series of words. In some cases, such as with idiomatic expressions, a translator may even need to substitute a different expression that is not a literal equivalent but which conveys the same idea. For example, the English expression "It's raining cats and dogs" gets substituted with "Il pleut des cordes" (= "It's raining ropes") when transferred into French. Translators may even decide to omit certain words (e.g., a cultural reference that will not be meaningful to the target audience) or to add in an explanation to clarify a concept that the target audience may have difficulty understanding.

Is it true that a good translator can translate a text on any subject?

Not on your life! Texts can be written on any subject, and no human being can know absolutely everything. For instance, you have probably had the experience of trying to read a document in your dominant language that you couldn't quite follow (e.g., a contract for a mobile phone plan, or an end-user licence agreement for a piece of software or an app). Every subject field has its own specialized concepts and terms, and it takes time and effort to develop this expertise. The authors of the original source texts are experts in their field, and, in order to do a good job transferring this specialized material into another language, translators likewise need to become very familiar with it. Many translators therefore choose to specialize in just a couple of areas, and an increasing number have pursued some kind of education in both their subject field specialization and translation (e.g., a bachelor's degree in law coupled with a master's degree in translation).

Is it true that there is one true or perfect translation for every text?

Absolutely not. Translation is actually somewhat subjective. As you've learned, languages contain many synonyms. For instance, you could describe very hot weather as "scorching" or "roasting". What's more, languages tend to have some degree of flexibility with regard to the ways that words can be combined. Although English speakers may find Yoda's way of speaking a little odd, there are some words that can be placed in different positions in a sentence without attracting a second glance. For example, many adverbs can be placed either at the beginning or end of a sentence without impacting the meaning (e.g., "Yesterday I went to school" and "I went to school yesterday"). In addition, it's possible to express the same basic idea using a positive or a negative construction (e.g., "I left" and "I didn't stay"). Given the numerous options available for expressing an idea, it is unlikely that any two translators will make exactly the same choices for every word and word combination in a text. Therefore, two (or more) translations can be valid, even if they are not identical.

Is it true that translation is actually impossible?

We've just established that there isn't one true or perfect translation for every text, so does this mean that translation is impossible? This question has been asked countless times throughout history, and there is even a well-known adage in Italian that states *traduttori traditori* (literally: "translators traitors"). In this case, the term "traitor" is being used in a metaphorical way rather than in a literal way. The idea being explored in this adage is that, because no two languages are identical, there will inevitably be some degree of loss – to the meaning, the form, or both – as part of the translation process, making it impossible for the translator to faithfully reproduce the source text in every respect. In other words, the translation process entails making some compromises. So translation is not about attempting an impossible task but about reducing and managing the inevitable losses and perhaps even compensating by introducing some gains in another part of the text to offset these losses. For instance, it may not be possible to preserve a rhyme when translating from one language to another, but maybe a translator could introduce a different type of wordplay instead (e.g., alliteration) to preserve the playful feel of the text overall and achieve an equivalent effect on the target audience. Seen from this perspective, we could say that translation is possible, although perfect translation is not. In the vast majority of cases, an imperfect translation can still be functional and meet a great many of our needs. We don't expect absolute perfection in most other areas of our lives, so it's very important for us to have realistic expectations about translation, too.

Is it true that computers are going to replace translators before too much longer?

It's complicated. There are already some very specific instances where computers can produce usable translations. For example, if you want to translate a friend's post on Facebook or Twitter or some other social media platform, an automatic machine translation tool, such as Google Translate, could be a perfectly good choice because it's fast, free, and convenient, and because the consequences of having a less-than-perfect translation are not likely to be too serious. However, in other contexts, such as in a hospital or in a court of law, using Google Translate or a similar tool may not be a good idea. The concepts in question are likely to be more specialized, and, if the translation is poorly done, the consequences could be quite serious (e.g., getting the wrong diagnosis, getting sent to jail). Chapter 6 is devoted to helping you improve your machine translation literacy by learning more about how automatic translation tools work, their strengths and weaknesses, and the situations in which they might be helpful or harmful. Another point worth mentioning is that it doesn't have to be an "either/or" situation because translators can (and do) use a wide range of computer tools, including automatic translation tools, as part of their workflow.

Concluding remarks

There's more to translation than meets the eye, isn't there? For starters, it takes a different skillset to work with written texts (i.e., translation) than it does with spoken or signed texts (i.e., interpreting). What's more, translators don't focus on translating words but rather on transferring the essential message from one language into another. This can mean paraphrasing ideas, rearranging the order of words, and even replacing culture-bound elements with concepts that are more familiar to the readers of the translated text. While it is completely normal for people outside the field of translation to have a limited understanding of what's involved, this chapter has attempted to dispel some commonly held misperceptions about translation. With this newfound knowledge in hand, you can now take the next steps in your journey to learning more about the fascinating world of translation and approach it with a deeper appreciation of some of the challenges involved and the skills required to overcome them. Up next in Chapter 2, we'll explore translation through the ages, looking at some key translation-related figures, events, and products that have helped to shape our multilingual society.

Key points in this chapter

- The word "translation" literally means "to carry across", and it is used as an umbrella term to describe the process of carrying a message from one language to another.
- "Translation" can also be used in a narrower sense, where it is usually contrasted with "interpreting". Translators transfer a written message from one language to another, while interpreters transfer a spoken or signed message from one language to another.
- The term "source" refers to the text, language, audience, or culture that is the *starting* point in the translation process (i.e., the original message), while "target" is used to refer to the text, language, audience, or culture that is the end point (i.e., the translated message). Source and target are therefore relative to one another, meaning that the *source* language for one job could be the *target* language for another job.
- Equivalence is generally understood to refer to the relationship between the source and target text, although equivalence can be sought at different levels (e.g., word, meaning, effect).
- Translators often have one dominant language (e.g., their native language or language of habitual use), and many translators translate only *into* their dominant language. In contrast, interpreters need to be able to work in both directions.

Basic concepts and terms in translation

- By convention, the source language is listed first and the target language second (e.g., from English into French is written as English>French).
- Translators translate ideas rather than words, although words are used to express ideas.
- Translation cannot be carried out using a word-for-word approach because languages present the world differently; sometimes one language has a word for a concept but another language does not.
- Different languages have different rules and conventions for the order in which words can be combined to form phrases or sentences.
- Translators need to consider both the content of the message and its form when transferring a text from one language to another, which may require making adjustments to both.
- Translation is a spectrum, with literal and free translation at its two extremes.
- A literal translation aims to keep as much of the structural form of the source text as possible while also conveying the meaning, while a free translation aims to convey the meaning of the source text but does so in a way that is less constrained by the source text's form.
- Translators may experience tension when trying to respect the words and message of the source-text author while also taking into account the needs of the target audience.
- Translation is a complex activity that includes both comprehension and production. Translators need to be very familiar with the subject matter of the source text to ensure a solid understanding of the content, but they must also be strong writers who can manipulate the target language to ensure that it aligns with target-audience expectations.
- There are quite a few commonly held misperceptions about translation, such as:
  - **All translators speak multiple languages.** (Some do, but others might work with just one source language and one target language. There is no single linguistic profile for a translator. Rather, translators (and interpreters) are a very diverse bunch!)
  - **All bilingual people make good translators.** (Knowing two languages well is necessary for translation, but it's not enough. Translators also need cultural and subject matter knowledge, among other things.)
  - **Translation and interpreting are interchangeable.** (Translation and interpreting are both concerned with transferring a message from one language to another, but in translation the message is written, while in interpreting the message is spoken or signed.)
  - **Translation is about substituting words in one language for words in another language.** (Word-for-word translations rarely work;

translation is about transferring a message using constructions that are natural in the target text.)
- **A translator can translate a text on any subject.** (No one can be an expert on every topic, and translators typically specialize in one or two subject fields.)
- **There is one perfect translation for every text.** (All languages have a certain degree of flexibility, which means that there are multiple ways to express the same idea. It would be very unlikely for two translators to propose exactly the same translation, yet both could be valid.)
- **Translation is impossible.** (Translation happens every day. Although there is no such thing as a perfect translation – and what in life is perfect, after all? – many translations are perfectly useful.)
- **Computers are on the verge of replacing translators.** (Computers can already produce translations that meet *some* of our needs, but they cannot genuinely understand the source text, the target audience's needs, or the translation's intended context of use. However, translators and computers working together can make a formidable team!)

Topics for discussion

As part of a class discussion, or as a prompt for an online discussion forum, consider the following:

- Beyond linguistic or language-related knowledge, what other type of knowledge does a translator most need to succeed?
- Has anything you've learned in this chapter caused you to think about translation or translators in a different way than you did before? Explain.
- What other potential myths have you heard about translation or translators? Based on what you've learned in this chapter, do you think they are true or false?

Exercises

- **Draw a mind map:** Create an initial mind map of the key concepts associated with translation that you have learned about in this chapter.
- **Create an elevator pitch:** Choose one commonly held misperception about translation and create an elevator pitch that you could give to friends, family, or colleagues to help set the record straight. A good elevator pitch needs to grab the listener's attention and explain a concept in such a way that they will understand it in a short period of time (e.g., in two minutes or less). An infographic could work too!

Find out more

Colina, Sonia. 2015. *Fundamentals of Translation*. Cambridge: Cambridge University Press.

- This textbook, and particularly Chapter 1, provides a clear and non-technical introduction to the basic and central concepts of translation.

Delisle, Jean, Hannelore Lee-Jahnke, and Monique C. Cormier, eds. 1999. *Translation Terminology*. Amsterdam: John Benjamins.

- This terminology collection presents and describes approximately 200 concepts that make up the basic vocabulary for the practical teaching of translation. The terms are included in four languages: English, French, German, and Spanish.

House, Juliane. 2018. *Translation: The Basics*. London: Routledge.

- This book provides an accessible introduction to foundational concepts in translation, including an explanation of the main approaches, a consideration of the role played by culture and society, the relationship between a translation and an original work, and the effects of globalization on translation.

Polizzotti, Mark. 2018. *Sympathy for the Traitor: A Translation Manifesto*. Cambridge, MA: The MIT Press.

- This book explores a number of misconceptions about translation and tries to sensitize readers to the many components that go into translation and the many challenges that can arise. Overall, the author attempts to sketch a portrait of the art and craft of translation and to help readers to see it not as a problem to be solved but as an achievement to be celebrated.

2 Brief history of translation

Translation has been practised for thousands of years. Although its precise origins are unknown, writings on the topic of translation can be traced far back in recorded history. For example, translation was discussed in the writings of Homer, a legendary author who lived and worked in Ancient Greece in the 8th century BCE and who is credited with creating the epic poems *The Iliad* and *The Odyssey* – two works that have themselves been translated many times. It would be impossible to provide an exhaustive history of translation in a single chapter, so instead this chapter assembles 17 examples that describe some of the key people, events, inventions, and texts that make up this rich history. Since translation is a global activity, this chapter draws on content that comes from different regions and traditions. Though they are presented as a series of independent and consecutive items, it is important to remember that translation activity was actually ongoing and happening simultaneously in different parts of the world. These 17 examples point to just a few of the many, many people and groups who contributed to the development of the field, but the exercise at the end of the chapter identifies additional figures and events, and you are encouraged to do some further investigation to learn more. Taken together, the individual elements in this mosaic will give you a glimpse into the history of translation and shine a light on some of the ways that translation has helped to shape our history – for better or worse – and led us to where we are today.

Tower of Babel

The biblical story of the Tower of Babel, which appears in the Old Testament book of Genesis, has long been associated with the notion of translation. According to the story, everyone on Earth used to speak the same language, which facilitated communication and collaboration. Working together, the people decided to build a city, including a tower that would reach the heavens. However, this angered God, who punished them by scattering them around the planet and making them speak different languages so that they could not communicate as easily. The incomplete city was named Babel, which means "confusion", since this was now the state of people when faced with others who did not speak the same language. And so it was the events at Babel that gave rise to the need for translators and translation, and, even to this day, the Tower of Babel is an image that is strongly associated with the translation profession.

> **Fun fact!** The International Federation of Translators publishes a journal of research in translation, and the name of the journal is *Babel*.

Septuagint (3rd century BCE)

The Greek Old Testament is often referred to as the Septuagint, which comes from the Latin for "seventy" (70). It is the earliest surviving Greek translation of books from the Hebrew Bible. The name Septuagint comes from the legend that the Hebrew Torah was translated into Greek at the request of the pharaoh Ptolemy II so that it could be included in the Library of Alexandria. According to the story, Ptolemy hired 70 Jewish scholars and installed them each in their own room before asking each one to translate the text. Each scholar worked completely independently and yet all produced an identical translation. As you learned in Chapter 1, translation is quite subjective because there are multiple ways of saying the same thing in a given language. Therefore, we would normally expect that translations of the same text produced by different translators would show at least some differences. It would indeed be miraculous for all 70 of the scholars to produce an identical translation, and so this was taken as an indication of God's hand at work.

> **Fun fact!** Holy books, such as the Torah, the Bible, and the Quran, are the most frequently translated books in the world.

Rosetta Stone (196 BCE)

The Rosetta Stone is a large fragment of granite that is carved with the same text in three different scripts. It was carved during the reign of the pharaoh Ptolemy V, and the text itself is a message that praises his rule. The top and middle sections of the stone contain the text written in two different Ancient Egyptian scripts – hieroglyphic and Demotic. The bottom third displays the same text in Ancient Greek. The stone was discovered in 1799 near the town of Rashid (known in English as Rosetta) in Egypt. At the time that the Rosetta Stone was discovered, no one was able to understand ancient Egyptian hieroglyphics. In contrast, Ancient Greek was widely known to scholars, and a few people were familiar with some elements of the Demotic script. By painstakingly studying the three scripts side by side for several decades, researchers were eventually able to decipher the previously unknown hieroglyphics. This in turn made it possible for us to deepen our understanding of Egyptian history.

> **Fun fact!** If you'd like to see the Rosetta Stone for yourself, you can find it in the British Museum in London, where it has been on display for over 200 years, and where it remains one of the most popular items in the collection.

St. Jerome (c. 342–420)

Born in what is now the northeast of Italy, St. Jerome was educated in Latin and Greek. Following his studies in Rome, St. Jerome became a hermit and spent several years living in the Syrian desert, where he began to learn Hebrew. Upon returning to Rome, St. Jerome was commissioned by the Pope to work as a translator. Between 380 and the time of his death in 420, St. Jerome produced a huge number of translations covering Church administration, monastic rules, theology, and letters, but he is best known for his translation of the Vulgate, a version of the Bible that he translated into Latin from Hebrew and Greek. The fact that St. Jerome referred to the original Hebrew source text rather than relying only on the Septuagint, which was itself a translation, set the Vulgate apart from other Latin translations. The Vulgate has since gone on to become one of the most influential translations of all time, and it is still currently used in the Catholic Church. Jerome is now recognized as a saint in the Catholic Church, where he is said to be the patron saint of translators. St. Jerome's feast day is celebrated on 30 September, which is the day that has since been chosen as International Translation Day.

> **Fun fact!** At some point in history, an apocryphal story emerged that, while St. Jerome was living in the desert, he tamed a lion by removing a thorn from its paw. As a result of this story, many of the paintings, engravings, and sculptures of St. Jerome that have been created throughout history picture him with a lion companion somewhere in the artwork.

Xuanzang (602–664)

Xuanzang lived in China in the 7th century and became a Buddhist monk in his early teens. For his work, he travelled through numerous provinces, preaching and learning sutras, but, at that time, the sutras were open to extremely diverse interpretations. Wanting to better understand the sutras, Xuanzang decided to travel to India, where Buddhism originated, so that he could study the original source texts. His epic journey lasted 25 years, during which time he visited many important temples, learned Sanskrit, and continued to study the sutras under the guidance of renowned monks. When he returned to China, Xuanzang recorded his experiences in a book called *Da Tang xiyu ji* (Great Tang Record of the Land to the West), which remains an important source in the study of Chinese-Indian communication. Xuanzang then devoted the remaining two decades of his life to translating Buddhist sutras into Chinese. He translated over 1300 works and established a large translation bureau, which attracted students and collaborators from across East Asia. Some of the original Sanskrit source texts were lost at various points in history, but, thanks to Xuanzang's extensive and careful translations of these texts into Chinese, it has been possible to recover the content of these lost Indian Buddhist texts by referring to the Chinese translations. Were it not for Xuanzang's translations, the content of these Indian texts would have been lost forever.

House of Wisdom (9th–13th century)

Founded in 830 CE, Bayt al-Ḥikmah ("House of Wisdom"), sometimes referred to as the Grand Library of Baghdad, was an institute of higher learning that also became one of the most celebrated translation centres in Arab history. In addition to an academy and library, the House of Wisdom also featured a translation bureau, where more than 60 translators worked to translate texts from Greek, Syriac, Persian, Sanskrit, and Aramaic into Arabic. The subject matter of the texts included philosophy, geography, astronomy, religious works, literature, science, medicine, and mathematics. The House of Wisdom existed as part of a major translation movement during the Abbasid Empire, and it is striking to note that translation therefore lay at the heart of one of the most important periods of intellectual activity in history. Beginning around the 12th century, the House of Wisdom began to experience a period of gradual decline until it was eventually destroyed by the Mongols during the Siege of Baghdad in the year 1258.

> **Fun fact!** One of the House of Wisdom's best and most prolific translators, Ḥunayn Ibn Isḥāq, translated over 100 works and was apparently paid in gold according to the weight of his texts. Allegedly, he wrote in large letters and left wide spaces between the lines in order to increase the page count. While this may have been motivated by greed, it paid off in an unanticipated way: the manuscripts remained intact and readable for centuries (Baker 1998a).

School of Toledo (12th and 13th centuries)

Beginning with Archbishop Raymond of Toledo, successive archbishops of Toledo in Spain sponsored or promoted translation activities that are now collectively referred to as the School of Toledo. During the 12th century, many translations were carried out from Arabic into Latin. One well-known and prolific translator from this period was Gerard of Cremona, an Italian translator who learned Arabic at Toledo and translated some 70 to 80 texts on mathematics, astronomy, philosophy, and medicine from Arabic into Latin. During the 13th century, the school attracted the attention of King Alfonso X of Castile, who funded numerous translations. During this period, Latin ceased to be the main target language and was replaced by Old Spanish, which in turn laid the foundations for the development of modern-day Castilian Spanish. After Alfonso's death, his successor was far less supportive of translation efforts, and, as a result, activities wound down as many translators relocated to work with patrons elsewhere.

Gutenberg press (c. 1440)

Few inventions throughout history have had a more dramatic influence than the Gutenberg press. A printing press is a mechanical device for applying ink to a surface such as paper or cloth. In around 1440, a German goldsmith named Johannes Gutenberg invented what is known as a movable-type printing press. This approach sped up the printing process considerably and ushered in the era of mass communication, which permanently altered the structure of our society. For instance, it led to a sharp increase in literacy, along with a corresponding demand for material to read – including translations! The first person to introduce a printing press into England is believed to be William Caxton (c. 1421–c. 1491) in around 1476. An Englishman, Caxton was working as a merchant in Belgium, but he also did some translation on the side. On a business trip to Germany, he observed how the printing industry was beginning to flourish there, so he decided to set up a printing press of his own. As a result, the first book ever to be printed in the English language was Caxton's own translation of a French work: *Recuyell of the Historyes of Troye*. Caxton went on to translate and then print more of his own works in English, as well as many works by other authors and translators, and he is credited with launching the standardization of the English language through his printing.

William Tyndale (c. 1494–c. 1536)

Translation was sometimes a dangerous business. William Tyndale was an English linguist and biblical scholar who became a key figure in the Protestant Reformation. Tyndale's translation of the Bible was the first English version to be printed on a printing press and also the first to draw directly from Hebrew and Greek texts. At that time in history, it was illegal for anyone to be in unlicensed possession of an English translation of the Bible, so Tyndale left England and went to the European mainland, where his translation was published and then smuggled back into England. The translation was condemned and Tyndale declared a heretic. He was captured in Belgium and then tried and convicted of heresy. To demonstrate just how seriously the state took the charges, they tied Tyndale to a stake and strangled him before burning his body. However, just a few short years later, the King of England approved the publication of English-language Bibles, and these were all based on Tyndale's work. Tyndale's translations had wide-reaching influence, and evidence of this can still be seen today in well-known versions of the Bible, such as the King James Version.

La Malinche (c. 1501–c. 1550)

Also known as Malintzin or Doña Marina, La Malinche was a Nahua woman from Mexico. She was enslaved and taken to another part of the country, where she learned a Mayan language. Later, La Malinche was one of 20 slaves given to the Spanish conquistador Hernán Cortés in 1519 upon his arrival in Mexico. One of Cortés's crew, Jerónimo de Aguilar, was a Spanish interpreter who also spoke Maya. When Cortés wanted to speak with people living in the Nahua region, he used de Aguilar and La Malinche as part of a chain. In other words, Cortés would speak in Spanish to de Aguilar, who would then speak in Maya to La Malinche, who would in turn speak in Nahuatl to the local people. The process would then be reversed to transfer the locals' response back up the chain to Cortés, who was thus able to understand local cultures and politics – information he would later use to conquer the Aztec Empire. As for La Malinche, she is viewed as a heroine by some and a traitor by others, and her reputation has undergone many shifts over time as people continue to assess her role in history.

Fun fact! Today, the process of interpreting from one language into another through a third language is known as *relay interpreting*, and it is sometimes used in large multilingual organizations, such as the United Nations, if interpreters are not available to work directly in all the necessary language combinations. A similar process can also be applied in translation, where it is usually referred to as *indirect translation* (Shlesinger 2010).

Anne Sullivan (1866–1936)

As a young child, American-born Anne Sullivan contracted an eye disease that left her partially blind and unable to learn to read and write. She was educated at a school for the blind and, at the age of just 20, became a teacher to Helen Keller, a child who was both blind and deaf and thus unable to communicate with other people. Sullivan first connected with the young Keller by finger spelling words into Keller's palm, and within a year Keller had learned over 500 words as well as the tactile writing system Braille. When Keller enrolled in university, Sullivan accompanied her and interpreted for her during class lectures. Sullivan remained a lifelong companion, teacher, and interpreter for Keller and was posthumously inducted into the National Women's Hall of Fame in the United States.

> **Fun fact!** Anne Sullivan's story became the subject of a play by William Gibson called *The Miracle Worker*, which was later adapted into a film with the same name in 1962.

Navajo code talkers (1942–1945)

The Navajo code talkers are the most well-known group of Indigenous Americans to have been recruited by the United States military to use their traditional language to send secret communications during the World War II. However, other groups of code talkers, including members of the Sioux, Comanche, and Cherokee nations, also participated in both World War I and World War II. Essentially, speakers of Indigenous languages were recruited to use them as the basis for a secret code that could be transmitted to and from the battlefield, where it could then be translated by other code talkers into English. If the coded messages were intercepted by enemies, these enemies would not be able to decode them. The work of the hundreds of code talkers was instrumental to the Allied Victory in World War II, although the irony of being asked to use their traditional languages was not lost on the Indigenous code talkers, many of whom had been subject to government-sanctioned programs where they were punished for using these languages. What's more, owing to the highly secretive nature of their work, the code talkers and their contributions were not made public until many years after the war.

United Nations (1945)

A key event in contemporary translation history was the establishment of the United Nations (UN). This organization was founded after World War II as a group of countries that wanted to ensure that future differences could be resolved peacefully rather than through wars or conflicts. Of course, resolving issues diplomatically requires an ability to communicate, and this need helped to elevate the profile of translation and interpreting. Today, the UN operates with six official languages: Arabic, Chinese, English, French, Russian, and Spanish. These languages were chosen in order to try to ensure the maximum possible coverage around the planet while still keeping logistics and costs to a manageable level. Official UN documents are made available in all six official languages. In addition, a delegate may speak in an official UN language and their speech will be interpreted simultaneously into the other official languages. Today, the work of the UN extends beyond peace and security to include work in the areas of human rights, humanitarian aid, international law, and other global issues. Owing to its highly international presence and profile, the UN is one of the world's largest employers of language professionals, including not only translators and interpreters but also terminologists, whose work will be explored in more detail in Chapter 4.

Nuremberg trials (1945–1946)

Another key event in the history of translation also emerged in the wake of World War II. Following the defeat of Nazi Germany, the leaders of the Allied Nations (France, the former Soviet Union, the United Kingdom, and the United States) agreed to convene a joint tribunal in the German city of Nuremberg. The International Military Tribunal tried the most important surviving leaders of Nazi Germany, but without translators and interpreters its work would have been impossible. For example, the main trial, which was conducted over a ten-month period, is sometimes described as "the trial of six million words" because the published transcripts of the material presented at the trial fills 42 volumes. That's a lot of text to be translated, especially if you consider that this was before word processors or the Internet had been invented! As impressive as the translators' contribution was, the work of the interpreters was even more remarkable. Prior to the Nuremberg trials, interpretation was done consecutively, meaning that a speaker would speak and then pause while the interpreter transmitted the message in another language. In the case of the Nuremberg trials, the Allied Nations had agreed that the trials should be carried out fairly and expeditiously, but in order to accomplish this the trials had to be conducted *simultaneously* in four languages (French, Russian, English, and German). It was necessary to include all four languages in order to be sure that all the judges, lawyers, and defendants could understand. Moreover, it was necessary to use the four languages simultaneously since repeating every item in all four languages consecutively would have been tremendously time consuming. Prior to the Nuremberg trials, some limited experiments had been done with simultaneous interpreting, but this approach was well and truly put to the test in Nuremberg. Certainly, there were challenges and even flaws in the system, but it changed the face of interpreting forever. New and improved tools and techniques have resulted in simultaneous interpreting becoming the predominant approach in institutions such as the United Nations, the European Parliament, and the Canadian House of Commons, not to mention at conferences and meetings around the world. You'll learn much more about the different modes of interpreting in Chapter 11.

Weaver's memorandum (1949)

Warren Weaver was an American engineer and mathematician who worked for the Rockefeller Foundation. During the 1930s and 1940s, his work brought him into contact with key innovators in the newly emerging field of computer science. Inspired by the success of code-breakers during World War II, who managed to decrypt messages sent using the Enigma machine, Weaver began to contemplate the idea of applying code-breaking techniques to the task of automatic translation. In 1949, he circulated a ten-page proposal entitled simply "Translation", in which he laid out his ideas for automatic translation based on his knowledge of statistics, logic, information theory, and cryptography. Since that time, the field of translation has never been the same. This text, which became known as "Weaver's memorandum", is generally credited as being the single most influential publication in the early days of machine translation. It was a major stimulus to research activity, and, in 1951, it led directly to Yehoshua Bar-Hillel's appointment to the Massachusetts Institute of Technology as the first full-time paid researcher in automatic machine translation. The free online machine translation tools that you may recognize and use today, such as Google Translate, might never have existed were it not for the research buzz generated by "Weaver's memorandum". In Chapter 6, we'll pick up the story of automatic machine translation and explore this subject in more depth.

> **Fun fact!** Although Warren Weaver was a mathematician by training, he was also a lover of words. He was particularly fond of Lewis Carroll's classic children's story *Alice in Wonderland*, and one of his hobbies was collecting copies of this work. His collection contained 160 different translations in 42 languages, and this inspired him to write a book about the challenges of translating the story, which was published in 1964 under the title *Alice in Many Tongues* (Bowker 2012).

International Federation of Translators (1953)

The International Federation of Translators (IFT) – often referred to by its French name or acronym *Fédération internationale des traducteurs (FIT)* – was established in Paris in 1953 with founding associations from France, Denmark, Germany, Italy, Norway, and Turkey. The IFT is an umbrella organization that brings together professional translators from around the globe, and it now has member associations on six continents (Africa, Asia, Europe, Oceania, and North and South America). Although its name specifies "translators", the IFT is concerned with the field of translation more broadly, which also includes interpreters and educators who are preparing the next generation of language professionals. The principal objectives of the IFT include bringing together associations of translators and promoting interaction and cooperation between them; facilitating the creation of such associations in countries where they do not yet exist; promoting research, training, and the harmonization of professional standards in the language industries; and generally upholding the interests of translators around the world. The IFT holds a World Congress once every three years to which all the member associations are invited to send delegates. The IFT also publishes the journal *Babel* and a quarterly newsletter, and it awards various translation prizes. To raise public awareness of translation and its importance in society, the IFT established International Translation Day in 1991, and this is now celebrated every year on 30 September, as part of which the IFT proposes a unifying theme. In recent years this has included "A World Without Barriers", "Translation and Indigenous Languages", "Promoting Cultural Heritage in Changing Times", and "Language Rights: Essential to All Human Rights". Local, regional, and national translators' associations host a variety of events corresponding to the theme in order to celebrate and raise the visibility of translation. This year, on 30 September, keep your eyes open for a celebration near you!

Fun fact! The day selected by the IFT as International Translation Day is the feast day of St. Jerome (30 September), the Bible translator considered to be the patron saint of translators.

Internet and World Wide Web (1980s to present)

Similar to the way that the Gutenberg press made it easier and faster to mass produce and share printed books, which in turn increased the demand for reading material (including translations), the Internet and World Wide Web have contributed greatly to knowledge sharing and an increased demand for translation. Although the early work of developing a network of networks dates back to the 1960s, it was not until the introduction of the World Wide Web by Tim Berners-Lee in the 1980s, and the availability of search engines and browsers to effectively find and display websites in the 1990s, that we fully entered the information age. The digital revolution has even led to the creation of new types of texts (e.g., websites) and services (e.g., streaming services) along with a demand to have them made available in other languages. These ideas will be investigated in more detail in Chapter 7

("Localization") and Chapter 10 ("Audiovisual translation"), among others. In addition, the digital revolution has brought us to the point where we have tools such as free online automatic translators (e.g., Google Translate) at our fingertips and can thus integrate translation into our daily lives more easily than ever before. Machine translation tools will be discussed more thoroughly in Chapter 6.

Concluding remarks

Though far from comprehensive, this very brief look at some key examples from the history of translation has nonetheless served to demonstrate the tremendous contribution that translators and translation have made to society throughout the centuries. The exchange and dissemination of knowledge, the unlocking and preservation of other cultures and traditions, the encouragement of literacy and reading and the development of literatures, the transmission of values, and the upholding of justice and human rights are all ways in which translation has helped to improve our society. Translation is not without its downsides, however. As the examples of La Malinche, the Navajo code talkers, and Weaver's memorandum show, translation can also be employed in situations of conflict, where it can be used to conceal or encode information, or to gain knowledge in order to take advantage of a situation. Indeed, at various points in history, translation has been used for nefarious purposes such as censorship or deliberately distorting a message as it passes from one language to another. As you will learn in Chapter 3, the translation community has developed professional codes of ethics to reduce the chances that translators will deliberately distort information. However, it's important to recognize that, while the overall benefits of translation do appear to outweigh the drawbacks, this practice can nonetheless be undertaken with less than noble goals in mind.

Key points in this chapter

- Translation has been practised around the world for thousands of years and has helped to shape our multilingual society in numerous ways.
- The Bible tells the story of the Tower of Babel, which alleges that all people once spoke a common language, and they collaborated to build a tower to the heavens. God punished the people by scattering them around the globe and giving them different languages, which led to the need for translation.
- One of the earliest translations of the Hebrew Bible is known as the Septuagint because legend says that 70 translators, working independently, produced identical translations, thus proving that the hand of God was at work during the process.
- The Rosetta Stone is a large stone tablet from Ancient Egypt that contains the same text written in three different scripts (hieroglyphs,

Demotic script, and Ancient Greek), which made it possible to decipher the meaning of the previously unknown hieroglyphic text.
- St. Jerome is possibly the most famous translator of all time. Known for translating the Vulgate (a Bible) from Hebrew and Greek into Latin, he is now the patron saint of translators and his feast day (30 September) is used to mark International Translation Day each year.
- Xuanzang was a Buddhist monk from China who travelled widely in India and translated over 1,300 works from Sanskrit into Chinese. Although many of the original Indian Buddhist texts were lost, Xuanzang's translations helped to preserve their content.
- The House of Wisdom functioned as an academy, library, and translation bureau during the Islamic Golden Age (around the 9th to the 13th century), placing translation at the heart of knowledge creation and dissemination.
- In 12th- and 13th-century Spain, successive archbishops promoted translation activities – mostly from Arabic into Latin – in what is known as the School of Toledo.
- Gutenberg's invention of the movable-type printing press made it easier and faster to distribute books. This boosted literacy levels, which in turn increased the demand for reading material, including translated texts. The first text ever to be printed in English was actually a translation from French by William Caxton.
- Biblical scholar William Tyndale translated the Bible into English and printed and distributed copies at a time when it was illegal to possess an English Bible. He was caught, tried, and executed for heresy, but just a few years later the King of England sanctioned the publication of English Bibles, many of which drew heavily on Tyndale's translation.
- La Malinche was an enslaved woman who was used by Spanish conquistador Hernán Cortés as an interpreter to communicate with Indigenous people in Mexico. It is believed by many that, without La Malinche's help, Cortés would not have been able to overthrow the Aztec Empire.
- Anne Sullivan was a teacher and interpreter for Helen Keller, a blind and deaf child who Sullivan initially taught to communicate through finger spelling.
- The Navajo code talkers were a group of Indigenous people who used their traditional language as part of a secret code to transmit communications to and from the battlefield during World War II.
- Following World War II, a group of countries that wanted to promote the peaceful resolution of any future political differences came together to form the United Nations, which has six official languages and uses translation and interpreting to promote multilingual communication.
- The Nuremberg trials that followed World War II incorporated simultaneous interpretation in French, Russian, English, and German as a method of ensuring that the surviving Nazi leaders could obtain a fair yet expeditious trial.

- Inspired by the code-breaking successes in World War II, mathematician Warren Weaver issued a proposal now known as "Weaver's memorandum" that launched research into automatic machine translation.
- The International Federation of Translators, an umbrella organization that brings together professional translator associations from around the world, was established in 1953 to promote interaction and cooperation between the various associations and to generally uphold the interests of all translators.
- The Internet and the World Wide Web ushered in the global information age and led to the creation of new types of texts and services that furthered the demand for translation.
- Translation has undoubtedly shaped our society in many positive ways, such as by acting as a vehicle for knowledge exchange, cultural preservation, and the upholding of justice; however, translation has also brokered interactions that have resulted in negative outcomes.

Topics for discussion

As part of a class discussion, or as a prompt for an online discussion forum, consider the following:

- One metaphor that has long been used to describe translation is that of a "bridge" (e.g., between two languages or cultures), and translators are likewise frequently described as "bridge builders", where bridge building is portrayed as having positive connotations. Given what you have learned in this chapter, do you think that the metaphor of "bridge builders" is a good one to describe translators? Why or why not? Can you think of other metaphors or descriptions that could apply?
- You have seen in this chapter that Holy books and other religious materials have been the most-translated texts throughout history. Why do you think this is the case?
- Which invention – the printing press or the World Wide Web – do you believe has had a greater impact on translation, and why?

Exercise

- **Research other historical examples:** The content in this chapter has only covered a few key examples in translation history. Do a little bit more research into some other important figures and developments in translation history. Some possible examples to explore include Cicero, Kumārajīva, John Wycliffe, Erasmus, Martin Luther, Margaret Tyler, Mathieu da Costa, Madame Anne Dacier, Sacagawea, Yan Fu, Vladimir Nabokov, Jorge Luis Borges, Valentin Berezhkov, Hitoshi Igarashi, Lia Wyler, Edith Grossman, and Erik Camayd-Freixas. Possible groups to investigate include the *benshi* in Japan, who interpreted silent films, or military interpreters involved in conflicts in the Middle East and elsewhere, while the Enigma machines used for coded communications in World War II were devices that inspired early attempts to develop automatic machine translation tools.

Find out more

Baker, Mona, ed. 1998b. *Routledge Encyclopedia of Translation Studies*. 1st ed. London: Routledge.

- The very first edition of this encyclopaedia contains a rich overview of translation traditions in many different regions of the world (from Africa to Turkey). This edition also includes entries on "Babel, tower of" (Robinson 1998) and the *Fédération internationale des traducteurs (FIT)* (Joly 1998), as well as short biographies of "Caxton, William" (Ellis and Oakley-Brown 1998a), "Ibn Ishaq, Ḥunayn" (Baker 1998a), "Malinche" (Bastin 1998), "Raymond, Archbishop of Toledo" (Pym 1998), "St. Jerome" (Kelly 1998), "Tyndale, William" (Ellis and Oakley-Brown 1998b), and "Xuan Zang" (Hung and Pollard 1998).

Delisle, Jean, and Judith Woodsworth, eds. 2012. *Translators through History*. Rev. ed. Amsterdam: John Benjamins.

- The authors explore the pivotal role of translators throughout history, noting their contribution to tasks as diverse as the invention of alphabets, the production of dictionaries, the development of national languages and literatures, the dissemination of knowledge, the spread of religion, and the transmission of cultural values.

Encyclopedia Britannica. Online version: www.britannica.com/.

- This resource contains summaries of many important people and events that have played a role in the history of translation. For example, you can find entries on subjects such as "code talkers", "Internet", "Johannes Gutenberg", "Rosetta Stone", "Septuagint", "United Nations", and "World Wide Web".

3 The translation profession today

In Chapter 2, you considered a number of figures, developments, and events – some dating back thousands of years and others more recent – that have helped to shape translation into the field of practice we have today. In this chapter, we are going to take a closer look at the contemporary translation industry and the language professionals who work in it. As you learned in Chapter 1, the term "translation", when used broadly, can also cover other practices that entail transferring content from one language to another. Therefore, the translation industry, broadly speaking, also includes interpreters (who work with spoken or signed language, see Chapter 11), terminologists and lexicographers (who produce resources such as dictionaries and term banks, see Chapter 4), localizers (who focus on translating digital content such as websites, videogames, software or apps, see Chapter 7), transcreators (who combine translation with creative copywriting to adapt marketing or advertising texts, see Chapter 8), and audiovisual translators (who do subtitling, dubbing, and voiceovers for films or series, see Chapter 10). In other words, the translation industry is very diverse, and it can be difficult to draw firm borders between the different activities within it since many people practise more than one. For instance, a translator may also do some terminology work and some localization work. To keep things relatively straightforward and easy to follow, this chapter will focus mainly on the work of translators, with occasional references to some of the other professions. More specific details about these other professions will then follow in later chapters.

In addition, the focus of this chapter will be firmly on the translation *profession* rather than on more informal translation activities. There are many examples of translation being practised by people who are not professional translators – in fact, you yourself might have done this if you have ever interpreted informally for a family member, subtitled your favourite anime, or used a free online machine translation tool (e.g., Google Translate). Informal translation is a perfectly valid activity that is carried out regularly in the everyday life of millions of people. However, for some people, translation is a profession. Knowing more about the translation profession – even if you don't plan to join it – will help to raise your awareness of the issues involved, the potential risks and mitigation efforts, the strategies that could

DOI: 10.4324/9781003217718-4

pave the way for successful translation, and the situations in which it might be preferable to turn to a professional rather than taking on the task yourself or trusting it to another person without specialized training.

What does it mean to be a professional?

Translation can be a fantastic hobby. Someone who likes playing with words, relishes the thrill of hunting for the *mot juste*, and gains satisfaction from crafting a well-written text might enjoy doing some translation on the side. Sometimes, this might even take the form of a small contract, and the translator will be paid for their work. But just as someone who enjoys baking – and even sells the occasional batch of cupcakes – is not usually considered to be a professional baker, someone who doesn't actually translate for a living is not usually considered to be a professional translator (even if their work is of very good quality).

A professional translator is usually understood to be a person who translates for a living. Hopefully this translator also enjoys translating, but simply loving something doesn't pay the bills, and a professional translator needs to earn money for their work. Doing something for a living, rather than as a hobby or occasional activity, introduces additional factors. For instance, time and cost take on considerable importance, alongside quality. While a hobby translator may be translating as a labour of love and able to take as much time as they need to get things just so, a professional translator needs to deliver the translation by the client's specified deadline and meet a daily quota of words in order to earn a decent living. In the business world, the expression "time is money" applies! Therefore, a good translator is someone who is reliable, works quickly, and has competitive rates, and we'll dig into these concepts a little more in the upcoming sections. A professional translator is also someone who takes professional pride in their work. So in addition to completing work on time, a professional translator needs to deliver a product that meets quality expectations while also deriving job satisfaction from the overall experience. This notion of professional pride will also be discussed more thoroughly later in this chapter. For the moment, though, let's zoom out to consider the industry as a whole.

What is the translation industry?

The translation industry has evolved significantly over time. At various points in history, translation was a personal effort conducted as a labour of love, an activity sponsored mainly by the Church, work that was carried out principally by scholars, and even a sort of cottage industry. Over time, translation has become more widely recognized as a specialized activity that often benefits from having practitioners who have received specialized training. In turn, this has led to the industry becoming increasingly organized. Most recently, as noted in Chapter 2, the development of the Internet and the

The translation profession today 41

World Wide Web dramatically accelerated the digital revolution. As it became increasingly common to create texts in digital form, and easier to share these texts widely, the demand for information, products, and services – in all languages – exploded. As a result, there is currently a huge demand for translation services, and a colossal industry has evolved to meet this demand. As pointed out above, a translator is just one type of professional who works with languages, so you may see references not only to the translation industry but to something broader, such as the language industry or the language services industry, which certainly includes translation as a core component, but which also encompasses interpreting, terminology, localization, transcreation, technical writing, editing, and even language teaching and testing.

Although we can see evidence all around us that the language industry is booming (e.g., multilingual websites, dubbed and subtitled series, localized videogames, food packaging in multiple languages), it's difficult to find precise and reliable figures that show the true scale, scope, and value of this diverse industry. Nevertheless, the following estimates suggest that it is extremely large:

- Focusing specifically on the translation services market, the company Verified Market Research (2021) valued it at $39.37 billion in 2020 and estimates that it will reach $46.22 billion by 2028, while the company Market Research Future (2022) forecasts that the value of the translation services market will reach $47.21 billion by 2030.
- Taking a broader view of the language services industry, Common Sense Advisory (DePalma et al. 2019) determined the value of the language services market to be $49.6 billion, while the *Nimdzi 100 – Language Services Industry Analysis* (Nimdzi 2019) estimated the market size for language services in 2019 to be $53.5 billion and predicts that this will increase to $70 billion by 2023.

In addition to the diversity of the activities that can fall under the umbrella of the language industry, another reason that it can be challenging to put a precise figure on the value of the industry is the variety of formats and job titles under which language professionals work. For instance, some organizations might have what is often referred to as an in-house language services department (although the size of such a department can vary enormously, from just a couple of people to hundreds). An in-house language services department could be housed in a large international organization such as the UN, a government (e.g., the Government of Canada's Translation Bureau), or even a private company that has branches in other countries or does a lot of international business (e.g., IBM, Deloitte). In such a case, a translator would formally be an employee of that organization and provide services to that organization in return for a salary and benefits. Note that these in-house departments often have a name that is broader than just translation, and they may provide services that go beyond translation (e.g., writing, editing, terminology, interpreting, or indeed anything that could be broadly construed as giving linguistic or cultural advice). Similarly, the job title of the person working for the in-house department could be translator, or it could be translator combined with another function (e.g., translator/terminologist, translator/reviser, translator/interpreter). Sometimes a person may carry out translation work but not even have translator as part of their job title (e.g., language advisor, bilingual writer). As an in-house employee, a translator becomes a specialist in the subjects and types of text handled by that organization. For example, a translator working for IBM would develop expertise in high-tech subjects and be able to translate user manuals, while a translator working for the UN would become familiar with administrative texts on subjects such as human rights and humanitarian aid.

> **Fun fact!** Translation is a popular second career. Many translators initially trained in another field (e.g., law, science, business) and later decided to obtain a qualification in translation. With training in both translation and another domain, these translators are well positioned to offer translation services in the field that corresponds to their previous studies and work experience.

In contrast to having an in-house position, other translators may work as freelancers. A freelance translator is essentially self-employed and so runs their own business. Organizations that do not have their own in-house language services department may hire freelance translators on a contract basis to translate a certain document. Some freelance translators build up a base of regular clients and receive steady work from them (e.g., translating quarterly reports or regular updates to user manuals). Other freelancers receive one-off jobs from many different clients. And, of course, many freelancers work for a combination of regular and one-off clients. Some freelance translators maintain their own independent status but still collaborate with other freelancers, such as by revising each other's work, recommending that colleague if they cannot take on a job themselves, or subcontracting part of a large job to them. Although they may have more than one client, most freelancers do develop an area of specialization. As noted in Chapter 1, translation can cover any subject, but no one person can be an expert in everything. It would take far too much time and be far too stressful to have to learn a new subject for every translation job, so most translators choose one or two areas in which to build up subject matter expertise, allowing them to work more quickly and confidently. One of the main advantages of working as a freelancer is flexibility, including flexibility in choosing clients and assignments, flexibility when working out schedules, and flexibility with regard to location (since much of the work can be organized and carried out remotely). However, being self-employed is demanding because, in addition to doing the translation work, a freelancer also needs to hustle to build and maintain relationships with clients, do their own marketing and tech support, purchase their own equipment, and manage the business side of things (e.g., billing, accounting). A freelancer needs to balance their own workload and schedule, and there may be no one to fall back on if they need to take sick leave or want to go on vacation. Freelancers also need to make their own arrangements for health insurance and retirement savings.

Beyond in-house employees and freelancers, there is another noticeable model in the language industry known as a translation agency or language services provider (often abbreviated to LSP). Essentially, a translation agency is an independent organization whose business is to provide translation services. An agency usually employs a group of staff translators but may also subcontract work out to freelancers as necessary. An agency usually has multiple clients and can bid for large contracts that would be beyond the capacity of an individual freelance translator but that can be worked on collaboratively by a team of translators. In addition to translators, whose collective expertise often covers multiple language combinations and subject matter specializations, an agency typically employs other types of personnel, such as project managers, translation technology experts, accountants, revisers, and terminologists. If the organization is a language services provider rather than an agency that focuses solely on translation, then other types of specialists may also be employed (e.g., interpreters, localizers). Unlike freelancers, staff translators may not have a lot of say in the assignments that they work on, and they are usually expected to meet a minimum quota of words to be translated per day. On the other hand, they are able to focus fully on translating, without the need to take on marketing, tech support, or accounting duties. The agency supplies the hardware, software, and resources needed by translators to do their job, and senior or experienced translators are often available to revise and provide feedback on the work of less experienced colleagues. The opportunity to focus on translating and to receive guidance from senior colleagues often makes working for a translation agency an appealing option for new translators, who may stay for a few years to gain some experience before taking the plunge and establishing themselves as freelancers.

How do translators work?

Obviously, each individual translator will develop a process that works best for them, but there are a number of commonalities that are likely to feature in the working process of the majority of translators, regardless of whether they work in-house, as a freelancer, or for an agency. One key element that all translators require to produce a successful translation is a brief from the client or work provider. A translation brief is a package of information and instructions that are relevant to the translation assignment. It can be short or long, depending on the client's needs, and is an essential starting point for any translation project. It includes relatively straightforward details, such as the language combination and direction as well as the deadline. But it should also include information about the purpose of the target text and how it will be used (e.g., published on a website), as well as a description of the intended target audience (e.g., Are they children, teens, or adults? Are they likely to have a certain level of education or a particular type of subject knowledge? Do they live in a particular region?). The client should specify whether a translator is expected to use any particular tools or resources (e.g., glossaries, reference materials) to produce the translation, and access to these should be provided, if necessary. The brief should also indicate if there are any formatting or layout requirements for the translated text.

The brief is key to the success of the project. As you learned in Chapter 1, a translator will be faced with many choices (e.g., choosing between two synonyms, choosing between a formal or informal style, choosing between regional variants). Translators therefore need to become master decision-makers, but the translation brief is the framework or reference document they will use to guide these decisions. Without a brief, the translator is more or less working in the dark, trying to guess which of the multiple options before them might be the best one. Although the translation brief should answer the most obvious questions that a translator might have, it may not answer everything. To ensure the best possible outcome, the translation brief should also include the contact details of someone in the client's office who will be available to respond to any additional questions that might arise during the course of the translation.

Another common feature of almost every translation project is the need to conduct research. As we have already emphasized, translated texts can cover almost every topic imaginable. Even though most translators specialize in just one or two areas, the knowledge in these fields is not static. New concepts are discovered, new tools and techniques are invented, disciplines borrow ideas from other fields, and companies try to set themselves apart from their competitors by offering original products and services or giving a new twist to existing ones. As summarized in Chapter 1, translators first need to comprehend the source text then formulate the target text. This means doing research on the concepts described in the source text in order to ensure that they have been properly understood, then doing research in the target language to determine the most appropriate terms or descriptions to express these ideas in the target text. We'll revisit this idea of research in Chapters 4 and 5 as part of a discussion on words and terms and the concepts that they represent. For the moment, the important thing to realize is that translators need to invest time in doing research in both the source and target language.

In the contemporary translation industry, it is inconceivable to imagine working professionally as a translator without the support of a range of technologies, many of which have been developed or customized specifically

The translation profession today 45

for this industry. We have already mentioned that translators need to meet deadlines and may have to meet daily quotas. Even if they don't have a specific quota to meet, the nature of the industry is such that a translator who works quickly can translate a greater volume of text and therefore earn more money. For most translators, the key to increasing productivity is making effective use of technology. Some basic tools used by translators are likely already familiar to you. These include text editors and word processors (e.g., Microsoft Word, Open Office Writer, WordPad, or Google Docs), which are commonly used to prepare a source text or deliver the final target text. However, in order to get from the source text to the target text, a translator may employ more sophisticated tools. One of the most frequently used translation tools is known as a translation memory, and it has become a cornerstone of the translator's toolkit.

Essentially, a translation memory tool works on the principal of recycling. A translator (or a group of translators) can store previously translated texts – alongside their corresponding source texts – in a database. The database stores the files in a way that links each source-text sentence to its equivalent target-text sentence. The database containing these linked pairs of sentences can then be searched by the translation memory tool. For example, when a translator has a new source text to translate, they can instruct the translation memory tool to search in the database for any sentences that are exactly the same as, or that closely resemble, sentences contained in the new source text. If the tool finds a match, then it displays this previous sentence, along with its linked translation, for the translator to consult (see Figure 3.1). If the translator thinks that the previous translation can be reused as part of the new project, then the tool can paste that sentence directly into the new target text. The translator can then edit the translation as necessary and move on to the next sentence, where the searching process can be repeated.

Translation memory tools are not perfect, however. For one thing, they are only likely to produce results if the database is very large, so a translation memory containing the previous work of a group of translators will be more effective than if it contained the work of just one. What's more,

New source-text sentence that needs to be translated	The filename is not a valid name.	Because the sentence in the new source text is exactly the same as the one stored in the database, the database entry would be retrieved as an **exact match**, which could then be pasted into the new translation.
Previously translated source-text sentence and its corresponding translation, which are stored as a linked pair in the translation memory database	EN: The filename is not a valid name. FR: Le nom de fichier n'est pas valide.	

Figure 3.1 An example of an exact match retrieved from a translation memory database.

New source-text sentence that needs to be translated	The specified file is not valid.	Because the sentence in the new source text is not exactly the same as the one stored in the database, the database entry would be retrieved as a **fuzzy match**, which the translator could then edit.
Previously translated source-text sentence and its corresponding translation, which are stored as a linked pair in the translation memory database	EN: The specified file is not a valid file. FR: Le fichier spécifié n'est pas un fichier valide.	

Figure 3.2 An example of a fuzzy match retrieved from a translation memory database.

apart from some special cases (e.g., translating a new version of an existing text, such as an updated user manual), there are not likely to be many exact matches. So most of the matches will be for similar sentences (known as fuzzy matches) rather than identical ones (known as exact matches) (see Figure 3.2). The usefulness of a fuzzy match will therefore depend on the degree of fuzziness. A match that has 99% similarity will likely be more useful than a match that has 50% similarity. If the match threshold is set too high, then useful information might not be retrieved from the database, but if it is set too low, then the translator may waste time examining, eliminating, or editing fuzzy matches that are not very helpful. Texts that are formulaic and repetitive (e.g., user manuals) tend to generate more matches than texts that are creative, where original turns of phrase are prized (e.g., advertising or marketing texts). Still, even with their limitations, translation memory tools have enabled many translators to work more quickly and to increase their productivity. Translation memory tools can also work in conjunction with other tools such as terminology management systems, which make it possible to search for matches at the level of individual terms rather than entire sentences.

Another tool that can be used either independently or in conjunction with a translation memory is automatic machine translation. Unlike a translation memory tool, which searches a database of translations done by a professional translator, a machine translation tool proposes its own translation. Google Translate is probably the best-known automatic machine translation tool available today, but other similar tools include Microsoft Bing Translator, DeepL Translator, Baidu Translate, Yandex.Translate, Systran, and Naver Papago. Chapter 6 is devoted entirely to automatic machine translation, so we'll take a much deeper dive into this subject there. For now, it is worth pointing out that computers cannot think and are not capable of understanding language or culture. As you'll learn in Chapter 6, these tools essentially work by trying to imitate other examples, but they do not always get it right. Sometimes, machine translation tools produce a text that sounds awkward and is difficult to read and understand, but other times they produce a text that may sound plausible but actually means something quite different to the message in the source text. Therefore, when professional translators work with automatic machine translation tools, they never trust the draft translation produced by the computer. Rather, they always double-check the content of that draft, and they almost always make changes to ensure that any errors are corrected and any inelegant language smoothed out. This process of validating and improving a draft translation originally produced by an automatic machine translation tool is known as *post-editing*, and it is becoming an increasingly common practice in the translation industry. Clearly, automatic machine translation tools are able to produce a first draft very quickly, giving professional translators a head start and the potential to increase their productivity. Another important point to recognize is that professional translators do not typically use the free online versions of machine translation tools that are available to regular users. Most of the developers of machine translation tools have a free version – which is the version that you have probably tried – and a paid version, which is usually accessed via a subscription. These paid versions are more secure (e.g., a client's confidential texts are not shared on the public Internet), and they can be customized in various ways to improve the quality. For example, they can be customized to work in specialized subject fields, to work for specific regional variants of a language (e.g., British English or Canadian French), or to use a client's preferred terminology or house style. Even though these customized versions offer a better-quality draft, a professional translator will still be sure to check and post-edit the translated version as necessary. As you will learn in Chapter 6, the free online versions of machine translation tools will probably produce a translation that is good enough if you just want to get the gist or overall meaning of a text (e.g., when translating an email from a friend), but it is risky to trust unedited machine translations in situations where the stakes are higher (e.g., when translating post-surgical care instructions from your doctor).

Translators who work in specialized areas of translation such as localization (i.e., the adaptation of websites, videogames, software, or apps, see Chapter 7) and audiovisual translation (i.e., the subtitling or dubbing of films or series, see Chapter 10) will also use additional specialized tools. For example, a localization tool will allow a translator to extract the translatable text from the surrounding computer code and reinsert the translated version back into the correct place. Meanwhile, a tool specialized for audiovisual translation will enable the translator to enter a subtitle's start and end times, or to specify the position of the subtitle (e.g., at the top or bottom of the screen).

A typical final step for all translators, regardless of their language combination, area of specialization, or tool selection, is to revise and proofread the translated text. Just as most of us don't usually submit the first draft of our writing (e.g., an essay or report) to our instructor or boss, translators don't submit their first draft either. For many translators, revision is an iterative process, meaning that they may revise an initial draft at several points throughout the translation process, but it is certainly essential for translators to do a final revision before sending the text to the client. This revision should be done with reference to the translation brief that was provided by the client at the beginning of the project to be sure that all the requirements and expectations have been taken into account in the final target text. Attention to detail is important, and translators often like to set the draft translation aside for a period of time then come back to it and revise it with fresh eyes, or work with a colleague to revise each other's texts.

What about pay and job satisfaction?

We've established that a professional translator is someone who earns their living by translating. As you might imagine, the typical earnings for a translator vary considerably from one region to the next, taking into account things such as cost of living, and supply and demand. An experienced translator will likely earn more than one who is just starting out, and a translator who has a highly specialized area of expertise (e.g., nuclear physics) or who works with less common language pairs (e.g., Danish to Greek) may be able to command a higher wage than someone who works with widely used languages (e.g., English to French) or in a common field (e.g., governmental or administrative texts).

In previous sections you've learned that there are different models of employment (i.e., in-house, freelance, or agency), which offer different advantages and drawbacks. These different models of employment also have different pay structures. For example, an in-house translator is likely to be a salaried employee, as is a translator who works for a translation agency or language services provider. In both these cases, there may be an expectation that the translator will translate a certain quota of words per day. In contrast, when agencies or freelancers bid on a translation contract, it is very common for the value of this contract to be calculated based on a rate per word – that is, a translator (or agency) receives a certain amount per word translated (which, again, will differ from one region to the next). This is often based on the source-text word count because the number of words is already known at the beginning of the job, so the price for the contract can be fixed in advance. But depending on the client and translator in question, the contract may specify that the price will correspond to the word count in the target text. As you know, languages use different words and grammatical constructions to express the same idea. Because translation is not a word-for-word process, the length of the target text will inevitably be either shorter or longer than the length of the source text. Whether it is shorter or longer will depend on the language pair and translation direction. For instance, if a source text is translated from English into French, the target text is likely to be longer, but if that same source text is translated from English into Korean, the target text is likely to be shorter.

You've also learned that the use of technology is now more or less essential to enable translators to keep up with the demand for translation, which has itself been largely driven by the introduction of other technologies (e.g., the Internet). This technologization of the translation profession has had a number of impacts, including on both pay and job satisfaction. A key issue is that some of the tools, including translation memories and automatic machine translation, can give a client or employer the impression that translation is an easy task: translators need only press a few buttons or make a few clicks and the job will be done. But as you're beginning to learn, translation is much more complicated than simply searching for a match in a database or pressing a "Translate" button. No existing translation tools are intelligent. They can look for and find patterns very quickly, but they do not actually understand language, and they certainly have no knowledge of culture or subject fields. In situations that require accurate and well-constructed texts, tools alone are not usually enough. Certainly these tools can help translators by enabling them to work more quickly and mechanizing some routine tasks (e.g., dictionary look-ups). However, translators bring a significant added value to the process because they can use their extensive linguistic, subject field, and cultural knowledge to verify whether the computer's proposals are accurate and appropriate for the needs of the target audience, and if they are not, then translators can make the necessary corrections and improvements.

Although tools can speed up the translation process, they have not been universally well-received by translators. For one thing, clients or employers – who don't usually understand all the complexities of translation – think that the tools make the job very easy, so they often want to pay less for the translation. Before tools such as translation memories and automatic machine translation became heavily used in the industry, a translator often had just one basic word rate. For instance, imagine that this rate is 15 cents per word. If the price per word is calculated using the word count in the source text, then a translator will be paid a total of $150 for translating a one-thousand-word text. However, following the introduction of translation memories and machine translation tools, clients began to argue that the rate per word should be lower because the tools were doing some of the work for the translator (e.g., by helping to identify sentences that could be reused or producing a first draft). However, clients do not always consider the fact that a translator still needs to critically evaluate the suggestions made by the tool, as well as to edit these as required and then read over and further edit the text as a whole to ensure that all of the individual pieces suggested by the tools actually work well together. Remember that a sentence is not just a string of words, and a text is not just a string of sentences. A text needs to be coherent, and it takes a translator, not a computer, to ensure that this is the case.

Now that technology has effectively lowered the going rate per word for translation, translators have become even more dependent on these tools because now, in order to earn the same income, they need to translate a higher volume of words. For instance, a translator who uses tools may now earn only 10 cents per word rather than the 15 cents they used to earn before these tools were introduced, meaning that they now need to translate 1500 words of text to earn $150. So in order to translate a higher number of words, the translator either needs to extend the length of their workday or work more quickly. Translators are therefore making increasing use of these translation tools to help them to improve their productivity. It is also becoming more common to see translators charging an hourly rate, or a flat rate for a project, as a means of drawing attention to the often-overlooked aspects of their work (e.g., evaluating the computer's proposals, revising the text for overall coherence), thereby ensuring that they earn a fair wage.

Clients are not the only ones who may be tempted to take advantage of automatic machine translation to put more money in their pockets. Some people who are not trained in translation may nonetheless advertise themselves as a translator and do little more than feed the source text into a free online machine translation system like Google Translate and then return the machine-translated text to the client with few or no corrections. What's more, these people often undercut the prices charged by professional translators, thus putting additional downward pressure on translation rates. In addition, these individuals tarnish the reputation of translators as a whole. This type of behaviour has been boosted by the so-called gig economy, along with the prevalence of websites such as Fiverr, Guru, or Upwork that advertise freelance services.

In addition to impacting pay, translation technologies can impact translators' job satisfaction in other ways. For instance, there is a difference between translating a text from scratch and post-editing proposals that have been suggested by a translation memory system or an automatic machine translation tool. Some translators find it both constraining and dissatisfying to post-edit texts because they have to work around the suggestions offered by the tool rather than having the freedom to come up with their own solutions. Yet, if they opt to translate from scratch or post-edit the suggestions too heavily, then they will most likely have a lower productivity and, in turn, a lower income. Translators may therefore experience tension as they try to balance the sometimes competing elements of job satisfaction and a fair wage.

Linked to job satisfaction is the issue of professional pride. Not only do some translators feel constrained by the text generated by their tools, but they also feel that the resulting computer-assisted translation is of an inferior quality compared to what they might have produced without the tools' input. Obviously a professional translator would not hand over a text to a client that contained outright errors, but the pressure to meet quotas or deadlines, combined with the need to earn a living wage by post-editing rather than translating from scratch, can result in translated texts that are less polished or elegant than what the translator would ideally like to submit. Faced with the choice of investing more time (and thus lowering their income) or submitting a translation that is acceptable rather than exceptional, a translator may need to opt for the latter, but it may not sit well with their professional pride, thus further detracting from their job satisfaction.

What are professional associations?

In Chapter 2, one of the important events in translation history was the establishment of the International Federation of Translators (IFT). The IFT is actually an umbrella organization whose members are other translators associations, to which individual translators may belong, from different countries and regions around the world. Some very large and well-known translators associations include the American Translators Association and the Institute of Translation and Interpreting in the United Kingdom. Note that even though the official name of many such associations specifies "translator" or "translation", this is often used in a broad way, meaning that these same associations often welcome other language professionals too, such as interpreters or terminologists. In addition, there is a separate international association specifically dedicated to conference interpreters: the International Association for Conference Interpreters, known more commonly by its French acronym AIIC. But what exactly is a professional association?

> **Fun fact!** Many translators associations welcome student members (for little or no cost) and contribute to mentoring and preparing this next generation for a successful career.

Essentially, a translators association is an organization that translators can join to be part of a professional community. A professional association is not exactly the same as a trade union, although they can share some characteristics. The specific membership requirements and services offered differ from one association to the next, but some of the more common features of a translators association include the following.

- **Offering an official certification status:** Some, though not all, professional associations administer and confer a professional certification on members able to demonstrate that they meet a certain quality standard (e.g., by passing a national translation exam, or by submitting a dossier of evidence that is evaluated by certified members). In some regions, this certified translator status (or, in some regions, sworn translator status) will help the translator to obtain work since it offers recognition of the translator's ability. Moreover, there are some types of documents (e.g., official documents such as birth certificates or university transcripts) that must be translated by a certified or sworn translator in order to be recognized as an official translation.

- **Promoting the recognition of professional translators:** The promotion of professional translators is an important responsibility of a professional association. This includes raising awareness of the profession and what it entails, as well as the benefits to be gained by entrusting work to a professional rather than to a machine translation tool or an untrained gig worker. The association gives its members a collective voice to negotiate working conditions (e.g., typical rates of pay in a region), and it allows its members to collectively showcase their professional pride.
- **Establishing standards and codes of ethics:** A key role played by many translators associations is the development of a code of ethics and professional practice to which its members are expected to adhere. For instance, a code of ethics could include an expectation to represent qualifications honestly (e.g., not accepting work in a language pair or subject field in which you are not competent), a commitment not to knowingly distort the meaning of a source text, or an agreement to keep client texts confidential. Such codes of ethics also offer a measure of protection to the public because a translator who violates the code of ethics can be sanctioned by the association.
- **Providing continuing education and professional development opportunities:** Translation is a career that requires lifelong learning, and professional associations can facilitate this by offering continuing education and professional development opportunities, such as workshops on new tools, refresher courses on tricky grammatical or stylistic issues, or even major conferences. Some associations even offer mentoring opportunities, where newcomers to the field can benefit from the guidance of more experienced members.
- **Creating a professional network:** Although translators associations welcome members who are in-house or agency translators, they provide a particularly valuable service to freelancers, who do not necessarily have any immediate colleagues with whom they can brainstorm solutions, debrief after a tricky assignment, pass along a referral, or even engage in conversation around the metaphorical water cooler. Translators associations help translators who are scattered throughout a region to stay in touch via newsletters, online discussion forums, social gatherings, and professional events.
- **Offering group benefits or discounts:** Since many translators work as freelancers, they do not receive employee benefits. Some translators associations therefore negotiate better rates for things such as group life insurance or professional liability insurance for their members.

Members may also benefit from other types of preferred rates (e.g., for trade magazines, hotels, and car rentals).

What kind of training do professional translators need?

Now that you know more about what it's like to work as a professional translator, you might be wondering what kind of training is needed to prepare for this career. Translator training is typically offered at either the bachelor's or master's level in most countries around the world. One widely recognized framework that is used as a reference for designing curricula for translator training programs is the *European Master's in Translation Competence Framework 2022* (EMT Board 2022), the influence of which extends beyond the European context. In programs adhering to this framework, students receive instruction and build experience in five main areas of competence:

- **Language and culture:** To succeed as translators, students must develop both general and language-specific linguistic, sociolinguistic, cultural, and transcultural knowledge and skills. Typically, students already have an advanced knowledge of at least two languages before being admitted to a translation program. Within the program, students will refine this knowledge, but it is not common for translation programs to offer beginner-level language training. Many translator training programs also include an opportunity to spend a semester or a year living and studying in another country to allow students to immerse themselves in their chosen language and culture.
- **Translation:** Not surprisingly, translation practice courses make up a large component of any translator training program. Students learn to conduct pre-translation tasks, such as source-text analysis, subject field research, and resource evaluation. They acquire theoretical knowledge and develop strategies and techniques for translating both general and specialized material in various fields and language combinations. They learn to analyze and explain their choices, and to revise and apply quality control measures to their own work and that of others.
- **Technology:** The earlier sections of this chapter emphasized the growing place of technology within the field of translation, and students need to acquire the knowledge and skills necessary to integrate present and future technologies into the translation workflow. This includes learning how to evaluate, select, install, use, and maintain tools and their associated resources (e.g., translation memory databases).
- **Personal and interpersonal skills:** This category, sometimes referred to as "soft skills", includes learning how to plan in order to manage time, workload, and stress. Other activities may include learning to work as

part of a larger team, learning to use social media in a responsible way for professional purposes, understanding workplace ergonomics, and understanding the importance of self-evaluation and lifelong learning, including where to find opportunities for updating skills.
- **Service provision:** Skills learned in this area include professional networking, working with clients (including negotiating working conditions), budgeting and project management, and complying with professional standards and codes of ethics. Many translator training programs incorporate a work-integrated learning opportunity (e.g., a work term, internship, or co-operative education placement) that allows students to gain hands-on experience with these aspects of translation service provision.

Although students might receive a basic introduction to some of the more specialized types of translation as part of their initial education program, they may go on to do more advanced training as part of a university program that specializes in an area such as localization (Chapter 7), audiovisual translation (Chapter 10), or conference or dialogue interpreting (Chapter 11). In addition, as noted above, professional translators associations may offer some targeted training opportunities (e.g., a workshop on a newly released tool) as part of their continuing education programming.

Concluding remarks

This chapter has given you something of a behind-the-scenes look at the vibrant translation industry, shining a light on what it means to be a professional who translates for a living rather than someone who simply enjoys playing with words. Translation has evolved considerably over the years, with technology acting as a driving force behind changes in the profession in recent times, affecting not only translation processes and products but also elements such as pay and job satisfaction. To help raise the profile of the profession and provide a collective voice for translators working in the language industry, professional associations have emerged to help set and manage the expectations of both translators and clients. Anyone wishing to work as a professional translator can follow university-level training, and, as a qualified translator, they will be able to bring significant added value to the table by applying their extensive linguistic, cultural, and subject matter expertise in ways that computers currently cannot.

Key points in this chapter

- A professional translator is one who translates for a living.
- Translating for a living, as compared to translating as a hobby, introduces some practical factors (e.g., time, price, tools) that must be taken into consideration.

The translation profession today

- The translation industry is a global business worth billions of dollars.
- Translators can work under different employment models, such as in-house as part of an organization's language services department, for a translation agency that provides language services, or as an independent freelancer.
- To set a translation project up for success, clients provide a detailed translation brief, which is a set of instructions or information about the target audience that can help a translator to make decisions that will best meet the needs of the audience.
- Translators tend to develop one or two subject field specializations, but they still need to do research to ensure that they understand the concepts and use appropriate terms.
- Translators use some common tools (e.g., word processors) but also more specialized tools.
- One very widely used tool is a translation memory system, which essentially allows translators to recycle sentences or parts of sentences from previous translations.
- Increasingly, translators also use automatic machine translation tools (e.g., Google Translate), but not the free online versions. Instead, they use the paid versions, which can be customized and are more secure, and they carefully check and post-edit the draft translation produced.
- Additional specialized tools are used by translators who work in particularly specialized areas (e.g., localization or audiovisual translation).
- Professional translators never submit a first draft but always revise and proofread the target text.
- The going rate for translation varies from one region to the next but may be influenced by the language combination or direction, the degree of specialization of the subject matter, and the translator's experience level.
- It is very common for freelance translators to be paid by the word, but translation tools are impacting on rates. For example, clients often want to pay less if a translator is using a tool. Often, there is a misperception that the tool is doing all the hard work and the translator is just pressing buttons, but the tools are not intelligent. Translators add significant value by verifying (and, if need be, correcting) the content and improving the overall coherence of the text.
- Untrained translators may also misuse machine translation and take advantage of gig work sites to sell unedited machine translation drafts to unsuspecting customers.
- To combat the lower rates, translators must increase their productivity.
- Technology can also impact translators' job satisfaction because translators may feel constrained by having to use the suggestions generated by translation memory or machine translation tools.

- Professional associations for translators serve several important functions, such as conferring certification status, promoting the profession, establishing codes of ethics, providing continuing education, creating a professional network, and offering group benefits or discounts.
- To prepare for a career in translation, students need to acquire competences in numerous areas through a university-level training program. Areas of competence include language and culture, translation, technology, personal and interpersonal skills, and service provision.

Topics for discussion

As part of a class discussion, or as a prompt for an online discussion forum, consider the following:

- Given the choice of translating a text yourself or editing a draft produced by an automatic machine translation system (e.g., Google Translate), which would you prefer, and why?
- In many regions, translation is now a semi-regulated profession thanks to the efforts of translators associations, which set quality standards and develop codes of ethics and professional practice for their members. Do you think that professional associations should continue working in this direction to bring more regulation to the profession? Or do you think that things have already gone too far and there are too many restrictions in place? Or perhaps you think that things are ideal the way they are currently (i.e., semi-regulated)? Explain your reasoning.
- Do you think that, as a manifestation of professional pride, translators should always strive to deliver the best possible translation, even if this means working extra or getting paid less? Explain your line of thinking.
- Do you think that free online automatic machine translation tools should be banned given the potential for these tools to be misused? Why or why not?

Exercises

- **Research a translators association:** Consult the list of member associations that belong to the International Federation of Translators (www.fit-ift.org/members-directory/).
  - Find an association in your region and explore its website, looking at the expectations held by this association for its members, as well as the benefits that it offers.

- Select an association from another region and compare what you find there with what you found for the association in your region. What are the similarities and differences?
- **Investigate a gig work site:** Visit a gig work site such as Fiverr (www.fiverr.com/) or Guru (www.guru.com/) and click on the tab for "Writing & Translation". Browse through the offers posted by people willing to do translation work. Based on what you have already learned about translation, analyze the various offers. Consider things such as language combination(s) and direction(s), subject matter, volume, timeframe, and price. Are there offers that look trustworthy? Do some seem a little suspect? Would you hire anyone from this site if you needed to have a text translated? Why or why not?
- **Try speed translation:** To get an idea of what it's like to translate under time pressure, find a short article or extract of approximately 300 words on a topic that interests you. As this will be the source text, you might want to find a text that is written in your less dominant language. Divide the text into thirds (i.e., three sections of approximately 100 words each).
  - Give yourself 3 minutes to translate the first 100-word section.
  - Next, give yourself just 2 minutes to translate the second section.
  - Finally, give yourself only one minute to translate the last section.
  - Compare your experiences translating under increasing pressure. Did your level of confidence and comfort diminish, improve, or remain unchanged? Did you use different strategies as the time available for translation became reduced? Looking at the translation you produced for each section, do you believe that the quality is comparable in each case or has it changed?

Find out more

Pattison, Ann, and Stella Craigie. 2022. *Translating Change: Enhanced Practical Skills for Translators*. London: Routledge.

- This book explores the impact of recent changes in society, culture, and language on the process and products of translation and interpreting. Topics addressed include technological change, economic uncertainty, and political developments, among others.

Robinson, Douglas. 2020. *Becoming a Translator: An Introduction to the Theory and Practice of Translation*. 4th ed. London: Routledge.

- This book explains how the translation market works and helps novice translators learn to navigate the profession, acquire the necessary social and transactional skills, and deal with potential challenges (e.g., technologies, stress).

EMT Board and Competence Task-Force. 2022. *European Master's in Translation Competence Framework 2022*. https://ec.europa.eu/info/sites/default/files/about_the_european_commission/service_standards_and_principles/documents/emt_competence_fwk_2022_en.pdf.

- This framework document outlines the standards for translator training and translator competence in the European Union (EU), but it is widely referenced beyond the EU in both academic contexts and the language industry.

4 Words, terms, and lexical resources

At first glance, it would be very easy to assume that translators translate words. After all, what is a text if not a series of words? Well, think back on some of the texts that you have written – maybe for one of your courses or your job. Did you just slap a bunch of random words down on a piece of paper and hand it to your instructor or boss? Probably not! Instead, you carefully chose the words that conveyed your *ideas*. At the end of the day, all texts are *about* something. Writers are usually trying to share their ideas with readers, even if the text in question is a sticky note with a message for your roommate (e.g., "We are out of milk!"). As you learned in Chapter 1, a translator's job is to understand and extract those underlying ideas or concepts from the source text and then find a way to effectively and accurately express those same ideas or concepts in the target language. So translators do not translate words; rather, they translate the ideas and concepts that are expressed or represented by words. And, of course, in order to convey those ideas in the target text, they need to repackage them appropriately, and the packaging consists of target-language words. Therefore, even though they are translating ideas, translators do need to know a lot about words. In particular, they need to learn how to identify the words that will make the most appropriate package for their audience.

Let's make an analogy to an activity in our everyday life. Imagine you have a gift to wrap. The gift is in the form of a gift card to a well-known online store with a diverse range of products. If you're giving this gift to your five-year-old niece as a birthday present, maybe you would choose pink wrapping paper decorated with rainbows and unicorns because these are currently some of her favourite things. But if the gift card is a Christmas present for your grandfather, would you make the same choice? Maybe you'd go with a tasteful green gift bag topped with red tissue paper. And if the gift is to thank your teenage neighbour for shovelling the snow from your driveway, perhaps a plain white envelope would do the trick (or, better yet, electronic delivery!). In all cases, the gift is the same, but different recipients appreciate thoughtfully selected packaging that meets their tastes. That's essentially what translators need to do. They need to figure out the very best way to package the gift – the gift of the author's ideas – for the intended

DOI: 10.4324/9781003217718-5

audience. At each stage, translators are faced with many different choices (e.g., paper wrapping or gift bag? Ribbon or bow? Glittery or plain?), and they have decisions to make. And while the essence of translating isn't really about translating words, we can't deny that words are essential to the process, so it definitely pays for a translator to be able to know how to identify the right ones and then use them effectively! In this chapter, we're going to learn more about two broad categories of lexical items: *words*, which are part of language for general purposes, and *terms*, which are part of language

	Language for general purposes (LGP)	*Language for special purposes (LSP)*
Area of interest	Everyday language	Language used by subject experts in specialized fields of knowledge
Lexical items of interest	Words	Terms
Products	Dictionaries	Glossaries (covering a single subject field) and term banks (covering multiple subject fields)
Languages covered	May be monolingual or bilingual	Often multilingual
Orientation	Word-based (i.e., in a dictionary entry, there is only one headword, but there may be multiple definitions)	Concept-based (i.e., in a term bank record, there will be only one definition because each record deals with only one specialized concept, but there may be multiple terms (in more than one language) that designate this concept)
Approach	Mainly descriptive (i.e., recording words as they are used without commenting on whether or not they should be used)	Often prescriptive (i.e., recommending which terms are preferred and which should be avoided)
Associated language profession	Lexicography (a subfield of linguistics)	Terminology (often viewed as a subfield of translation)
Associated language professional	Lexicographer (who may have received initial training in linguistics)	Terminologist (who often receives initial training in translation)

Figure 4.1 Some of the differences between lexical resources in language for general purposes and language for special purposes.

Words, terms, and lexical resources 61

for special purposes. Let's begin by taking a high-level look at some of the differences between these two categories before exploring these ideas more deeply in the upcoming sections (see Figure 4.1).

What is the difference between language for general purposes and language for special purposes?

Language for general purposes (LGP) refers to the everyday language that we use to describe ordinary things or to discuss everyday situations. If you are a native speaker of a given language, you will be able to converse easily with other speakers of that same language using LGP. The collection of words that make up LGP can be found in a type of lexical resource called a *dictionary*. For example, a well-known dictionary for the English language is the *Oxford English Dictionary*, while *Le Grand Robert* is a widely recognized dictionary for French, and Duden's *Vollständiges Orthographisches Wörterbuch der deutschen Sprache* is undoubtedly familiar to German speakers.

Although we often speak about "the" dictionary, there are many competing products that come from different publishers (e.g., for English, there are dictionaries from publishers such as Cambridge, Oxford, Macmillan, Merriam-Webster, and more). In addition, different kinds of dictionaries have been developed for different purposes and user groups. For instance, some dictionaries focus on the words used in a particular region, such as the *New Zealand Oxford Dictionary* or the *Dictionnaire du français acadien*. Respecting the linguistic preferences of target audiences in different regions is particularly important in localization, which will be explored in more detail in Chapter 7. Meanwhile, other dictionaries, such as the *Cambridge Advanced Learner's Dictionary* or *Langenscheidt Großwörterbuch Deutsch als Fremdsprache*, support people who are learning a foreign language by focusing on the most frequently used words in that language and offering clear explanations of their most common meanings. Bilingual or multilingual dictionaries also exist and can be helpful for tasks such as translation (e.g., *Le Robert et Collins Dictionnaire Français-Anglais* or the *Langenscheidt Großes Schulwörterbuch Lateinisch-Deutsch*). Finally, there are a few dictionaries that focus on the language used in a particular subject field, such as the *Cambridge Business English Dictionary* or the *Merriam-Webster Medical Dictionary*. However, when we talk about the language that is specific to a particular domain of knowledge, then we begin to cross into the realm of language for special purposes (LSP). As indicated in Chapter 3, the majority of translators do specialize in one or two subject fields, so they need to work with the specialized language of that field.

Imagine you are at a dentist's office and you overhear a dentist saying, "I need a referral to an orthodontist for a patient who has a class 3 malocclusion". Would you truly understand what the dentist was saying? You would very likely understand some of the words, such as "referral" and "patient", because these words are part of our everyday language. You might even get the gist of "orthodontist" as being a more specialized type of dentist, even if you don't know exactly what an orthodontist does. But what about "class 3 malocclusion"? This lexical item does not belong to LGP. Instead, it belongs to the specialized vocabulary of the field of dentistry. When a lexical item is part of an LSP, it is referred to as a *term*, rather than a *word*. More precisely, we could say that terms are used to designate concepts in a specialized field of knowledge. A specialized field of knowledge could be associated with a profession (e.g., dentistry, law, engineering, chemistry), but it could also be associated with a sport, hobby, or other activity since these also have specialized concepts. For instance, the sport of golf has terms for its specialized equipment (e.g., *driver*, *putter*, *wedge*, *tee*), while the hobby of knitting has terms for different types of stitches (e.g., *garter*, *rib*, *seed*, *basketweave*). If you are enthusiastic about any subject – whether for work or leisure – and you want to discuss it with other enthusiasts, then you will need to learn the LSP of that field. In fact, you have recently had some experience in this regard when you learned some of the terms that are relevant to the field of translation, such as *source language, target text*, and *equivalence*, back in Chapter 1.

So in general, words belong to LGP, which covers ideas that are familiar to most people because they are part of our everyday lives. In contrast, terms belong to LSP, which deals with concepts that are familiar only to a certain portion of the population with a particular interest in that subject. Of course, the distinction between words and terms is not always clear cut because the border between LGP and LSP is fuzzy. For example, sometimes it might be possible to describe the same concept using both a word and a term, creating a sort of pseudo-synonymy. This is the case for when a person's lower jaw juts forward and their bottom teeth overlap their top teeth: the LSP term for this concept is *class 3 malocclusion*, while the general language word for it is *underbite*. Even though these two lexical items both refer to the same concept, a dentist will have a much more detailed understanding of the situation than an average person. For instance, the dentist will be able to understand what caused it, how serious it is, how to treat it, etc. In contrast, an average person probably won't know these things. Because a specialist's knowledge goes deeper, they often need terms that allow them to discuss the situation with other experts in a more nuanced and detailed way. So in the case of dentistry, there are many types of malocclusions (e.g., *class 1 malocclusion, class 3 division 1 malocclusion, pseudo class 3 malocclusion*), and malocclusions are related to other specialized concepts, such as *bruxism* (which may cause malocclusion) and *temporomandibular joint disorders* (which may result from malocclusion). A translator who encounters the concept of a lower jaw jutting forward in a source text must choose whether to use the word *underbite* or the term *class 3 malocclusion* in the target text. As discussed in Chapter 3, information from the translation brief, such as the intended target audience (i.e., patients or dentists), will help a translator to make this decision.

Words, terms, and lexical resources 63

Confusion between LGP and LSP can also be caused when the same string of characters can represent either a word or a term. This linguistic phenomenon, where a lexical item can have more than one meaning, is known as polysemy. For instance, the noun *work* is part of our general language, where it can refer to a creative product, such as a book, song, or painting (e.g., a work of art). However, in the field of physics, *work* is a term with a different and very specialized definition (i.e., the energy transferred to or from an object via the application of force along a displacement). It is only by considering a polysemous lexical item such as *work* in the larger context of a sentence or text that we can establish whether it is being used as a word or a term and determine its intended meaning. It is crucial for a translator to understand the intended meaning in the source text because the target-language equivalent might differ depending on the meaning. For instance, *work* in the sense of "work of art" would be translated as *oeuvre* in French, while *work* in the field of physics would be translated as *travail*.

Another reason why it is not always possible to distinguish clearly where LGP stops and LSP begins is that knowledge is not static. Sometimes, knowledge first emerges within a specialized field, but then some of the concepts may migrate into our general knowledge, at least to some degree, creating a grey area between LGP and LSP. This is the case for the term *orthodontist*, for example, which many people understand to some degree, although they may not understand all the nuances. The Covid-19 pandemic provided some other good examples of this phenomenon. Prior to the pandemic, terms such as *mRNA vaccine* and *R number* were not part of most people's general knowledge, but during the pandemic the public health officers in many regions began to use and explain these terms to the wider public. The process whereby terms move from a specialized field to our general knowledge is known as *de-terminologization*. It is in these grey areas that we sometimes see dictionaries that are semi-specialized. For example, the *Merriam-Webster Medical Dictionary* presents terms from the field of health, but the target audience is not doctors, nurses, or other healthcare providers. Rather, the target audience consists of average people, and the goal of the dictionary is to help them become informed healthcare consumers. Therefore, the concepts are explained in a way that is accessible and less detailed than would be the case in a dictionary aimed at medical professionals. In contrast, lexical resources that are aimed at subject field experts are most typically referred to as *glossaries* (rather than dictionaries). A glossary tends to focus on one particular subject field, while an online database that covers multiple subject fields is usually known as a **term bank**. Like dictionaries, glossaries can be either monolingual or bilingual, while the majority of term banks are multilingual. As you will learn in the upcoming sections, multilingual term banks are a particularly valuable resource for translators.

Although the type of lexical item – that is, word or term – is one of the main features that distinguishes LGP from LSP, there may also be grammatical or stylistic differences, and this idea will be picked up again in Chapter 5.

64 *Words, terms, and lexical resources*

For now, let's keep our focus on words and terms and the lexical resources in which they appear.

What's in a dictionary?

As noted above, the collection of everyday words for a given language can normally be found in a type of lexical resource called a dictionary. The practice of compiling dictionaries is known as *lexicography*, and the people who make official and reputable dictionaries are known as *lexicographers*. Lexicography is a branch of linguistics, and lexicographers may have prior training in linguistics. But just as you learned in Chapter 3 that some gig workers may do translation without being trained to do so, some people who are not trained in lexicography may create unofficial dictionaries and post them online. We'll talk more in Chapter 5 about evaluating resources (particularly free online resources), but in this chapter, our focus is on those lexical resources that have been produced by language professionals. In the case of dictionaries, these tend to come from major publishers, such as the ones mentioned above for English (e.g., Oxford, Merriam-Webster), French (Robert, Larousse), and German (Duden, Langenscheidt). While not every language (or language variety) has one or more professionally produced dictionaries, many do, and these are usually quite well known and often pointed out as trusted sources by school teachers or language instructors. If you are unsure which dictionary is a trusted source for your language, ask your instructor for advice.

An important part of a lexicographer's job is deciding what should go into a dictionary and what should be left out. On the one hand, this includes deciding which words to incorporate into a dictionary, and, on the other hand, it involves determining the type and amount of information used to describe each word in its entry. No dictionary can ever be complete because language is constantly evolving, just as the world around us – and our understanding of it – evolves. Once again, we can look to the Covid-19 pandemic for examples. For instance, it inspired people to come up with new words (known as *neologisms*) to describe aspects of living in a pandemic (e.g., *covidiot* or *quarantini*). It also led to de-terminologization, meaning that some concepts and their associated terms began to move from LSP to LGP (e.g., *contact tracing, rapid antigen detection test*). Some of these words might end up in a dictionary, while others may not. Some may get a detailed entry, while others may get a briefer description. How does a lexicographer decide?

Fun fact! Samuel Johnson, a lexicographer who published *A Dictionary of the English Language* in 1755, once famously described a lexicographer as "a harmless drudge that busies himself in tracing the original, and detailing the signification of words". However, the 1998 non-fiction book by Simon Winchester, titled *The Professor and the Madman: A Tale of Murder, Insanity, and the Making of the Oxford English Dictionary*, reveals that the history of this profession has had moments of mayhem! In 2019, this book was adapted into a film called *The Professor and the Madman* starring Mel Gibson and Sean Penn. Meanwhile, in another book entitled *The Dictionary Wars: The American Fight Over the English Language*, author Peter Martin recounts how a movement to gain cultural independence from Britain devolved into a full-scale battle between lexicographers, scholars, and publishers who were vying for dictionary supremacy. So much for harmless drudgery!

It's important to recognize that it is *not* a lexicographer's job to judge words as being "good" or "bad". Lexicographers try to describe words as they are actually used, rather than trying to tell us what we should or should not say. But even though lexicographers are not gatekeepers who try to dictate how we use words, they still need to make choices about what to include in a dictionary in order to make that dictionary as useful as possible. The criteria typically applied by lexicographers to decide whether or not to include a word in a dictionary are as follows: there must be **significant evidence** that a word has been **in use** over an **extended period of time**. First, the word needs to be *in use*, which means that people are actually saying or writing it. What's more, in order to reflect general usage, the word must be spoken or written *a lot* rather than just a few times. Finally, the word should not be just a short-lasting fad but must have *staying power*. Of course, these criteria are a little bit vague. At what point does the number of times a word is used become significant, and when does a word pass through the stage of being a fad to being in regular use? There are no hard and fast answers to these questions, so lexicographers must draw on their experience and professional judgement to make these decisions. They also make their decisions based on data or evidence, which has become much easier to gather and analyze in the age of digital texts and the Internet. Historically, lexicographers identified new words by reading as many books as possible, and while reading is still an important part of their work, the Internet makes it easier to access a wide variety of sources, while tools known as corpus analysis tools (see Chapter 5) make it easier to search through and analyze digital texts. Of course, this is only true in cases where a language has a written script or where there are digital documents in that language. For languages that have a primarily oral tradition, or for which there is no digital typeface for the characters, the job of monitoring that language and extracting information to put in a dictionary becomes much more challenging. This is the case for some Indigenous languages, for example, although initiatives such as UNESCO's "Languages 4 All" are seeking to redress these imbalances by encouraging the development of tools and resources in these languages.

The words that are included in a dictionary are known as *headwords*, and they are presented in their most basic form. For instance, if a headword is a noun, it will be shown in the singular form rather than the plural, while if the headword is a verb, it will be shown in the infinitive form rather than in a conjugated form. For languages that are marked for grammatical gender (e.g., French, German, Spanish), the masculine form is used for the headword. The complete list of headwords is used to structure the dictionary's content. The conventional way of organizing a dictionary is according to alphabetical order. A main advantage of alphabetical order is that it is widely understood and therefore relatively easy to use, although it can occasionally present a challenge if a user is unsure of how to spell a word. Another advantage is that no separate index is required to access the entries.

> **Fun fact!** Alphabetical order is all around us, yet it remains curiously invisible. If you'd like to learn more about the history of alphabetization – from the Library of Alexandria to Wikipedia – check out Judith Flanders' intriguing book *A Place for Everything: The Curious History of Alphabetical Order* (New York: Basic Books, 2020).

In addition to deciding on the overall list of headwords to be included in a dictionary, lexicographers must also prepare an entry that presents a selection of information about each headword. The type and volume of information provided can vary from one dictionary to the next, depending on a variety of factors. For example, a so-called pocket dictionary will contain less information than an unabridged dictionary, while a dictionary that is in electronic form can use features such as hyperlinks and audio files, which are not feasible in a printed dictionary. In addition, monolingual dictionaries do not contain exactly the same type of information as bilingual or multilingual dictionaries.

In monolingual dictionaries, it is common to find the following types of information:

- **Pronunciation:** There is often a guide to the word's pronunciation, either in the form of a phonetic transcription, an audio file (in online dictionaries), or both. Some dictionaries may even provide pronunciation guides for more than one regional variety of a language (e.g., British and American English).
- **Grammatical information:** Typical types of grammatical information include the headword's part of speech, gender, and any non-standard plural form or conjugated form.
- **Definition(s):** A much-used feature of a monolingual dictionary entry is the definition of the headword. Language is polysemous, meaning

that a given word can have more than one meaning. Sometimes these meanings are closely related, and other times they are more distant, but a definition for each meaning or sense of a headword will be included in the entry. Definitions play the important role of linking a word to the concept that it designates.

- **Example(s):** Some dictionaries also include one or more short examples that show how a headword can be used in a phrase or sentence.
- **Usage labels:** If the headword has any special usage features, such as being typical of a particular region or subject field, or being figurative, old-fashioned, informal, or pejorative, this information may also be included in the entry.

With regard to bilingual dictionaries, a main difference is that these do not tend to contain definitions. Instead, they present one or more equivalents for the headword in another language. Bilingual dictionaries may also be bidirectional (see Chapter 1). A bidirectional dictionary will have two halves or two volumes – one for each direction. For instance, if the two languages in question are Portuguese and Spanish, the first half of the dictionary will be organized alphabetically according to the Portuguese headwords, and the entries will contain equivalents in Spanish (i.e., Portuguese>Spanish), while the second half of the dictionary will contain the headwords organized alphabetically in Spanish, and the corresponding entries will present equivalents in Portuguese (i.e., Spanish>Portuguese).

What's in a term bank?

While dictionaries contain information about general language words, term banks are lexical resources that contain information about terms and their corresponding concepts in specialized fields of knowledge. The practice of compiling a term bank is known as *terminology work*, and the people who make term banks are known as *terminologists*. Strictly speaking, terminology work can be carried out in just one language; however, the vast majority of term banks are multilingual, and translators are one of the major user groups of this type of lexical resource. What's more, most people who work as terminologists received their initial training in translation, so terminology work is often regarded as a subfield of translation.

From an organizational perspective, one key difference between dictionaries and term banks is that dictionaries are organized around headwords, while term banks are organized around *concepts*. While a dictionary has one entry for each headword, a term bank has one term record for each concept. This means that, in a dictionary, an entry for a polysemous word will have multiple definitions – one for each meaning that the word can have – and these definitions are listed one after the other in the same entry. In contrast, a specialized concept can have only one definition, so there is never more than one definition in a given term record. If two different concepts are designated by the same term, then there will be two different records (one per concept). However, if a single concept can be referred to by more than one term (e.g., by synonyms or by equivalents in multiple languages), then all of these appear on the term record for that concept. Although polysemy and synonymy can occur in specialized fields of knowledge, this is actually much rarer in LSP than in LGP. Because a key goal of LSP is to facilitate clear and precise communication between experts in a specialized domain, terminologists and subject experts try to avoid having multiple terms for the same concept or using the same term to designate more than one concept, because these practices can create confusion. In other words, terminology often seeks to standardize elements of a specialized language so that there is a one-to-one relationship between a concept and a term. So while lexicography is more of a descriptive activity, where lexicographers record how language is used, terminology work is often more prescriptive in nature, and term banks may suggest which terms are preferred and which ones should be avoided.

If we compare the content of these concept-based term records with the content of typical dictionary entries, we can note that there are both commonalities and differences. Again, the content will vary somewhat from one term bank to another, but some of the most commonly found types of information contained in a term record include:

- **Subject field:** This is the specialized field of knowledge to which the concept and term belong.
- **Term(s):** Terms are the linguistic designations for the concept covered by the record. Usually, the preferred term is displayed first, and, if necessary, this is followed by synonyms, spelling variants, and abbreviations.
- **Equivalent(s):** In a bilingual or multilingual term bank, the equivalents in other languages are also displayed. Again, the preferred term in each language will be displayed first, followed by any synonyms, spelling variants, and abbreviations.
- **Grammatical information:** The most typical grammatical information displayed is the part of speech, and for languages that are marked for grammatical gender, this information is also included. Information about number is included only in cases where this deviates from the normal pluralization rules.
- **Usage labels:** Usage labels can be used to indicate that a term is used only in a particular geographic region or within a specific organization. They can also be used to indicate frequency (e.g., rare, obsolete), formality (e.g., familiar), connotation (e.g., pejorative), official status (e.g., approved, unofficial), and acceptability (e.g., correct, avoid, Anglicism).
- **Definition:** There will be only one definition (per language) on each term record. The definition is the link between a concept and the term used to designate this concept.

- **Context:** A context is a short segment of text (often a sentence but sometimes a paragraph) that shows a meaningful example of a term in use. Contexts may be provided for each language.
- **Observations:** Additional information that helps to explain the concept, term, or any restrictions on its use.
- **Sources:** A term record documents the sources in which the terms and equivalents were identified, as well as the sources for the definitions and contexts.

Because term banks are online resources, the question of how the content is organized is less relevant than in the case of printed resources. In the past, the content of printed glossaries was often organized thematically rather than alphabetically. In other words, related concepts were grouped together in the same section of the glossary, which helped to make the relationships between the concepts clear. In online resources, search functions allow users to access the contents using keyword searches, so the records are not grouped as part of the overall organization of the term bank. However, some term banks still try to capture the relationships between different terms because there is a pedagogical value in understanding a concept as part of a larger system of concepts. One effective way of presenting these relationships in an online term bank is to display a visual concept map where the concepts are displayed as nodes, and arrows show the relationships between them.

While dictionaries tend to be monolingual or bilingual, many term banks are multilingual, and many also cover multiple subject fields. Some well-known and widely used term banks that are recognized as high-quality resources include:

- **Inter-Active Terminology for Europe (IATE):** A term bank administered by the Translation Centre for the Bodies of the European Union that contains term records in the 24 official languages of the European Union as well as Latin (https://iate.europa.eu/home).
- **UNTERM:** A term bank that covers subjects relevant to the United Nations in its six official languages (Arabic, Chinese, English, French, Russian, and Spanish) as well as in German and Portuguese (https://unterm.un.org/unterm/portal/welcome).
- **WIPO Pearl:** A term bank maintained by the World Intellectual Property Organization (WIPO) that contains records for scientific and technical terms derived from patent documents in ten languages: Arabic, Chinese, English, French, German, Japanese, Korean, Portuguese, Russian, and Spanish (www.wipo.int/reference/en/wipopearl/).
- **TERMIUM Plus:** A term bank maintained by the Government of Canada's Translation Bureau that covers subjects relevant to the Government of Canada and the Canadian public in English and French. A limited number of entries are also available in Spanish and Portuguese (www.btb.termiumplus.gc.ca/).

- **Le Grand dictionnaire terminologique (GDT):** A term bank maintained by the *Office québécois de la langue française (OQLF)* in Canada that covers a wide range of subject fields. The term records are primarily in French and English, but some records also include Catalan, Galician, Italian, Latin, Portuguese, Romanian, and Spanish (https://gdt.oqlf.gouv.qc.ca/index.aspx).

How are lexical resources useful for translation?

As discussed in Chapter 1, translation has two main phases. First, translators need to understand the message in the source text. Next, they need to produce that same message in the target language. Different types of lexical resources can help with different aspects of the translation task.

When a translator is working to comprehend the meaning of the source text, monolingual source-language dictionaries can explain LGP words, while term banks can offer definitions of specialized concepts. At the language transfer stage, when a translator needs to carry an idea from one language into another, a bilingual dictionary or term bank can be very helpful for suggesting a possible equivalent. A translator can then take these possible equivalents and look them up in a monolingual target-language dictionary (or in a term bank with records in the target language) in order to confirm that the potential equivalent does indeed have the same meaning as the word or term used in the source text. Definitions are extremely important in the context of translation because, in order for a source-language lexical item and a target-language lexical item to be considered as equivalent, they need to mean the same thing. By comparing the definitions in source- and target-language resources, a translator can ensure that both lexical items are referring to the same concept. Because bilingual dictionaries do not tend to contain definitions or provide much in the way of context, it can be very risky to select a target-language equivalent based solely on the information provided in a bilingual dictionary. Instead, bilingual dictionaries can be used as a source of potential equivalents and a launching point to guide further research using other resources.

When it comes to the production phase of translation, when a translator is working to create a target text, lexical resources can provide some support, but they may not be entirely sufficient. The goal in the production phrase is to create a target text that not only conveys the message accurately but also presents it in a form that is natural and appropriate in the target language. Both dictionaries and term banks contain some usage information, but this is limited. For instance, there may be usage notes that can advise whether a particular lexical item is region specific, informal, or field specific, but often what translators want is to see how the word is actually used by looking at examples. In many cases, the examples provided in lexical resources are insufficient because they are usually quite short (no more

Words, terms, and lexical resources 71

than a sentence), and there is often a limited number of examples for a given lexical item. Therefore, once again, lexical resources can provide a starting point for translators, but they may need to go further and conduct additional research using other types of resources to get a better idea of how to use lexical items effectively in the target text. One popular type of resource for exploring usage is a corpus, and we will look at corpus-based resources in more detail in Chapter 5.

What other contributions do lexicographers and terminologists make?

Since this book is primarily about translation, this chapter has focused on lexicography, terminology, and their respective products – dictionaries and term banks – mainly from the perspective of how they can be useful in the context of translation. However, lexicography and terminology are fascinating disciplines in their own right, and their influence extends far beyond translation. For instance, dictionaries have played a very important role in helping to standardize spelling, while term banks have done the same for specialized terms, thus facilitating communication. Meanwhile, terminologists and lexicographers have made enormous contributions to the field of *language planning*, particularly for less widely used languages. Because English has become such a dominant language in scientific research and development, as well as in popular culture, many new concepts are named in English when they are first discovered or invented. Terminologists and lexicographers work to propose equivalents in other languages to ensure that these languages continue to thrive and don't simply resort to borrowing from English all the time. But proposing new lexical items that will be accepted by speakers of another language is not as easy as it sounds! Lexicographers and terminologists must strive to ensure that their proposals are accurate and transparent, but they also need to follow the existing rules (e.g., for plural formation or conjugation) and be pronounceable and fit in well with the language overall. Some examples of regulatory bodies that work to propose and recommend new words and terms as part of language planning and preservation efforts include *An Coiste Téarmaíochta*, the Irish Terminology Committee, which is an agency specifically charged with the production of terminology in the Irish language, and the *Office québécois de la langue française* (OQLF), whose mission is to develop and implement policy pertaining to linguistic officialization, terminological recommendations, and the francization of the language used in the public and private sectors in Canada's primarily French-speaking province of Quebec. As you can see, lexicographers and terminologists can have a great deal of influence in how general and specialized language is used, both as part of and beyond translation efforts.

Concluding remarks

Translators are charged with transferring a message from one language to another, but the content of this message – in both the source and target language – is expressed through a combination of general language words and specialized terms. Lexical resources such as dictionaries and term banks, which can be monolingual, bilingual, or multilingual, can provide translators with essential information that helps them to understand the concepts in question, identify potential equivalents in another language, verify the equivalence, and, to some degree, use the lexical item correctly in the target language. In combination with other resources and tools (see Chapters 5 and 6), dictionaries and term banks are key components in a translator's toolkit. Beyond creating lexical resources, lexicographers and terminologists also play important roles in the field of language planning and language policy development.

Key points in this chapter

- There are two broad categories of language: language for general purposes (LGP) and language for special purposes (LSP).
- The lexical items that belong to LGP are called *words*, and those that belong to LSP are called *terms*.
- The words of a language are recorded in a dictionary, while specialized terms are recorded in a term bank.
- Although it is convenient to discern between LGP and LSP, there is some overlap between the two, such as the case of de-terminologization, where specialized terms migrate into general language. However, LGP users may have a more superficial or limited understanding of the de-terminologized lexical item than do subject experts.
- The profession concerned with making dictionaries is known as lexicography. The people who do this work are called lexicographers, and they often have a background in linguistics.
- Lexicographers do not decide whether a word is good or bad; their job is to describe words as they are actually used.
- Lexicographers need to make decisions about what to include in a dictionary, and commonly used criteria are that words must actually be in use, and they must be used a lot and over a long period of time.
- Lexicographers base their decisions on data gathered from surveying vast quantities of (mainly online) text with the help of corpus analysis tools.
- It is very challenging to develop lexical resources for languages that have a mainly oral tradition or no digital typeface.
- Dictionaries are conventionally organized alphabetically.
- Different types of dictionaries have been developed for different purposes and user groups (e.g., dictionaries for various regional language varieties, dictionaries for language learners, bilingual dictionaries).

Words, terms, and lexical resources 73

- Some types of information commonly found in monolingual dictionary entries include pronunciation guides, grammatical information, definitions, examples, and usage labels.
- Bilingual dictionaries do not usually contain definitions but rather equivalents in another language; bilingual dictionaries are often bidirectional.
- The profession concerned with making term banks is known as terminology. The people who do this work are called terminologists, and they often have a background in translation.
- Although terminology work can be carried out monolingually, it is more often multilingual, and translators make up the main group of term bank users.
- While dictionaries are organized around headwords, term records are based on concepts.
- To facilitate precision in specialized communication, there is often a one-to-one relationship between a concept and a term, while synonymy and polysemy are discouraged.
- Whereas lexicography is principally a descriptive activity, terminology work often has a prescriptive element that seeks to standardize and recommend preferred terms.
- Some types of information commonly found in term bank records include the subject field, term(s), equivalent(s), grammatical information, usage labels, definition, context, observations, and sources.
- Term banks are online resources that are searchable by keyword. In order to present the relationships between concepts, which have a high pedagogical value, some term banks include visual concept maps.
- Translators need to be very sure that they have understood the concepts in the source text, so resources that provide definitions (e.g., monolingual dictionaries, term banks) are critical for the comprehension phase of translation.
- Bilingual dictionaries can provide inspiration or leads, but to ensure that terms are truly equivalent, it is essential to verify that they are referring to the same concept. This can be done by comparing definitions from a monolingual source-language dictionary and a monolingual target-language dictionary, or from the different sections of a multilingual term record that has definitions in both languages.
- In the translation phase of crafting a target text, the usage information provided in both dictionaries and term banks can be instructive, but a limitation of lexical resources is that they focus mainly on lexical items in isolation, or they show them only in a limited number of examples, which are often short. To see how lexical items are used in texts, other resources such as corpora offer an excellent complement to lexical resources.
- Lexicographic and terminological products (i.e., dictionaries and term banks) are valuable resources for translators, but lexicographers

74 *Words, terms, and lexical resources*

and terminologists also play an important role in language planning, including for less widely used languages.

Topics for discussion

As part of a class discussion, or as a prompt for an online discussion forum, consider the following:

- If you had the choice of working as a lexicographer or as a terminologist, which would you choose, and why?
- Many languages have some kind of regulatory body that oversees the development and reform of that language, including its words and terms. For example, for French there is the *Académie française*, for Spanish there is the *Real Academia Española*, and for German there is the *Gesellschaft für deutsche Sprache*.
  - There is no similar regulatory body governing the English language. Why do you think this is?
  - Is there a regulatory body governing aspects of your dominant language? Do some research online to find out if one exists and what type of activities it undertakes, or explore one of the organizations mentioned above to learn more about what is involved in language planning.

Exercises

- **Expand your vocabulary:** There can be no doubt that translators need to be masterful wordsmiths who are in possession of an excellent vocabulary. The Government of Canada's Language Portal contains a wealth of vocabulary quizzes. Why not explore the site and expand your vocabulary too!: www.noslangues-ourlanguages.gc.ca/en/jeu-quiz/vocabulaire-vocabulary-eng.
  - In the *Neologisms* section, see if you can identify some of the new terms that have entered the English language in fields such as technology or the environment.
  - In the *Thematic vocabulary* section, see how familiar you are with the terms used in fields such as gardening or vegetarianism.
- **Differentiate between words and terms:** The Government of Canada's Translation Bureau created the *Pavel Terminology Tutorial* in English and French and then collaborated with other organizations to make this resource available in Arabic, Dutch, Italian, Portuguese, and Spanish. Although the tutorial is meant to support the training of people who want to become professional terminologists, it begins with a very gentle introduction to the field and contains a variety of interactive exercises (along with answers and explanations). For example, Section 1.2.4 explores the difference between *words* and *terms*. Explore the *Pavel*

Words, terms, and lexical resources 75

Terminology Tutorial and learn more about the work of terminologists and how they create products for translators: www.crtl.ca/Pavel/Pavel%20Terminology/www.bt-tb.tpsgc-pwgsc.gc.ca/btb66a0.html.
- **Compare the content of dictionaries and term banks:** Lexical items can have different meanings when used in general language and specialized language, or when used in different domains of a specialized language. Look up the following lexical items in both a general language dictionary and a specialized term bank and compare the information you find in the two resources. Beyond the definitions, take the time to fully explore the other types of information available in the various resources.
    - Look up "catfish" in the *Merriam-Webster Dictionary* (www.merriam-webster.com/) and in IATE (https://iate.europa.eu/search/standard).
    - Look up "friend" in the *Collins English Dictionary* (www.collinsdictionary.com/dictionary/english) and in UNTERM (https://unterm.un.org/unterm/portal/welcome).
    - Look up "sandbox" in the *Cambridge English Dictionary* (https://dictionary.cambridge.org/) and in WIPO Pearl (https://wipopearl.wipo.int/en/linguistic).
    - Look up "swish" in the *Macmillan English Dictionary* (www.macmillandictionary.com/) and in TERMIUM Plus (www.btb.termiumplus.gc.ca/).
- **Explore concept maps:** Although dictionaries tend to be organized alphabetically, there is a pedagogical advantage to presenting the concepts from a particular subject field as part of a visual concept map to highlight the relationships between them. One term bank that has a visual concept map is WIPO Pearl. Explore this concept map at https://wipopearl.wipo.int/en/conceptmap. You will see a number of bubbles on the screen that represent clusters of related concepts. Click on any bubble and the screen will show a second layer of bubbles in which concepts are clustered into narrower categories. Click on any second-level bubble and a detailed concept map will open showing individual concepts and their relations to one another.

Find out more

Antia, Bassey E. 2000. *Terminology and Language Planning: An Alternative Framework of Practice and Discourse*. Amsterdam: John Benjamins.

- This book situates terminology work in the context of language planning and policy development and considers the socio-political, cultural, and technological factors that can influence the development of specialized language and its applications, such as language promotion and preservation.

Bowker, Lynne. 2021. *Translating for Canada, eh?* University of Ottawa. https://ecampusontario.pressbooks.pub/translatingforcanada/.

- Chapter 2 of this free Open Educational Resource introduces the notion of term banks and explains how they can be used to support translation. The examples used are TERMIUM Plus and *Le Grand dictionnaire terminologique* (GDT), two free online term banks from Canada. The chapter includes practical exercises for working with these term banks.

Fuertes-Olivera, Pedro, ed. 2018. *The Routledge Handbook of Lexicography*. London: Routledge.

- The volume provides a comprehensive overview of the study of general language words and the process of dictionary making. It also discusses different types of dictionaries, including dictionaries for translation (Giacomini 2018), as well as lexicographic traditions in a wide range of languages, such as Arabic, Chinese, English, French, German, Hindi, Indonesian, Portuguese, Russian, and Spanish.

Kockaert, Hendrik J., and Frieda Steurs, eds. 2015. *Handbook of Terminology*. Amsterdam: John Benjamins.

- This volume introduces the fundamentals of terminology and also contains chapters that specifically explore the relationship between terminology and lexicography (Kageura 2015) and between terminology and translation (Bowker 2015).

Martin, Peter. 2019. *The Dictionary Wars: The American Fight Over the English Language*. Princeton: Princeton University Press.

- The author recounts the true story behind the creation of the first dictionaries of American English, exploring the lives of lexicographers Noah Webster and Joseph Worcester and the heated competition between them in their efforts to produce a definitive national dictionary.

Winchester, Simon. 1998. *The Professor and the Madman: A Tale of Murder, Insanity and the Making of the Oxford English Dictionary*. Harper Collins.

- In this historical non-fiction book, the author unveils the obsessions of the two men at the heart of the *Oxford English Dictionary* – James Murray, the scholar and dictionary editor, and William Minor, a former surgeon who had committed murder and was jailed in an asylum for the criminally insane. From his prison cell, Minor contributed nearly 10,000 citations to the dictionary. The book was adapted into a film in 2019.

5 Other tools and resources

In earlier chapters, it has been emphasized that translators need to develop keen research skills to ensure that they both understand the source text and can produce an appropriate target text. In Chapter 4, you learned that lexical resources such as dictionaries and term banks are an important component of a translator's toolkit, but because these resources tend to focus on words and terms in isolation, and because they concentrate largely on providing information about meaning and only to a lesser extent about usage, translators need to turn to other tools and resources to help fill the gaps. In addition, in Chapter 3, you learned that the translation profession has become highly technologized in recent decades and that, in order to keep up with the increasing demand for translation, today's translators use some specialized tools, such as translation memories, to increase their productivity while also maintaining good quality in their translations. Translation memory tools help translators to recycle chunks from previous translations, and although they make up another key element in a professional translator's toolkit, these tools are most helpful for people who translate a high volume of text, particularly in fields that have a formulaic or repetitive style. Some translation memory tools are available only for purchase, while others are free but may still require a user to invest a significant amount of time in order to become proficient since these tools have many sophisticated features. For the most part, people who translate only on occasion or for non-professional reasons (e.g., on language courses, for friends or family) will not benefit greatly from using translation memory tools. So what other tools and resources are available and of potential interest to non-professional translators?

How can I tell if a tool or resource will be useful?

Before considering any specific tools and resources, it is worth discussing the importance of evaluating sources of information. Chapter 4 focused on dictionaries and term banks that have been produced by professional lexicographers and terminologists. When a product is professionally produced, it is usually considered to be of high quality. However, in our digital world, where it has become increasingly easy to create and share

DOI: 10.4324/9781003217718-6

information online, the quality of available sources varies greatly. Therefore, translators need to learn how to distinguish between resources that are trustworthy and those that may be less reliable. In fact, being able to evaluate the quality of a source is relevant not only to translation but to any activity that requires research, so these evaluation skills may be transferable to other activities too, such as work related to your courses or your job.

If you are carrying out translation for non-professional reasons, then you will most likely be looking for sources that are low cost and convenient, meaning those that are freely available online via the World Wide Web. In the past, cost was often a factor that could be used to distinguish between higher- and lower-quality sources. If a source was being sold as a commercial product, this usually indicated that it had been produced in a professional way with quality control measures in place, while a free resource often signalled a low-quality item. However, cost is no longer a reliable predictor of quality when it comes to information. For instance, more and more educational institutions, organizations, and even private companies are supporting the Open movement, which seeks to make a wide variety of content, including educational materials, scientific research, software and more, available for free or at a very low cost. As a result, a growing volume of free high-quality content is now available, but it is still necessary to learn how to distinguish between this content and other less reliable material. This has become more challenging as we see an increase in the spread of misinformation and disinformation (e.g., fake news, fake science). It is therefore essential for a translator – or any researcher – to develop a critical mindset and to take the time to evaluate their sources.

Another important point is that just because a tool or resource is useful for translating one text does not mean it will be the best choice for translating a different one. So it's not necessarily helpful to try to categorize tools and resources as being absolutely "good" or "bad". Instead, it's important to evaluate each tool or resource for its potential to assist with the job at hand. In other words, each time you sit down to translate a new text, you need to re-assess the tools and resources that are available to you and determine how well they can help you to translate the text in front of you at that moment. Therefore, it's important to build up a toolkit that contains many different options.

Some criteria that can be used to determine whether or not a tool or resource will be useful for your purposes include the following.

- **Relevant:** Information can be packaged for many different purposes and audiences. Think back to the idea of the translation brief discussed in Chapter 3. A brief is a set of instructions that a client provides to a translator to help them make decisions as they translate. The brief should contain information about the translation's intended purpose and its target audience. If you are translating in a non-professional context, then you will not likely receive a formal brief, but you may nonetheless have some information about who might be reading your translation and what it is intended to achieve. Keep this information in mind when evaluating a source to see if the source seems relevant. For instance, if you are translating a text for an adult, will a site aimed at children be a useful source? If you are translating for a layperson, will a site that contains highly specialized jargon be of much help? Remember also that the same lexical item might have different meanings in different contexts. In English, the word "bar" means something very different in a legal context than it does in the context of the hospitality industry or a sport such as gymnastics. It's not enough to find a resource that contains the word – it needs to contain information about the relevant concept, too.

- **Credible:** There is a big difference between a source that has been produced by a credible author or group and one that has been produced by an individual or group that lacks expertise in the field. Anyone can post information online, but there are clues that can help you to determine whether or not something is likely to be credible. One possible indicator is the domain name or web address. If the web address shows that the page was created by an organization such as a higher education institution (e.g., .edu), a government department (e.g., .gov), or a known national or international organization (e.g., .org), then this could be a sign that the information was verified before being posted. In contrast, information that has been posted by an individual or a private company (e.g., .com) may need to be scrutinized further. Some individuals and companies may be well known and have established themselves as experts, while others may be posting simply to stir up trouble or to promote their own products. Study these sites carefully (e.g., check the "About" page) to see if the owner appears to be a genuine expert, and cross-check the content on another site to try to verify what you have found.
- **Up to date:** Remember that both knowledge and language are dynamic rather than static. In other words, our understanding of concepts evolves over time, and the words and terms that we use to describe them do too. Most of the time, you are likely to be translating content that reflects the current state of knowledge, so it makes sense to choose sources that are also relatively current rather than sources that were produced many years ago. Check to see if the website or source that you are consulting is current or updated regularly. If it contains a lot of stale links or refers only to information that you know is old or outdated, then it may not be the best choice.
- **Accurate:** If you are researching a topic because you don't know much about it, then it may be challenging to know whether or not a source is accurate. However, even relatively superficial signs, such as spelling errors or sloppy grammar or presentation, can signal problems. After all, if an author doesn't pay attention to relatively straightforward issues

such as spelling, then perhaps they are not paying attention to other more important details, such as the accuracy of the content.
- **Objective:** To try to determine if a source seems objective, you can check whether it presents a balanced view of the subject or whether it seems more oriented to promoting one particular viewpoint. Ask yourself if the source is promoting a particular product or otherwise attempting to persuade you of something. Check to see if it provides facts that can be verified elsewhere or whether it is mainly appealing to your emotions using only vague generalizations.

This list of evaluative criteria is not foolproof, but it might at least help you to rule out some obviously problematic sources. Honing your judgement takes practice, and it is always a good idea to pause and reflect on the appropriateness of a source rather than rushing to use it without a second thought.

What kinds of resources are useful for translators?

As we have already established, translations can deal with every topic imaginable. Therefore, almost any type of resource can be useful for a translator at some point. The choice of resource will depend very much on the task in front of you, but, as you've already learned, translation involves both text comprehension and text production, meaning that translators may need to consult some resources that deal with the subject matter and other resources that deal with language.

Subject matter resources are essentially texts on the same topic as the one covered in the source text. If the source text is in your less dominant language, then you might like to do some background reading on the topic in your dominant language too, just to make the learning process easier and also to get familiar with the relevant terminology in the target language. If you are tackling a topic that you don't yet know much about, then it could be useful to start with an introductory text on the topic, such as a Wikipedia article. Once you have acquired the basics, it will also be very helpful to cross-check key details elsewhere, such as by reading one or more texts in the target language that are comparable to the source text (i.e., texts aimed at a similar audience or that have a similar purpose). For example, you might have to carry out a translation exercise for a language course. If the exercise involves translating a newspaper article on topic X, then read some newspaper articles on that same topic in the target language. Or if your parent asks you to translate a recipe from your heritage language into the language used in your current community so that a neighbour can try preparing the dish for their own family, then begin by reading some recipes in the target language to get a feel for the typical format and style. Looking for examples of target-language texts whose purpose and target audience are similar to the purpose and target audience of your translation will help you to get a feel for the expectations and norms you should strive to meet.

Reading these comparable texts will give you a global sense of the type of text you should aim to produce, but it may not provide you with the solutions to specific translation challenges in your source text (e.g., source-language phrases for which you don't know the target-language equivalent). For this, you may need to do some research in linguistic sources. We have already discussed lexical resources in Chapter 4, but there are other types of language resources too, which will be presented in the upcoming sections.

How can I find linguistic resources for translation?

It is highly likely that you are already familiar with search engines (e.g., Google search, Microsoft Bing, Baidu). We won't review general search engines here, although you may be able to improve your searching skills by learning how to use the more advanced features of your favourite search engine. If you want some tips, try asking a librarian at your university or public library for ways to become a power searcher. However, one resource that may not yet be familiar to you, but which can help you to locate a range of language-related resources quickly and easily, is MagicSearch (https://magicsearch.org/).

MagicSearch is a multilingual metasearch engine that provides a sort of one-stop shopping experience for language resources. In other words, MagicSearch allows you to search multiple sources (e.g., dictionaries, term banks, bilingual concordancers, discussion forums, machine translation engines) with a single search, which can be a great time saver. Just select a language pair, enter a search term, and click the Search button. MagicSearch will return the results as a single scrollable page showing what was found in each of the sources. If you want to investigate the contents of any resource further, you can click on the link for that resource and it will take you directly to it. Although MagicSearch proposes an initial set of sources to search, along with the order in which they will be displayed, you can customize this by adding or removing sources and changing the order in which the results will be displayed (e.g., to put your preferred sources near the top). Depending on the language pair you select, you may see some familiar resources listed, including some of the dictionaries (e.g., Collins, Larousse) and term banks (e.g., IATE, GDT, TERMIUM Plus, UNTERM) that were presented in Chapter 4. In addition, you will see some other types of resources, such as bilingual concordancers (e.g., Linguee, Glosbe, TradooIT), discussion forums (e.g., WordReference, ProZ.com), and automatic machine translation tools (e.g., Google Translate, DeepL Translator; see Chapter 6). Don't forget to adopt a critical mindset and to evaluate the usefulness of each resource in relation to your current translation task.

What are online bilingual concordancers?

Although monolingual dictionaries and term banks can be very useful for understanding concepts (e.g., through definitions), and bilingual dictionaries and term banks can help to identify possible equivalents in another language, sometimes the lexical item or expression that a translator needs may not be included in these resources, meaning that the translator must conduct additional research elsewhere. Other times, a translator may have an idea of which word or term they would like to integrate into their translation, but they first want to see it in context in order to better understand how to use it properly in the target text. In such cases, a free online bilingual concordancer can be very helpful because it displays multiple examples of a search term and its possible equivalent(s), each in a larger context.

In some ways, a bilingual concordancer is similar to the translation memory tool described in Chapter 3, but it is simpler to use because it is not integrated as part of a more sophisticated tool suite. A free online bilingual concordancer can be accessed through a web browser, and it will allow you to search through pairs of source and target texts to see lexical items and their equivalents as they appear in sentences. The source and target texts come from a wide variety of sources, and they are usually taken from bilingual or multilingual websites. For example, the website of the World Health Organization has information available in Arabic, Chinese, English, French, Portuguese, Russian, and Spanish, while the websites of the European Union are available in the 24 official languages of its member countries. The source and target texts are then broken down into sentences, and the corresponding sentences from the source and target texts are linked together, as shown in Figures 5.1 and 5.2.

Of course, what is shown in Figures 5.1 and 5.2 is just a short extract from a single text. In reality, the free online bilingual concordancers gather together thousands and thousands of source and target texts from many different multilingual websites, and they create linked pairs of sentences from each of these texts. Then, if you would like to see how a term such as *air pollution* has been translated into Spanish, the bilingual concordancer will search through the English-language collection of texts, identify every sentence in which the term *air pollution* occurs, and display all these sentences alongside their corresponding sentences from the target texts. The tool also indicates the original source that each sentence was taken from (with a link back to the complete text). This way, you can quickly see the term and its translation in a series of short sentences, but if you'd like to see more context, you can pull up the text from which a sentence was extracted. Figure 5.3 provides an extract that shows how the results from a bilingual concordancer are typically displayed.

By looking at the contexts provided by a bilingual concordancer, you can see how the lexical item that you have queried is used in the source

Source text from the World Health Organization's website (www.who.int/health-topics/air-pollution)	Target text from the World Health Organization's website (www.who.int/es/health-topics/air-pollution)
Air pollution	Contaminación atmosférica
Air pollution is contamination of the indoor or outdoor environment by any chemical, physical or biological agent that modifies the natural characteristics of the atmosphere.	La contaminación del aire (tanto el exterior como en de interiores) es la presencia en él de agentes químicos, físicos o biológicos que alteran las características naturales de la atmósfera.
Household combustion devices, motor vehicles, industrial facilities and forest fires are common sources of air pollution. Pollutants of major public health concern include particulate matter, carbon monoxide, ozone, nitrogen dioxide and sulfur dioxide. Outdoor and indoor air pollution cause respiratory and other diseases and are important sources of morbidity and mortality.	Los aparatos domésticos de combustión, los vehículos de motor, las instalaciones industriales y los incendios forestales son fuentes habituales de contaminación de aire. Los contaminantes más preocupantes para la salud pública son las partículas en suspensión, el monóxido de carbono, el ozono, el dióxido de nitrógeno y el dióxido de azufre. La contaminación del aire exterior y de interiores provoca enfermedades respiratorias y de otros tipos y es una de las principales causas de morbimortalidad.

Figure 5.1 An English-language source text from the World Health Organization's multilingual website alongside its corresponding target text in Spanish.

language, as well as how it can be translated in the target language. Of course, Figure 5.3 shows an extract with just a few examples, but in an actual online bilingual concordancer, you are likely to retrieve many more examples (depending on your search term and language pair). Note that the Spanish-language sentences in Figure 5.3 contain two different possible equivalents for "air pollution". Four of the sentences use *contaminación del aire*, while one sentence contains *contaminación atmosférica*. Studying the contexts may help you to decide which option best meets your needs. For instance, you can see that *contaminación del aire* appears to be more common, and that *contaminación atmosférica* is used as part of an official title for a specific agreement.

Another advantage of a bilingual concordancer is that it allows you to look up phrases or expressions that might not be included in a conventional lexicographic resource because they are not words or terms per se. For instance, as shown in Figure 5.4, you could enter a Spanish phrase such as "darlo por hecho" into the search box and see the different ways

Air pollution	Contaminación atmosférica
Air pollution is contamination of the indoor or outdoor environment by any chemical, physical or biological agent that modifies the natural characteristics of the atmosphere.	La contaminación del aire (tanto el exterior como en de interiores) es la presencia en él de agentes químicos, físicos o biológicos que alteran las características naturales de la atmósfera.
Household combustion devices, motor vehicles, industrial facilities and forest fires are common sources of air pollution.	Los aparatos domésticos de combustión, los vehículos de motor, las instalaciones industriales y los incendios forestales son fuentes habituales de contaminación de aire.
Pollutants of major public health concern include particulate matter, carbon monoxide, ozone, nitrogen dioxide and sulfur dioxide.	Los contaminantes más preocupantes para la salud pública son las partículas en suspensión, el monóxido de carbono, el ozono, el dióxido de nitrógeno y el dióxido de azufre.
Outdoor and indoor air pollution cause respiratory and other diseases and are important sources of morbidity and mortality.	La contaminación del aire exterior y de interiores provoca enfermedades respiratorias y de otros tipos y es una de las principales causas de morbimortalidad.

Figure 5.2 The source and target texts aligned sentence by sentence.

that this phrase has been translated into English by others (e.g., "take that for granted", but also "consider it done" and "make that happen"). These options can inspire you and help you to determine an appropriate way to express this idea in your own target text.

Earlier in this chapter, we discussed the importance of evaluating sources, and this advice also applies to the contents shown in a free online bilingual concordancer. The texts that are gathered and processed by a free online concordancer are not necessarily reviewed or pre-evaluated before being included in the collection, so it's up to you as a user to consider the sources for the sentences displayed and to use your good judgement about whether a given source appears to be reliable and appropriate in relation to your translation task.

Two popular and free online bilingual concordancers are Linguee (www.linguee.com/) and Glosbe (https://glosbe.com/). Both these tools contain additional features beyond the concordancer, including a dictionary feature. However, it is important to recognize that these dictionaries are not as carefully curated as the resources discussed in Chapter 4. While the latter are compiled by professional lexicographers and terminologists who use computer aids, the dictionary features of tools such as Linguee and Glosbe may

Other tools and resources 85

First among the causes that trigger asthma and asthma attacks is air pollution. www.europarl.europa.eu/	La principal causa desencadenante de asma y crisis asmáticas es la contaminación del aire. www.europarl.europa.eu/
Imagine you are reporting on air pollution in your country. www.america.gov/	Imagine que usted va a informar sobre la contaminación del aire en su país. www.america.gov/
Neither the Protocol, nor the Convention on Long-range Transboundary Air Pollution, contains definitions of the terms used in this statement on exemptions. www.pops.int/	Ni en el Protocolo, ni en el Convenio sobre la contaminación atmosférica transfronteriza a larga distancia se ofrecen definiciones de los términos utilizados en ese texto sobre las exenciones. www.pops.int/
Major groups discussion papers on energy for sustainable development, industrial development, air pollution and climate change. daccess-ods.un.org/	Documentos de debate presentados por los grupos principales sobre la energía para el desarrollo sostenible, el desarrollo industrial, la contaminación del aire y el cambio climático. http://daccess-ods.un.org/
The revenue would be used to clean up air pollution around the port. www.4children.org/	Los ingresos se usarían para limpiar la contaminación del aire en los alrededores del puerto. www.4children.org/

Figure 5.3 An extract of the results from a bilingual concordancer for the search term "air pollution".

Ya no podemos darlo por hecho y debemos defender a Internet desde el punto de vista político, y respaldar su vitalidad personalmente. www.icann.net/es/	We can no longer take that for granted and we must advocate for the internet politically, and support its vitality personally. www.icann.net/en/
Si tenemos en stock puede darlo por hecho. www.storexservidores.es	If we have it in stock, we can make that happen. www.storexservidores.es
Cuando se trabaja con Dasco, usted puede "Darlo por Hecho". http://dascoinc.com/es/	When you work with DASCO, you can "consider it done". http://dascoinc.com/en/
PERO, no peude darlo por hecho. http://facetsite.com/	But, it cannot be assumed. http://facetsite.com/

Figure 5.4 An extract of the results from a bilingual concordancer for the search string "darlo por hecho".

have less direct oversight by language professionals and incorporate more automated techniques and crowdsourcing (see Chapter 7). However, the clear benefit offered by the bilingual concordancers is the extensive set of examples that illustrate lexical items and their equivalents in contexts of use that have been taken from actual texts.

Both Linguee and Glosbe also offer the option to translate a lexical item, phrase, or even a text using an automatic machine translation tool. This feature can be useful if no examples of the item can be found in the dictionary or concordancer, but automatic translation tools must be used with caution, and this will be explored in detail in Chapter 6.

> **Fun fact!** Concordancers were used for linguistic research, language teaching, and lexicography before they eventually caught the attention of translators.

What are translation communities and discussion forums?

Sometimes, the best resource for finding an answer to a question might be another person. Recall that, in Chapter 3, you learned that a large number of translators work as freelancers, meaning that they don't have colleagues working in the next office or down the hall. Nevertheless, the Internet makes it possible to connect quickly and easily with people all around the planet, so a number of different sites have been established that allow individuals to ask translation-related questions and receive advice or suggestions.

Translators Café (www.translatorscafe.com/cafe/) and ProZ.com (www.proz.com/) are two online community sites that have been created by and for translators. Some aspects of these sites are specifically aimed at professional translators, such as the areas where potential clients and professional freelancer translators can make contact and discuss job opportunities. As a non-professional translator, you will not likely be seeking work via these sites, but each of these communities also has a discussion forum where people can pose questions and respond to the queries of others. Some threads in the discussion forum are quite specialized, but others are more general and open to less experienced translators (e.g., the "Beginners: Ask Here!" thread on Translators Café). If, after conducting your own research, you are unable to find a solution to a translation problem, or if you don't know how to interpret the information you find in a language resource, then you might consider posting a question to a discussion forum on a translation community site. Before posting your query, it would be useful to scroll through some of the existing threads to get a feel for which types of queries are appropriate and which are not. Members of the translation community are typically generous with regard to sharing their knowledge, but it would not be appropriate to ask someone on the discussion forum to do your homework for you, or to answer a question that you have not made an attempt to research yourself first.

Another language resource that includes a discussion forum more oriented to non-professional translators is WordReference (www.wordreference.com/). The WordReference site contains a number of tools and resources, including a series of bilingual dictionaries, grammar references, and verb conjugators, but the language forums are one of its most well-used features. The people who post to the WordReference language forums are a more diverse group that may include some professional translators but also language teachers, language students, and others who are simply language enthusiasts. These forums can be a good place to seek advice on whether a phrase or expression that you are considering using in your translation sounds natural or conveys its intended meaning. Once again, it would be a good idea to check out the "Terms and rules" section of the language forums page for advice on what types of queries are permitted, as well as guidance on how to formulate a post so that it generates helpful responses.

What tools can support revision?

In Chapter 3 you learned that professional translators always include a revision phase in their work, and this is good practice for any type of writing you intend to share with someone else (e.g., an essay for a course, a report for your boss). Tools such as spelling and grammar checkers can be helpful for verifying that no typos or subject–verb agreement problems have slipped into your text. This can be particularly useful if you are writing in, or translating into, a language that is not your dominant one, but mistakes can happen even in your dominant language, so it never hurts to double check.

Many word processing tools include some spellcheck and grammar checking features, but there are additional standalone tools that can be accessed online. In many cases, these tools offer a basic version for free, with the option of paying for a more advanced version. Tools that offer a free online version include Grammarly for English (www.grammarly.com/), Bon Patron for French (https://bonpatron.com/), and Spanish Checker for Spanish (https://spanishchecker.com/). Try searching online for a similar type of tool in the languages that you work with.

Another technique that may help you to catch errors or determine whether your text sounds natural is *prooflistening* (rather than, or in addition to, proofreading). Sometimes your eye might skip over errors, but if you use a text-to-speech computer tool to read your text out loud, those errors might jump out at you as you listen. One such tool that is available in multiple languages is Speechify (https://speechify.com/), which has a free version with limited features and a paid version with more options.

While some of these tools can help you with the revision process, it's important to remember that no tool is foolproof, and, at the end of the day, you must take responsibility for the final version of your text.

Concluding remarks

It might not be the first thing that comes to mind when you think of translation, but having top-notch research skills is essential for translators. Whether its researching subject-related content or linguistic usage, translators need to know where they can look for the required information, as well as how to evaluate what they find. Very few resources can be described as categorically "good" or "bad". A resource might provide information that is very useful for translating one text but turn up nothing helpful for another. Each text has its own characteristics, including its intended purpose and target audience. This is why the translation brief (see Chapter 3) is so important to keep in mind when selecting the sources, and why it's essential to build up a robust toolkit. Even if you are not a professional translator, you may translate informally on occasion, so it can still be useful for you to be able to find and evaluate potential resources against your needs and to use tools that could help with translation-related tasks. One relevant approach is to identify some target-language texts that are comparable to the source-language text. This will give you a feel for how such texts are normally constructed in the target language. A multilingual metasearch engine can save you time by enabling you to carry out the same search in multiple resources at the same time, while a bilingual concordancer can allow you to see how source-language words, terms, or expressions are used in context, and also how these have been translated in other texts. While online tools and resources may contain the information you need, human resources can sometimes answer questions that computers cannot. Discussion forums make it possible to seek advice from others who may have the linguistic insights you need. A human–computer combination can also be a great approach when it comes to finalizing your text – tools can help you to catch silly mistakes, but remember that it's ultimately your responsibility to create a quality product. You'll find more on this important topic of human–computer interaction in the field of translation in Chapter 6, which deals with automatic machine translation tools.

Key points in this chapter

- Lexical resources (e.g., dictionaries and term banks) are helpful for learning about isolated lexical items, but translators must complement these with other types of tools and resources.
- Professional translators use translation memory tools, but these are less useful to non-professional translators.
- The Internet has made it easier to create and share information, but material found on the web can be of varying quality and must be evaluated.
- To evaluate potential resources for translation, assess whether they are relevant, credible, up to date, accurate, and objective. Remember to keep

Other tools and resources   89

the translation's purpose and intended audience in mind while making this assessment.
- Comparable texts are target-language texts that have a similar content, purpose, and target audience to those of the source text. These comparable texts can allow you to get a feel for the typical format and style of this text type in the target language.
- To find linguistic resources for translation, try using a metasearch engine, which will allow you to search multiple resources with a single query.
- Bilingual concordancers share some features with translation memory tools, but the free online concordancers are easier to access and use.
- Free online bilingual concordancers gather sets of source and target texts from multilingual websites and align them on a sentence-by-sentence basis.
- You can search for a lexical item or expression in the source language, and the bilingual concordancer will display many examples of source-text sentences containing that search term alongside target-language sentences that contain an equivalent. This lets you see both the search term and its equivalent(s) in authentic contexts.
- Free online bilingual concordancers also provide a link to the full text from which the sentences have been extracted, allowing you to see a broader context and to evaluate the quality of the source.
- Discussion forums allow you to consult people – either language professionals or language enthusiasts – to seek advice on how to translate a term or use an expression correctly in the target language. Be sure to check the forum's rules or guidelines before making a post.
- Revision is an important final step in any translation (or writing) project, and tools such as grammar checkers or text-to-speech tools (which read your text out loud) can help you to catch unintended errors in your target text. However, tools are not foolproof, and you must take final responsibility for the quality of your text.

Topic for discussion

As part of a class discussion, or as a prompt for an online discussion forum, consider the following:

- Which tool or resource would you recommend to a friend to help with a translation-related task? Don't recommend something that's really well known or already covered in this book, and don't be afraid to think outside the box! For instance, it doesn't have to be a text-based resource but could be a video, a podcast, or a piece of software. And it doesn't have to deal with language but could address some other aspect of translation work (e.g., subject-matter knowledge, time management, text editing, dictation, professional development). As part of your recommendation, tell us (a) the name of the tool or resource, (b) where we can find it (e.g., link), (c) what it does, and (d) its strengths and weaknesses. Together, we can identify a whole range of tools and resources that could make handy additions to a translator's toolkit.

Exercises

- **Write a love letter or break-up letter to a tool or resource:** Design thinking is an approach that companies use to determine how users feel about their products. One design-thinking technique involves writing either a love letter to a product we appreciate or a break-up letter to one we don't and explaining why. Temporarily viewing tools or products as though they are people can help us to better understand their context within our lives. Writing a letter is a great way to tap into the emotional connections we have with our tools or resources and find ways to promote their best attributes or suggest ways to fix the features that don't work so well.
  - Select a tool or resource that can be used to support a translation task (e.g., it could be one of the lexical resources mentioned in Chapter 4, one of the tools or resources discussed in this chapter, or another one of your choosing).
  - In 250–300 words, write a letter to that tool or resource explaining why you adore it or why you won't be using it again. If you have mixed feelings, you can express these too.
  - As an optional step, you can make a short video in which you read your letter aloud.
- **Explore MagicSearch:** The MagicSearch (https://magicsearch.org/) multilingual metasearch engine offers a sort of one-stop shopping experience for language resources. Explore the options available for your language pair(s). Examine and compare the results shown in different resources for the same search term. Are there some resources that you think will be more helpful than others for the comprehension phase of translation? How about for the production phase?
- **Play with a bilingual concordancer:** Try out a free online bilingual concordancer such as Linguee (www.linguee.com/) or Glosbe (https://glosbe.com/) in your preferred language pair by searching for terms or expressions that you are not quite sure how to express in another language. Remember to adopt a critical mindset when evaluating the suggestions by carefully considering the sources that the examples come from.
- **Explore the discussion forums:** Browse through some of the discussion forums on Translators Café (www.translatorscafe.com/cafe/), ProZ.com (www.proz.com/), and WordReference (www.wordreference.com/). How do the topics in the first two, which are more oriented to professional translators, compare to those in WordReference, which targets a

broader community of language enthusiasts? Which do you think you would be more likely to consult, and why?
- **Experiment with a grammar checker or read-aloud tool:** Try the free online version of one of the grammar checkers or text-to-speech tools suggested earlier in this chapter or search for one in your own language. Do you think these tools could facilitate your revision work?

Find out more

Bowker, Lynne. 2021. *Translating for Canada, eh?* University of Ottawa. https://ecampusontario.pressbooks.pub/translatingforcanada/.

- Chapter 3 of this free Open Educational Resource introduces the notion of bilingual concordancers and explains how they can be used to support translation. The example tool used is TradooIT, a free online bilingual concordancer that works in English and French. The chapter includes practical exercises for working with TradooIT.

Chan, Sin-wai, ed. Forthcoming. *Routledge Encyclopedia of Translation Technology*. 2nd ed. London: Routledge.

- This encyclopaedia contains a range of introductory articles on various tools that can support translation activities, including bilingual concordancers.

Koskinen, Kaisa, and Minna Ruokonen. 2017. "Love Letters or Hate Mail? Translators' Technology Acceptance in the Light of their Emotional Narratives". In *Human Factors in Translation Technology*, edited by Dorothy Kenny, 8–24. London: Routledge.

- In this article, the authors use the design-thinking approach of asking translators to write love letters or break-up letters to technologies used in the translation profession. The results reveal that technology is a central and, for the most part, positive aspect of translators' work, but that poorly functioning tools or tools with low usability are a source of frustration since these hinder productivity.

6 Machine translation

In Chapters 4 and 5, you learned about some different tools and resources that you can turn to for help when translating texts, such as online term banks (e.g., TERMIUM Plus and IATE) and online bilingual concordancers (e.g., Linguee). In this chapter, we'll take things a step further by exploring a type of tool (e.g., Google Translate, DeepL Translator, or Baidu Translate) that attempts to automate the core elements of the translation process more fully. In the world of professional translation, these tools are referred to as *machine translation systems*, where the term "machine" is a sort of throwback to the early days of computers, when they were referred to as *computing machines*. Nowadays, we typically just say *computers*, but, in the world of translation, this older term *machine* has become embedded as part of the term *machine translation*. Sometimes, in the popular press or more general language discussions, you might see or hear the term *automatic translator* rather than machine translation. Essentially, however, whether it is called a machine translation system or an automatic translator, this type of technology attempts to carry out the whole task of translation without any help from the user. Sometimes the user might participate after the draft translation is produced to fix up the text, but the computer has at least made an attempt to produce a complete draft. In the rest of this chapter, and elsewhere in the book, we'll use the term *machine translation (MT)*, which is now very established in the field, to describe the type of tool that attempts to produce a complete draft translation automatically. However, this doesn't mean that users (such as you and me!) have no role to play whatsoever. As you'll find out, it's critical for users to be thoughtful in their use of this technology and to apply good judgement and critical thinking to decisions such as whether or when to use MT.

We'll begin with a quick overview of the history of MT, which provides some important context for how these tools have developed over time, as well as how they have become embedded in our society. By understanding the underlying approaches used in these tools, you can better comprehend their strengths and weaknesses and make more informed decisions about when it makes sense to rely on these tools and when it would be a better idea to choose another option. As you'll find out, these tools are now actually

DOI: 10.4324/9781003217718-7

very easy to access and use, but this doesn't mean that you should depend on them in all circumstances. Using critical judgement to assess the risks and decide whether or not to proceed with MT, or how much to trust the resulting translation, is part of what we refer to as *MT literacy*. In brief, using MT is easy, but using it critically requires thought. Therefore, much of this chapter will focus on helping you to become a savvy MT user by enhancing your MT literacy skills.

What is machine translation's origin story?

The field of MT is older than you might think. Although MT tools did not become popular or widespread until Google released the first version of its free online tool Google Translate in 2006, this technology dates back to the period just after World War II. As you learned in Chapter 2, in 1949, an American mathematician named Warren Weaver released a twelve-page double-spaced document that became known as "Weaver's memorandum". In it, Weaver proposed the idea of using computers – which were a very recent invention at that time – to translate between languages such as English and Russian. Some of Weaver's ideas were inspired by the success of cryptographic or code-breaking techniques used during the war. This relatively modest document is now regarded as one of the most influential texts ever written about MT, and it was essentially responsible for launching research in this field around the globe. Wow!

Early efforts: Rule-based MT

The initial attempts to build MT systems using basic cryptographic techniques such as substitution ciphers did not work out because, as you've already learned in Chapter 1, translation is *much* more complex than simply substituting a word in one language with a word in another. But the idea of getting computers to translate was still very exciting. The ball was rolling! In 1951, the Massachusetts Institute of Technology (MIT) hired Yehoshua Bar-Hillel as the world's first full-time MT researcher, and in 1952 he organized an international conference that brought together people from all around the world who were interested in working on the challenge of getting computers to translate. This led to the Georgetown-IBM experiment in 1954, where a small-scale Russian-to-English MT system was developed and demonstrated publicly to encourage governments to invest in MT research. The demo was carefully controlled because the MT system could only translate about 60 sentences, but it did the trick of generating a buzz and attracting funding.

For the next decade, researchers continued working on this so-called rule-based MT, or RBMT, which essentially tried to map out a detailed series of grammatical rules and paired these with very large bilingual dictionaries. Obviously, grammar and vocabulary are very important components of language, so the RBMT systems did have some limited success. However, as discussed in Chapter 1, people use much more than just grammar and vocabulary to communicate successfully. For example, to interpret the intended meaning of a text, people also draw heavily on their real-world knowledge and on contextual clues. For example, the French word *"avocat"* can be translated into English as either *"lawyer"* or *"avocado"*. Look at the following sentence:

>J'ai mangé l'avocat.
>[I ate the ____.]

How do people figure out the correct translation of *"avocat"*? Well, they certainly don't rely only on grammar. They also rely on contextual clues, such as *eat*, and on their knowledge of the fact that avocados are a type of food, whereas lawyers are people. And we don't eat people! So the correct translation in this sentence pretty much has to be "avocado".

But what if we said something like, "That judge eats lawyers for breakfast"? Here, we need to know that "to eat somebody for breakfast" is an idiomatic expression that is used figuratively, not literally (because we still don't actually eat people, do we?). How on earth can we expect a computer – which is not intelligent and has no real-world knowledge – to figure this stuff out?!

A bump in the road: The ALPAC report

As it turns out, we can't expect computers to figure things out in the same way that people do. Despite working hard on the problem of MT for over a decade, researchers were unable to get computers to successfully translate texts that contained anything more than straightforward literal meanings or pre-programmed exceptions. Understandably, the funders who had invested large sums of money into MT research were frustrated, and in 1964 the US government established a committee of scientists known as the Automatic Language Processing Advisory Committee (ALPAC) that was tasked with evaluating the current state of MT research and making recommendations for the future. After looking into the situation, the committee produced a report in 1966 that became known as the ALPAC Report. It essentially said that the committee members judged MT to be slow, expensive, and of poor quality, and they recommended that researchers look into developing computer-assisted translation (CAT) tools (such as the ones discussed in Chapter 5) rather than continuing to work on fully automatic MT. As a result, the funding for MT research dried up, and there was very little activity for the next couple of decades.

One exception was the METEO project, which began at the Université de Montréal in Canada in the 1970s. This MT system was specifically designed to translate weather forecasts from English into French, and it was quite successful. Of course, it's important to remember that a weather forecast is very limited with regard to both the range of vocabulary needed and the way that sentences are structured (e.g., Chilly tonight. Sunny this afternoon. Clouding over tomorrow). Because of its restricted grammar and vocabulary, this sublanguage of weather forecasts turned out to be an ideal candidate for MT. However, this really is an exception, and to this day researchers have not been able to identify another sublanguage that works as well. Besides, most people don't want to only translate texts about the weather. They want an MT system that can translate texts on many different topics of varying levels of complexity.

A new way of thinking: Data-driven MT

Although research activity in the field of MT was very limited during the 1970s and 1980s, computer technology was still advancing. By the 1990s, computers were smaller, faster, and more powerful. At the same time, people were beginning to create more and more texts in electronic form using tools such as word processors. The growing popularity of the Internet and World Wide Web in the 1990s also made it easier to share and access electronic documents. These advances opened the door to thinking about MT in an entirely new way. Early attempts to build MT systems had focused on using grammar rules and dictionaries, but because they could not easily be supplemented with the type of real-world knowledge that people have, these linguistic resources were not enough to produce successful translations. Clearly, computers are not equipped to process language in the same way as people do. So researchers began to consider what types of tasks computers *are* good at. As it turns out, computers excel at tasks such as pattern matching and rapid mathematical calculations. Could it be possible to apply these approaches to translation?

In the next phase of MT development, researchers decided to use the strengths of computers to come up with *data-driven* approaches to MT. In a data-driven approach a computer is given many, many, many examples of texts that have *already* been translated by human translators. These examples can be used to train an MT system. For instance, an MT system can use pattern matching to find all the examples of a particular phrase in the source language, then it can count how many times this phrase has been translated by X or by Y. The MT system can then do complex statistical calculations such as calculating the probability that the source text should be translated by X rather than by Y in a new text.

Because computers are so good at tasks such as pattern matching and rapid calculations, the results of these statistical machine translation (SMT) systems were surprisingly good. They soon produced better results than the older RBMT systems, leading researchers such as G. A. Fink, F. Kummert, and G. Sagerer (1995) to ask the cheeky question, "With friends like statistics, who needs linguistics?" Indeed, from the mid-1990s until about 2016, statistical MT prevailed as the dominant approach.

When Google released the first version of Google Translate in 2006, this tool employed a statistical approach to MT, and it did not take long for this free online MT tool to become popular. To celebrate the tool's ten-year anniversary in 2016, the company released some interesting facts on their blog *The Keyword*, noting that Google Translate had grown from supporting two languages to 103 languages, and from hundreds of users to 500 million users (Turovsky 2016). The year 2016 also marked another interesting turning point for MT because it ushered in yet another data-driven way to approach the task of getting computers to translate: neural machine translation (NMT).

Where are we today? Neural MT and an emerging need for MT literacy

The popularity of free online MT tools continues to soar. *The Keyword* blog reported that, by 2021, there had been more than one billion downloads of the Google Translate app on Android phones alone (Pitman 2021). In addition to the obvious benefits of being free and online, another key reason that Google Translate and similar tools have become so popular is that the neural approach to MT has also delivered another major jump in translation quality.

NMT is a data-driven approach to MT that uses an artificial intelligence technique known as machine learning. Once again, this requires that an extremely large sample of texts and their human translations be provided to the MT system as training material. In the case of NMT, the tool contains an artificial neural network that consults this training corpus and, based on the patterns identified in the training data, learns how to translate new texts. Although the translations produced by NMT systems are not perfect, they are usually of a much higher quality than texts produced by RBMT systems, and NMT systems typically outperform SMT systems also. Having said this, it is important to recognize that NMT systems – and the translations that they produce – are not perfect.

In fact, the improved quality of the translations, combined with the ease of access to free online MT systems and their straightforward user interface, has contributed to an emerging need for MT literacy. When tools are very easy to access and use, you can slip into a sort of auto-pilot mode where you don't necessarily think too hard about what you are doing. In the case of free online MT systems, anyone with an Internet connection can access these tools easily. And the way to interact with tools such as Google Translate or DeepL Translator is very simple: go to the website (or app), select the target language, type or paste the text that you want to translate, and voilà! – the translation appears. In some cases, a translation widget might even be embedded in a social media platform (e.g., Twitter or Facebook) or into a web browser (e.g., Google Chrome or Microsoft Edge), so the translation actually happens behind the scenes without the user needing (or even

Machine translation   97

choosing) to initiate it. In such cases, you may not even realize that the text you are reading has been translated automatically!

Indeed this seemingly magical aspect of MT is frequently emphasized in the popular press, which is probably the main source of information about MT for users who are not professional translators (Vieira 2020). When journalists present MT as making translation easy, they gloss over the reality of how these tools actually work (i.e., the tools draw on the results of many high-quality translations painstakingly carried out by professional translators), as well as the potential risks involved in using them.

So what types of things should you, as a user of free online MT, know about these tools? Keep reading to get some tips and improve your MT literacy.

What is machine translation literacy?

You have already learned – and probably experienced – that using free online MT tools is very straightforward. The interface is simple, as is the process. So MT literacy is not really concerned with the "how to" aspect of using MT. Rather, it's about helping users to increase their understanding of how the tools work, to assess when and where they can be usefully employed, and to learn how to work with them more effectively to get better results. If you don't have a good level of MT literacy, then the speed and convenience of these tools may cause you both to underestimate the intricacies of translation and to overestimate the tools' capabilities, which could lead to a misuse of MT. Are you ready to improve your MT literacy and become a more savvy user of free online MT tools? If so, keep reading.

> **Fun fact!** Using machine translation is easy; using it *critically* requires thought.

What are some implications of data-driven approaches?

As previously mentioned, current MT systems are NMT systems that take a data-driven approach. It is not necessary for users to understand every detail of how an artificial neural network works in order to use MT, just as it is not necessary for a driver to understand every detail of how an internal combustion engine works in order to drive a car. However, some understanding of how a car works is essential in order to operate the vehicle safely and effectively. For example, it's essential for a driver to know that pressing down on the brake pedal will cause the car to slow down or stop. It also helps to know that, when the fuel gauge reaches empty, the car will cease to function, so it's best to keep the fuel tank at least partly filled. Likewise, it's important to know that indicator lights can occasionally burn out, that objects in the mirror are closer than they appear, and so on. Knowing at least some aspects of how a vehicle works can help you to get the most out of it while also ensuring that you and those around you remain safe. Although the specifics of how NMT works are very different to how a car works, the general principle still applies. Understanding some of what is happening under the hood of NMT will help you to appreciate the strengths and limitations of this technology and empower you to use it in a responsible and effective way. So what exactly does data-driven mean in the context of NMT, and why is this important?

Well, in some ways you can think of an NMT system as a child: initially, it doesn't know anything, but it can learn to do some things by seeing examples. In the case of NMT, the examples that it needs to see in order to learn how to translate are previously translated texts and their original source texts. These two types of text – the original source texts and their translations – are stored together in a *parallel corpus*, where they are typically aligned so that each sentence in the source text is paired with its corresponding sentence in the translated text.

In order to be useful as a training corpus for an NMT system, the parallel corpus needs to be HUGE. Although children can often learn to do something by seeing just a few examples, computers are not actually intelligent, so machine learning requires many, many examples in order to provide the computer with enough data to be able to approximate a task. As you've already learned, translation is a complex task, so a training corpus for an NMT system needs to contain thousands, or even tens of thousands, of examples of previously translated texts. As a general rule, the more examples an NMT system can consult, the more it will learn and the better the resulting translation will be. This has notable implications because some languages are more widely used than others, meaning that it is easier to put together a large parallel corpus for some language pairs than for others.

For instance, English and French are both widely used languages. Moreover, there is a lot of translation activity between these two languages. For example, they are the official languages of Canada, meaning that there is a lot of translation between this pair within the federal government. English and French are also official languages in a number of other organizations, such as the European Commission, the United Nations, and the World Health Organization, to name a few. This means that it is relatively easy to find many examples of previous translations between English and French that can be compiled into a training corpus. Therefore, in the world of data-driven MT, both English and French are known individually as high-resource languages, and together they are a high-resource language pair. And when there are lots of resources (i.e., previous translations) to use for training purposes, the quality of the translation produced by an NMT system can be relatively high.

However, not all languages or language pairs are widely used. For example, languages such as Icelandic and Welsh have relatively few speakers and are used primarily in geographically restricted areas of the world. Therefore, it is much harder to find language resources in Icelandic than it is in English, so Icelandic is considered to be a low-resource language. What's more, if we take two low-resource languages (e.g., Icelandic and Welsh) and look for examples of translation between them, it is unlikely we will find many. So now we are dealing with a very low-resource language pair. If there are not enough examples to train an NMT system, then the resulting translations are likely to be of a much lower quality than the translations for a high-resource language pair. To try to get around this issue, some tools adopt what is known as a pivot language strategy. In this case, instead of translating from Icelandic directly into Welsh, the translation is divided into two separate steps and goes through a high-resource pivot language, such as English.

Direct translation: Icelandic to Welsh
Indirect translation through a pivot language: Icelandic to English then English to Welsh

The idea behind the pivot language strategy is that it will likely be easier to build corpora of translations between Icelandic and English and between English and Welsh than it will be to find translations between Icelandic and Welsh directly. However, the indirect translation approach does open the door to other potential problems. For example, by translating the text twice, there are twice as many opportunities to introduce errors. Moreover, if there is a translation error in the first stage (i.e., when translating between Icelandic and English), then this error will be carried forward to the second stage (i.e., when translating between English and Welsh).

Another point to consider is that some languages have more than one regional variety. This idea will be explored in more detail in Chapter 7, when we investigate an area of translation known as *localization*, but for now it's enough to recognize that a language such as English, French, Arabic, or Chinese may have more than one variety (e.g., US versus UK English, Canadian French versus Belgian French, Levantine Arabic versus Maghrebi Arabic, Mandarin versus Hakka). So while it may be relatively easy to compile a training corpus for a major or dominant language variety, it could be more challenging for a less widely used variant. Therefore, it is still uncommon to see free online MT systems that allow users to select a particular regional variety rather than simply a language, although this could change in the future.

So we could say that bigger is better when it comes to data-driven approaches. However, quantity alone is not sufficient to produce good translations. In addition to providing a large volume of data, it is also important to include the right kind of data in a training corpus for an NMT system. But what kind of data is the right kind?

When it comes to the issue of high resource and low resource, it's also relevant to think back to Chapter 4, where we explored the difference between general language and specialized language. In order to be able to successfully translate a text from a particular domain (e.g., health, law, economics, engineering), MT systems need to see enough examples of texts from this domain. If an NMT system is trained using a parallel corpus of general language texts, it is unlikely to perform well when it comes to translating a more specialized text. Similarly, if the tool is trained using texts from a single, specialized domain (e.g., law), it may have difficulty producing a good translation of a text in another domain (e.g., health). So the question of resources applies not only to languages but also to text type and domain. If an NMT system has not seen enough examples of a particular specialized term, or a particular type or genre of text (e.g., contracts, reports, patents), then it will not have enough data in this area to generate a high-quality translation.

If we begin to combine some of these notions, it quickly becomes apparent that creating training corpora for high-resource languages and very general domains is much easier than finding resources for combinations of low-resource languages in more specialized fields. It would likely be quite challenging to identify a substantial corpus of Icelandic to Welsh translations on dentistry or aeromechanical engineering, for instance.

Training corpora can reveal other issues too. For example, it is now quite well known that Google Translate can sometimes produce sexist language. Some languages, such as Turkish, have third-person singular pronouns that are not marked for gender. So the Turkish pronoun "o" is used to refer to "he", "she", or "it". But when translating out of Turkish and into English, it is necessary for the NMT system to make a choice. How does it make this choice? Well, it looks at the examples in the corpus, and it learns from these. That sounds pretty reasonable, doesn't it? Well, it may interest you to know that Google often translates the gender-neutral Turkish pronoun "o" as "he" when the surrounding context contains words such as "doctor" or "intelligent", but it translates that same gender-neutral pronoun "o" as "she" when the surrounding context contains words such as "nurse" or "beautiful"! What is going on here?

Remember previously how we said that, in some ways, an NMT system is like a child? Well, any parent can confirm that children often learn things by observing other people and imitating them. Sometimes this means that children learn things we wish they wouldn't! A well-known example is swearing. If a child overhears a parent using a curse word, the child might repeat that word, much to the parent's dismay. In the case of an NMT system, it looks at the examples in the training corpus to see how things have been translated before. As it turns out, most of the examples in the corpus that contain the words "doctor" and "intelligent" also contain the pronoun "he" rather than "she". As a result, Google Translate has learned to associate the male pronoun with this group of words and to select that male pronoun whenever it encounters a context containing "doctor" or "intelligent". The root of the problem here is not really Google Translate but rather the data in the corpus. It points to a wider problem in society where we have historically encouraged men to pursue certain professions while women are steered towards others. This behaviour eventually gets encoded into our documents, and, in turn, these documents become learning material for NMT systems. So just like a small child can learn to swear by hearing examples of curse words, an NMT system can learn and amplify sexist language. Similar issues can arise with regard to other types of bias in text, such as racial or religious bias.

So what does all this mean for users of free online MT systems? Clearly, users do not have any control over the data used to train these tools. However, it's important to be aware of these issues because they teach us that MT cannot be generalized as simply "good" or "bad". Rather, it's necessary to recognize that if you are working with high-resource languages, then your chances of having a reasonable quality output are improved. In contrast, if you are working with low-resource languages, then you should be mindful of the fact that, in general, NMT systems will not perform as well. And while users cannot control the data bias that may manifest itself in the MT output, you can at least be aware of the possibility, keep an eye out for it, and correct it, if necessary.

Another key point to realize is that each tool – Baidu Translate, DeepL Translator, Google Translate, Microsoft Translator, Naver Papago, Reverso, Systran, Yandex.Translate, and so on – has been trained using a different corpus. Each of these tools is produced by a different company, and each company has collected a different training corpus with which to train their tool. This means that each tool will learn different things, so each will produce different results. That's right – no two tools will produce exactly the same results! Many people tend to use only one tool – often Google Translate – without having tried any others. Depending on the language pair or subject field that you are working with, it could be worth your while to experiment with a few other tools to see if another one produces better results for your needs. Also, keep in mind that these tools are constantly learning, so don't rule out using a particular tool just because you once got disappointing results. Wait a few weeks then give it another try because it may have learned something new!

Why is transparency important?

Now that you are aware of some of the potential issues associated with data-driven approaches to MT, you can also see the value of knowing whether a particular text has been produced using MT, and, if so, with which system. For example, having access to information such as the source language, the MT system used, and whether or not the translated text was checked over or edited by a person can help a reader to gauge how much confidence to place in a particular translation. This is why transparency around MT use is important. Transparency involves making users aware of the conditions under which a translated text is produced. Without a clear statement or label, readers might simply assume that a text has been translated or verified by a professional translator, so they might trust the content implicitly. However, if the text is actually a raw or unedited machine translation, then it may contain some errors. It does not mean that we should avoid using MT altogether because these tools have the potential to be very useful when used wisely! However, in order to be able to judge how cautious you should be, you need information. Therefore, if you are using MT to produce a text that you intend to share with someone else, be sure to clearly and visibly label the translated text with details about the source language, MT system used, any quality control measures taken (e.g., verified/edited or not), and date of production. By providing this type of information, you empower the readers to decide for themselves how much to trust the content. If you don't provide this information, then the readers have no information on which to base their decision, and they may end up placing too much faith in a poorly translated text.

For students, transparency around the use of an MT system may also extend to coursework. Students may wonder whether or not the use of MT is considered cheating in an academic context. While there is no definitive answer to this question, it may be useful to consider it through the lens of transparency. First, it would be helpful if instructors could provide a clear policy about MT use. If your instructor has not provided a policy, you could ask if they have one that they can share. If a policy exists, you should follow it, or consult the instructor if you have any concerns. If there is no policy, you might consider how well the use of MT aligns with the learning objectives of the course. For example, if you are taking a language learning course, then it might go against the spirit of the course to simply write full texts in your dominant language then use an MT tool to translate the complete text into the language you are learning. However, you could potentially employ MT in a more targeted way (e.g., to translate shorter segments) or to verify your efforts (e.g., through back translation). In contrast, if the course is not a language course but rather a course on another subject that is being taught through another language (e.g., a course on geography or science taught in a language other than your dominant one), then using MT to help you understand course materials or write assignments in another language may be less controversial. In either case, if you do decide to use MT, it could be helpful to be transparent about which tools you have used and how (e.g., looking up terms, translating short segments, translating entire passages). This way, you and the instructor are on the same page, and if the instructor has concerns, they can address them with you in a constructive fashion.

Another key point to remember when using MT in connection with coursework is that proper referencing and citation are still essential. If you refer to ideas taken from another author, you still need to reference the original source of those ideas, even if you paraphrase or translate them into another language. Transparent acknowledgement of the source still matters, regardless of the language in which you are writing or preparing your work.

What's involved in risk assessment?

In the preceding sections on data-driven approaches and transparency, the notion of risk awareness has been raised. For example, you've seen that a text translated between two high-resource languages is more likely to be of good quality, while a text translated between two low-resource languages, whether directly or through a pivot language, may be of lower quality and therefore warrant a more cautious use. You've also learned that being transparent about MT use, such as by labelling a text as a product of MT, along with details such as the source language, MT system used, and any quality control measures taken, can empower readers to decide how much confidence to place in a text. These are important elements in risk assessment in the context of MT, but there are additional considerations.

One important consideration has to do with the intended purpose and context of use of the translated text. For example, if you are using MT to help you understand song lyrics, a manga comic book, or a friend's social media post, then these are low-stakes situations because a mistranslation is unlikely to have serious consequences. In contrast, if you are using MT to translate information from your doctor about after-care following a surgical procedure or to fill out immigration forms, then these are higher-stakes scenarios because a poor translation could have more serious repercussions on your health or future.

A related concept is understanding that translation can be undertaken for different purposes (e.g., comprehension versus production). For instance, an unverified or unedited machine translation may be useful for helping you to understand a text in a familiar field, where your own domain knowledge can help you to fill in any blanks. However, MT may be less appropriate for a purpose such as publishing a text on your company website, where a poor translation could affect the company's image or reputation.

Sometimes external factors such as time or budget may come into play when deciding the extent to which MT could be a good choice. If there is a sense of urgency, where information must be shared quickly, then it may make sense to use MT – at least to produce an initial draft that could then be verified or edited in less time than it would take to produce a translation from scratch.

Finally, there can be another type of risk associated with free online MT. While you may think that the text you enter into a free online MT system will simply disappear when you close the window, this is not always the case. Many tool providers (e.g., Google, Microsoft) specify in their terms of use that they have the right to keep this data and reuse it for other purposes (e.g., for additional training for machine learning systems). Once text has been entered into a free online MT system, it is not possible to take it back out again. It is therefore important to think carefully about the nature of the text and to take care not to enter any information that is sensitive or confidential.

How can we interact with MT?

A final way to improve your MT literacy is to consider how you can interact with these tools in order to improve their usefulness. Typically, this can be done either before or after you send the text to the MT system, and it may depend on whether you are using the tool to help you prepare a message that you want to share with other people or whether you are using it to help you understand a text that has been written by someone else. If you are only using MT to help you understand a text written by someone else, then you probably won't need to edit it. However, if you are using MT to produce a text that is destined to be read by others, then you may want to do some editing of both the source text and the resulting translation.

If you are the author of the text to be translated, then you can actually influence the quality of the translation by ensuring that the original text is well written. In computer science, there is a well-known expression that says, "Garbage in, garbage out" (GIGO), and this idea applies very well to translation too. A source text that is unclear or poorly written is hard to understand, and if a translator can't understand the source text, then they are not likely to produce a high-quality translation. By taking the time to express your ideas clearly in the source language, you will help to set the scene for a more successful translation. So what does translation-friendly writing look like? Well, the qualities of a good text may differ from one language to the next, but the key aim of translation-friendly writing is to reduce ambiguity. Some possible ways to achieve this when writing in English include:

- Keeping sentences relatively short (e.g., 15–25 words).
- Using the active voice rather than the passive voice.
- Using terminology consistently (e.g., not introducing synonyms unnecessarily).
- Repeating key nouns instead of using pronouns.
- Punctuating sentences correctly.
- Avoiding long strings of modifiers.
- Avoiding idiomatic or culture-bound expressions.

Once you have prepared your source text in a translation-friendly way, you can run it through the MT system to obtain a draft translation. If you have some command of the target language, you might even be able to spot places in the target text where the translation is a little rough. If so, you can return to the source text and try refining those parts, then send the improved source text through the MT system again. These steps can be repeated as many times as necessary until no further improvements can be made. The advantage of working in this way is that it allows you to focus on manipulating the source text, which is most likely in your dominant language, rather than forcing you to make corrections in the target text, which is probably in your additional or less dominant language.

Of course, even after working hard to reduce ambiguities in the source text and make it as translation friendly as possible, you may still end up with a translation that requires a bit of editing. If your own knowledge of the target language is good enough, you may be able to undertake this editing work yourself, but if you are not very strong in the target language, then it may be a good idea to ask a speaker of that language to look the text over before you distribute it more widely.

The level of editing required depends on what the target text is going to be used for. If the translation is for internal use or a low-stakes task, then it probably only needs to be good enough to get across the essential meaning of the original text. In this case, the most important thing is to ensure that the translation is accurate, even if it sounds a bit awkward or inelegant. However, for some higher-stakes tasks, a greater degree of editing may be required in order to ensure that the text is not only accurate but also reads well. This higher level of editing may be desirable if the text is going to be shared publicly, for example. Once again, it is difficult to give specific tips for post-editing as these may differ depending on the language or language pair in question. However, some general tips for producing a "good enough" quality translation for a low-stakes task include:

- Correcting errors of meaning.
- Ensuring that no information has been accidentally added or left out.
- Fixing any offensive, inappropriate, or culturally inappropriate content.

Taking the editing a step further in order to bring it up to a publishable quality, additional steps include:

- Ensuring that relevant conventions or rules for spelling and grammar are applied.
- Restructuring sentences to improve the natural flow of the text.

Once all meaning errors and stylistic problems have been addressed, the translated text can be shared with the intended audience.

Concluding remarks

MT is a technology that is now widely accessible, easy to use, and improving in quality. At the same time, our world is becoming increasingly multilingual, meaning that MT is probably among the most common ways that people outside the language professions will come into contact with or experience translation. Although free online MT tools are easy to use, it's still important to view them in a critical way and to make informed decisions about whether, when, and why to choose MT over or in combination with another option (e.g., using concordancers, post-editing MT output, hiring a language professional). By improving your MT literacy skills, you will become a savvy user who can assess the benefits and risks involved in using MT, and you will be able to use this technology in a responsible and effective manner.

Key points in this chapter

- The term *machine translation* (MT) is a throwback to when MT research initially began, not long after "computing machines" were first invented.
- MT tools attempt to automate the core elements of the translation process and produce a complete translation.
- Early approaches to MT, now known as rule-based MT, used large bilingual dictionaries and detailed sets of grammar rules to try to process language in a way that partially resembles the way humans process language; however, this approach had very limited success because computers do not have access to real-world knowledge and context.
- As computer technology advanced and people began creating texts in electronic form, MT developers began to consider data-driven approaches to language processing that used techniques that computers are good at (e.g., pattern matching, rapid calculations).
- Early data-driven MT used statistical analyses, but, more recently, neural MT has begun to employ artificial neural networks coupled with machine learning.
- Although MT tools are easy to access and use, users still need to have good MT literacy skills in order to apply these tools responsibly and effectively.
- One facet of MT literacy involves understanding the essentials of how data-driven approaches work, including the fact that they are data sensitive.
- Data-driven MT works best for high-resource languages, which means languages and language pairs that are widely used; languages, language pairs, and language varieties that are less widely used are known as low-resource languages, and data-driven MT systems tend to produce lower-quality translations for these languages.
- In addition to requiring a very large volume of data, data-driven approaches also need the right kind of data. In translation, this could mean texts from a specific domain or texts of a particular genre.
- Different free online MT systems have been trained using different parallel corpora, meaning that no two systems will produce identical translations. Don't be afraid to try more than one system to see which

one works best for your needs. In addition, these tools are constantly learning, so try them again regularly as they may have improved.
- It's important to be transparent about MT use, such as by identifying texts that have been produced using MT and specifying the source language, tool, and any quality control checks that have been applied. This allows readers of the text to judge how much confidence they want to place in its content.
- Students who use MT should also be transparent, consider how well the use of MT aligns with the goals of the course, and remember to use proper referencing and citation even when translating ideas.
- Risk assessment is a key part of MT literacy, and it includes evaluating whether a given translation task is high stakes, which may have serious consequences if the translation quality is poor, or low stakes, for which the repercussions of a poor translation would be minimal. MT may not be the best choice for high-stakes tasks, but it may be sufficient to meet the needs of users in a low-stakes situation.
- Do not enter sensitive or confidential information in a free online MT system.
- Texts written in a translation-friendly way will be easier for an MT system to translate.
- Depending on the purpose of the translation, the text produced by an MT system may need to be checked and corrected or edited by someone who speaks the target language before being shared more widely.

Topics for discussion

As part of a class discussion, or as a prompt for an online discussion forum, consider the following:

- What is the most surprising or novel thing that you've learned about MT in this chapter (i.e., something related to MT that you didn't know before or hadn't previously thought about)?
- Using MT for coursework is a type of academic fraud. Do you agree or disagree, and why? (Note: this topic can also be used to set up a more formal debate, where one group of students argues for and another against).

Exercises

- **Analyze representations of MT in the media:** Find one or two short articles on MT in the online press in your region. Read the articles and reflect on the way that MT is portrayed. Given what you now know about MT, does the way that it is represented seem accurate? Fair? Balanced? Biased?

108 *Machine translation*

- **Compare different MT systems:** For your preferred language pair, find two or more free online MT systems (e.g., Baidu Translate, DeepL Translator, Google Translate, Microsoft Translator, Naver Papago, Reverso, Systran, Yandex.Translate) and use them to translate the same text. Compare the translations produced by each MT system. Which passages are similarly translated? Which are different? Try the exercise again using a different type of text (e.g., one that is more specialized or from a different subject field). Does one system seem to do a better job for the type of text that you want to translate?
- **Try translation-friendly writing:** Take an extract from a text that you have written in your dominant language for one of your courses. Using a free online MT system, translate your text into another language that you know well and analyze the output. Are there areas in the translation that don't seem to be quite right or which could be improved? Return to your original text and study the parts that were not well translated. Can these segments be re-written in a way that is simpler or clearer? Modify the text to try to improve its clarity and then re-translate it. Is the re-translation better than the first one?
- **Try post-editing:** When you have achieved as many improvements as you can through translation-friendly writing, revise or post-edit the translated text to try to further increase its quality.
- **Reflect on ethics:** What ethical issues can you identify in these mini case study scenarios? What might have changed if the instructor or student had made different decisions?
  - **Scenario 1:** Jenny is an English-speaking university student in the United Kingdom taking an intermediate-level course in Italian. For a graded assignment, students in the class have to write a few paragraphs in Italian about their most and least favourite foods. The instructor does not give any instructions about which tools or resources can be used to produce the assignment. Because the deadline has almost arrived, Jenny decides to write the text quickly in English first then translate it into Italian using DeepL Translator. Jenny doesn't have time to revise the work, so the text produced by DeepL Translator is the version that gets submitted. The instructor gives Jenny a grade of zero for the assignment.
  - **Scenario 2:** Yingjie is a Chinese-speaking international student studying business at a university in the United States. For an assignment, the instructor asks the students to read three English-language articles on a business topic and to summarize the articles in English. Yingjie begins by using Baidu Translate to translate the original English articles into Chinese. Yingjie reads the translated versions and prepares a summary in Chinese. Using Baidu Translate, Yingjie translates the Chinese summary into English. To check that

the meaning of the English summary is correct, Yingjie translates it back into Chinese using another MT tool (Google Translate). There are some problems, so Yingjie reworks some sections of the Chinese text to make it clearer and easier to understand before repeating the translation and back-translation process again. Once satisfied with the text, Yingjie adds a note to the assignment explaining the translation tools and process that were used to complete the assignment. The instructor gives Yingjie a satisfactory grade for the assignment.

- Puzzle it out:
  - Crossword puzzle: Try the interactive crossword puzzle on the MT Literacy Project website: https://sites.google.com/view/machinetranslationliteracy/home/teaching-resources.
  - Jigsaw puzzle: Complete an online jigsaw puzzle to reveal an infographic about MT literacy on the MT Literacy Project website: https://sites.google.com/view/machinetranslationliteracy/home/teaching-resources.

Find out more

Bowker, Lynne, and Jairo Buitrago Ciro. 2019. *Machine Translation and Global Research*. Bingley, UK: Emerald.

- This book introduces the notion of MT literacy and explores ideas for translation-friendly writing.

Kenny, Dorothy, ed. 2022. *Machine Translation for Everyone: Empowering Users in the Age of Artificial Intelligence*. Berlin: Language Science Press. https://langsci-press.org/catalog/book/342.

- This free open access resource presents information on ethical considerations for machine translation use, how neural machine translation works, how to write for machine translation, how to post-edit machine translation output, and how to use machine translation for language learning.

Nitzke, Jean, and Silvia Hansen-Schirra. 2021. *A Short Guide to Post-editing*. Berlin: Language Science Press. http://langsci-press.org/catalog/book/319.

- This free open access resource provides some practical tips on how to post-edit machine translation output, including a discussion of risk assessment and risk considerations.

Poibeau, Thierry. 2017. *Machine Translation*. Cambridge, MA: MIT Press.

- This is a concise and non-technical overview of the development of automatic machine translation tools, including the different approaches and major highlights in the history of MT.

Vieira, Lucas Nunes. 2020. Machine Translation in the News: A Framing Analysis of the Written Press. *Translation Spaces* 9, no. 1: 98–122.

- A discussion of how the media can reflect and influence the public perception of machine translation.

7 Localization

Up to this point, we've been focusing on the idea that translation and interpretation activities deal with transferring a message from one language, such as English, to another language, such as French. However, many languages have more than one regional variety. In the case of English, there are well-known varieties such as British English and American English, but there are others too: Canadian English, Australian English, New Zealand English, South African English, Hiberno-English (Irish English), and more. And English is not unique in this respect. Arabic speakers from the Maghreb region (e.g., Morocco, Algeria, or Tunisia) use dialects that differ from those used by Arabic speakers in regions further to the east (e.g., Egypt, Sudan, or Saudi Arabia). In addition to the French spoken in France, there are other varieties used in Belgium, Switzerland, Canada, Haiti, Algeria, and the Congo. Differences also exist between the German used in Germany, Austria, and Switzerland. Meanwhile, the variety of Portuguese that you hear in Portugal is not the same as that which you hear in Brazil, and Peninsular Spanish (from Spain) likewise differs from the varieties of Spanish found in the Americas.

Sometimes, it is not enough to translate into a given language. If the text is intended for an audience that speaks a particular language variety, then a language professional may need to go beyond translation and engage in an activity known as *localization*. In this chapter, you'll have a chance to learn more about how languages and cultures can differ from one region to the next, and how these differences can be addressed through localization.

What is GILT?

Although the focus of this chapter is on localization, this activity is part of a sphere of related activities, and it's important to understand how these various activities relate to and feed into one another. As shown in Figure 7.1, there are four closely related activities that together are referred to by the acronym GILT: Globalization, Internationalization, Localization, and Translation. In some ways, these sound like similar concepts, and, indeed, some people use them interchangeably. However, each of these activities plays a subtly distinct role in the overall process of expanding a product or service beyond regional

DOI: 10.4324/9781003217718-8

112 *Localization*

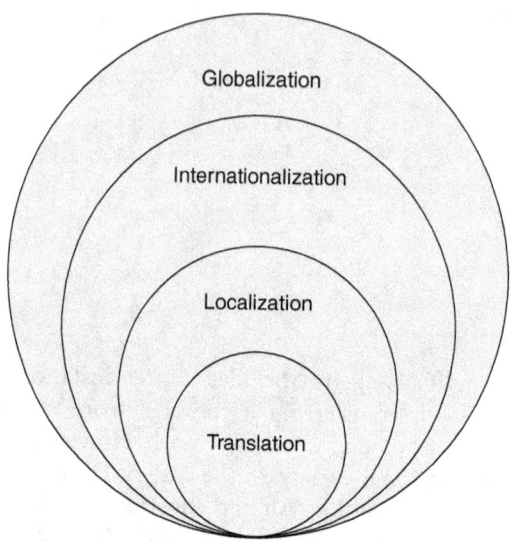

Figure 7.1 Relationship between the four activities of GILT.

borders. Let's take a quick look at each of these four concepts in turn before going on to conduct a more in-depth exploration of localization.

Globalization: Globalization is primarily a business concept, and it refers to the processes that a company uses to make its business or products available to customers around the world. As an example, think about a company such as Amazon, which makes it easy to buy products from businesses or individuals across the planet. Yet even when buying products that have been sourced or produced in another country, most customers can still interact with the Amazon website in their own language. Globalization offers many benefits for both companies and customers; however, it requires a lot of preparation to "go global" properly. Two of the most important steps for successful globalization are internationalization and localization.

Internationalization: Once a company has made the business decision to globalize, the next step in the process is internationalization, which is the practice of designing products and services in a way that makes them adaptable to international markets. This often requires working with different types of subject experts beyond translators. For example, when internationalizing software or websites, it is important for the software or website to be Unicode-enabled so that it can represent characters from non-Latin alphabets, such as Russian, Chinese, or Hindi. If the software uses the traditional ASCII encoding rather than Unicode, then

Localization 113

it will only be able to represent characters from the Latin alphabet. Another way to internationalize software or websites is to design parts of the user interface, such as buttons or drop-down menus, in a way that allows them to automatically expand or contract to fit the text. As you already know, it can require a different amount of space to convey the same idea in different languages. A simple example is the word "Save" in English as compared to its French-language equivalent "Sauvegarder". The English word has just four characters, while the French equivalent is almost three times as long with 11 characters. This means that the space allocated for a menu or button in French needs to be wider than it does in English. A computer programmer can internationalize the user interface by designing it in such a way that the width of the menu or button will grow or shrink as necessary depending on the length of the word. If the product is not internationalized, then there is a risk that a long word such as "Sauvegarder" would get chopped off because the menu or button can only accommodate the shorter word "Save". Finally, as part of the internationalization process, a company might separate out the localizable content from the computer source code (e.g., HTML code), which should not be translated. Sometimes a company might even internationalize the content itself, which entails writing the content in a way that is as culturally neutral as possible. For example, the English-language expression "hit it out of the park" is an allusion to baseball, where an exceptional player could hit the ball hard enough that it would land outside the stadium. In a country where baseball is not a common sport, this culture-bound reference would need to be adapted. To facilitate the localization process, the original content could first be internationalized by writing in a culturally neutral way, such as by saying "did an exceptional job".

Fun fact! The terms *globalization, internationalization, localization,* and sometimes even *translation* can be abbreviated to numeronyms by making reference to the number of characters between the first and last letter in each word:

- Globalization = G[lobalizatio]N = G11N: "G" is the first character in the word, "N" is the last character, and there are 11 other characters between them, which get represented by the number 11.
- Internationalization = I[nternationalizatio]N = I18N: "I" is the first character, "N" is the last character, and there are 18 other characters in between.

Based on the pattern shown above, what would the numeronyms for *localization* and *translation* be?

Localization: After a product has been internationalized, the next step in the process is localization, which consists of adapting the product or service to a specific target market. A target audience usually has both linguistic and regional preferences that they would like to see in their target text, and this combination of language and region is referred to as a locale. Each locale is described using two two-letter codes for the language and territory of use. For example, the locale identifier for English-speaking users in the United States is en_US, while the locale identifier for English-speaking users in Canada is en_CA. Meanwhile, French-speaking Canadian users would be represented with the locale identifier fr_CA, while the locale identifier for French-speaking users in Belgium is fr_BE. You may be wondering why it is necessary to include both language and region in the locale identifier. The short answer is that a language can have more than one variety (e.g., Portuguese and Brazilian Portuguese), and the differences can extend beyond purely linguistic features to include other types of preferences or conventions (e.g., units of measurement, time and date formats, currencies). Identifying a locale is not always straightforward, however. For example, although there are many Spanish speakers in the United States, there is no locale for es_US since there is no single US-specific variety of Spanish. Rather, there are many different varieties of Spanish spoken as a heritage language in this country (e.g., people who immigrated from Mexico, Cuba, or Puerto Rico will speak the variety from their homeland). It is therefore difficult to localize into Spanish for a US market. Locales and localization will be explored in more detail in the upcoming sections. For now, it is sufficient to emphasize that the localization process is complex, and that, while translation plays an important role in localization, it is necessary to go beyond translated content to achieve success in local markets.

Translation: As we have learned throughout this book so far, translation essentially means converting the content (usually of a written text) from a source language into a target language. It's not a word-for-word process, but it does strive to transfer the essential meaning of the source text while respecting the grammatical rules and other conventions of the target language.

So how, then, is localization different from translation? We can say that translation changes the language of a text, but localization goes further to offer a more comprehensive adaptation that affects elements such as visual content, layout, and more. Localization accounts for not only languages but regional varieties of languages, as well as the associated cultural preferences of those regions. When taken as part of the GILT framework, translation is just one step in the overall process, and it is essential to have a good team that includes not only translators but also local consultants and marketing experts (to make sure that the cultural aspects of each target market are respected), software engineers (to ensure that the code behind a website or videogame is properly internationalized), project managers (to keep projects on track and on budget), and more. Successfully going global requires a true team effort!

Why does localization matter?

If localization is more complex than translation and requires a bigger team and more planning, you may be wondering why it's important or whether it is worth the extra effort. Think about your own experience with online shopping, using a streaming service such as Netflix, or even going to a restaurant such as McDonald's. Do you feel more confident or satisfied when you can use your own language to interact with these services? Many businesses have found that regular translation is not always sufficient to enable them to succeed in local markets. Instead, these businesses have discovered that localizing their content helps them to gain the trust of the local public, who are then more prepared to buy the product or service.

Selling in another country means more than overcoming language barriers. It means coming up with a customized message that has been developed especially for each local audience. To globalize a business successfully, the company must localize for each country in line with local culture. At the same time, the company wants to keep a unique voice that will enable the public to identify their brand all around the world. Therefore, localization is a real balancing act that involves not only translation but also a cultural approach. It is not enough to simply translate a website; people need to understand and identify with the company's message before they buy their products. Therefore, a localization expert must reshape it so that it fits in with local values and customs and leaves the local audience feeling as if the content has been produced especially for them. By tailoring their marketing to meet local expectations, a company can increase the engagement level of potential customers and thus improve their chances of increasing sales and growing their business internationally.

What gets localized?

In the 1980s, desktop computers began to appear, making computer tools available to a wide range of users who were not experts in computer science. Of course, user-friendly software then became necessary, so programs were developed for common activities such as document creation (e.g., word processing tools) and financial management (e.g., spreadsheets). Soon after, computers began to be used for leisure activities also (e.g., videogames), and this market continues to grow (e.g., virtual reality). In the 1990s, the widescale adoption of the Internet and the World Wide Web made it possible to communicate and to share information more easily across a vast network, leading to new digital genres (e.g., websites). And as computer technology continues to advance and to become smaller and more powerful, we now have tablets, smartphones, watches, fitness trackers, navigation systems, and more that also run software (e.g., mobile apps), not to mention virtual assistants that can answer our questions (e.g., Google Home, Amazon's Alexa, Apple's Siri).

These digital genres – software, videogames, virtual reality, websites, mobile apps, virtual assistants – can be found all around us, and they have dramatically transformed the way that we shop, play, communicate, collaborate, study, and work. As we learned in the previous section, people are typically more comfortable carrying out these activities in their own language, meaning that a new market emerged to make these products and services available in other locales. Because there is often a need to go beyond translation and to include extensive cultural adaptations, localization (rather than translation) has become the preferred approach for bringing these products and services to new markets.

Another reason why localization has emerged as a profession distinct from translation is that localizers need to deal with issues and constraints that do not typically apply to translation more generally, so localizers develop a specialized skillset. For example, localization is often affected by space constraints, such as the size of the screen where the digital content is to be displayed. In addition, the textual content in software or videogames does not always follow a linear, sentence-by-sentence structure. Instead, the content is often stored digitally in resource files, and users interact with the program and select their own reading path, which means that individual text strings must be able to be combined in different ways and still make sense. As such, localization requires distinct skills and, as noted above, it is often carried out by a team rather than by an individual. Let's now take a look at some of the language-related issues and non-linguistic elements that a localization specialist might need to deal with.

How do languages vary from one region to the next?

You have undoubtedly had the experience of reading or listening to a language variety that is different from the one you are most used to hearing. For example, you might have read a social media post or watched a film that originated in another country, or perhaps you may have travelled abroad or met someone from another country who is travelling in your region. What tell-tale signs have you noticed that indicate that one language variety is different from another?

> **Try it!** To hear some different pronunciations of British and American English, try looking up the words "tomato", "bottle", or "ladder" in online dictionaries such as the *Collins English Dictionary* (www.collinsdictionary.com/) for British English and the *Merriam-Webster Dictionary* (www.merriam-webster.com) for American English. Click on the speaker icon beside each word to hear the pronunciation.

One of the most noticeable differences between varieties of the same language is the way that words are pronounced. In cases where localization specialists need to provide voiceovers for videogames, multimedia websites, or virtual assistants, it is important to take pronunciation into account and to provide the content using a local accent that corresponds to the target region (e.g., American, Australian, or South African English).

Another noticeable difference is at the lexical level, meaning that different language varieties might use different words or terms to refer to the same concept. Figures 7.2, 7.3, and 7.4 give some examples of well-known vocabulary differences between different language varieties. Can you think of some others?

Spelling and the use of diacritics (i.e., accents on letters) are other ways in which language varieties can differ (see Figures 7.5 and 7.6).

Sometimes there may even be grammatical differences between varieties of the same language. For example, in British English it is common to say "I have eaten dinner already" (using the present perfect construction "have

American English	British English
candy	sweets
dessert	pudding
elevator	lift

Figure 7.2 Vocabulary differences between American English and British English.

French	Canadian French
audio à la demande	baladodiffusion
administrateur de site	webmestre
filoutage	hammeçonnage

Figure 7.3 Vocabulary differences between French and Canadian French.

Portuguese	Brazilian Portuguese
rebuçado	bala
chávena de chá	xícara de chá
tu/vós	você/vocês

Figure 7.4 Vocabulary differences between Portuguese and Brazilian Portuguese.

American English	British English
center	centre
color	colour
organize	organise

Figure 7.5 Spelling differences between American English and British English.

Portuguese	Brazilian Portuguese
camião	caminhão
equipa	equipe
género	gênero

Figure 7.6 Spelling and diacritic differences between Portuguese and Brazilian Portuguese.

eaten"), while in American English it would be typical to hear "I ate dinner already" (using a simple past construction). In another example, in the variety of English spoken in Ireland it is common to use the adverb "after" followed by a present participle (-ing verb) to mean that an action has recently been completed. So the sentence "I'm after having my dinner" in Irish English means the same as "I just had my dinner" in American English.

Pronunciation, vocabulary, spelling, and grammar are important elements to consider when localizing content, but there are many others that can be adapted to make a website or videogame speak more directly to people from another culture and improve their experience of using a product or service. Let's consider some of these non-linguistic elements now.

What non-linguistic elements differ in language varieties?

Because localization involves not only linguistic but also cultural adaptation, a localization specialist might need to make changes or adaptations to a text that go beyond words or terms in order to provide a better experience for the user. For example, date and time formats can differ from one region to another. In the United States it is most common to use the order month/day/year, while in the United Kingdom dates are usually written in the order day/month/year. Therefore, a date such as 12/4/2022 would correspond to December 4 in the US but to 12 April in the UK! Similarly, some regions prefer to write times using the 12-hour clock, e.g., 11:30pm, while others opt for the 24-hour clock, e.g., 23:30. Presenting dates and times in the format that is typical for the region helps customers to interpret the information correctly. Other types of number-related conventions that can differ from region to region include telephone number formats and decimal separators, such as using a point versus a comma (e.g., 10.7 versus 10,7).

Currency is another good example of a unit that may need to be changed as part of the localization process. Not only could there be a difference in the type of decimal separator used, but the unit of currency could change as well. For example, a text for an audience in France or Belgium would show prices in euro (€); a text for an audience in French-speaking Canada would need to show prices in Canadian dollars (CD$); and a text for a French-speaking Swiss audience would display prices in Swiss francs (CHF).

When it comes to units of measurement, some English-speaking countries (e.g., Canada) use the metric system, meaning that kilometres and kilograms are preferred. In contrast, other English-speaking countries (e.g., the United States) use a system of measurements based largely on the imperial system, where units such as miles and pounds are preferred. Meanwhile, yet other English-speaking regions, such as the United Kingdom and Ireland, use a hybrid of the metric and imperial systems, meaning that distances may be measured in miles, but weights are often provided in kilograms (while beer still comes in pints!). Meanwhile, temperatures in Canada are recorded using the Celsius scale, while the Fahrenheit scale is preferred in the United States.

If you are translating a text with visual elements, such as a website or videogame, then it may be necessary to change the colours or images. For instance, in some cultures the colour red is considered to be lucky, while in others it represents danger. Likewise, icons or symbolic images may have cultural significance. For example, a picture of the Washington Monument will be quickly recognized by an American audience, while an image of Tower Bridge will be more familiar to British people. If visual content is meant to represent a given region, then it will be more effective if the people in the image are from ethnic groups found in that region. Similarly, the scenery, wildlife, climate, and landscapes should also be selected in accordance with the region they are meant to represent. It would be strange to use a snowy landscape to represent a Caribbean island, just as it would be odd to select a mountain scene to represent the Netherlands. Meanwhile, bald eagles usually make us think of the United States, beavers are strongly associated with Canada, kangaroos leave us in no doubt that Australia is being represented, and pandas immediately make us draw a connection with China.

Punctuation and layout may also need to be adapted for different languages and regions. For instance, quotation marks are written one way in English (" ") but another way in French (« ») and in German („ "). What's more, in some regions it is standard to read from left to right, in others from right to left, and in yet others from top to bottom. These differences may determine where information should be placed on a page or screen in order to make it appropriately visible. What's more, as we learned in the discussion of internationalization above, some languages take up more space than others, which can also impact how information is organized.

There's definitely a lot to keep track of in localization. However, as noted previously, it is most often a team effort, so it may not be the sole responsibility of the translator to make all the adaptations, such as changing colours, substituting images, or adapting layout. However, it is important for all the elements to work together. It would be really confusing for a reader if the text referred to a red button that was actually blue, or it described an eagle but the accompanying image was of a kangaroo! Therefore, it's important for all team members to have an overall understanding of the different elements that can be localized and to make sure that, in the final version, all of these elements are coherent with one another and best suited to the intended target audience.

What tools and resources can help with localization?

Given the complexity of localization, sophisticated tools and platforms have been developed to support localization activities. However, unless you go on to work as a professional localizer, you are unlikely to encounter many of these tools because they are expensive and specialized. For example, one handy feature of a localization tool is that it can extract the source-language text strings from the surrounding computer code (e.g., HTML tags or programming language) so that the localizer can focus on adapting the text without worrying about accidentally deleting or modifying an important piece of code. Then, when the text has been localized, the tool can automatically insert the translated version back into the appropriate place in the computer code. Because this book is not aimed at preparing professional localizers, we will not explore these professional tools any further here, but you can find more information in the resources listed in the "Find out more" section at the end of this chapter.

Even if you don't wish to work as a localization professional, you may still need or want to adapt texts to different language varieties. For example, you might decide to take advantage of crowdsourcing, which is a technology-enabled approach or business model. Essentially, crowdsourcing refers to the practice of enlisting a large number of people (usually via the Internet) to do a task that was traditionally done by employees or suppliers. Crowdsourcing can be applied to many activities, including translation and localization. In a crowdsourcing model, lots of people make a small contribution, which together add up. So a given individual might translate only one sentence, but if there are many individuals who each translate one sentence, then an entire product (e.g., software interface, website, videogame) can be translated relatively quickly. Facebook and Twitter are two well-known companies that have used crowdsourcing to localize their respective user interfaces.

Sometimes crowdsourcing participants may be paid, but often they are not. Instead, companies may rely on the fact that users want the product to be available in their language, that they are being asked to make only a small contribution, or that they simply enjoy translating. As is the case for any model, there are pros and cons to crowdsourcing localization. From the company's perspective, the option of free or low-cost labour is attractive, and it's a good way to leverage the knowledge of people who are speakers of the desired language variety. However, it's also important for the company to implement quality control measures to ensure that the work of the non-professional localizers will meet the needs of the target audience. From the perspective of the participants, some of the benefits of contributing to a crowdsourced localization project may include non-monetary incentives (e.g., gamification rewards such as badges) or the promise that the product or service will become available in their language variety.

If you are someone who wants to participate in crowdsourcing, or if you have other localization-related needs, then having access to resources and tools that allow you to explore different regional variants may be of interest. As discussed in Chapter 5, term banks such as TERMIUM Plus or IATE make a special note on a term record if the term in question is used mainly in a specific geographic region. For instance, on the record for the term "self-isolation" in the IATE term bank, it is noted that the equivalent "auto-isolement" is used in Canada and Switzerland, but the equivalent "isolement à domicile" is used in other varieties of French.

It is also possible to use an online bilingual concordancer, such as Linguee, to research regional preferences. As you learned in Chapter 5, Linguee displays the source for each sentence that it displays. This source most often takes the form of a web address or Uniform Resource Locator (URL). In many cases, the final segment of the web address contains an indication of the country hosting the web page. For example, .pt indicates that a web page is from Portugal, while .br indicates that it is from Brazil. By noting the source of a given example, you can get some idea of whether that term is used in a particular region.

While it is possible to investigate regional preferences for terms using term banks or online bilingual concordancers, these resources do not always facilitate quick comparisons of the way that terms are used in different varieties of a language. However, there is a tool that allows you to make such comparisons easily. Diatopix (http://olst.ling.umontreal.ca/diatopix/) is a free online tool that was conceived by Patrick Drouin (a professor at the Université de Montréal in Canada) and programmed by Benoit Robichaud. Diatopix allows a user to enter a term or pair of terms and to see how frequently these terms are used in different regions of the world. For varieties of English, the regions available for comparison are Australia, Canada, Ireland, New Zealand, the United Kingdom (UK), and the United States (US). Meanwhile, the different varieties of French that can be compared are those used in Belgium, Canada, France, Luxembourg, and Switzerland. In addition, Diatopix also works for several varieties of Spanish and Portuguese.

How does it work? As explained on the website, Diatopix allows users to see in a graphical format (e.g., a bar graph or pie chart) the way that terms or expressions are distributed on the web. To do this, Diatopix uses the Google search engine's custom search and categorizes the results according to the main countries where that language is used (Australia = .au, Canada = .ca, Ireland = .ie, New Zealand = .nz, etc.). For instance, a user can enter the term "wellington boots" and Diatopix will return an easy-to-read visual display showing that this term is not used very often in any region other than New Zealand, so it would not be a good choice for an audience in Canada. Similarly, a translator could enter two different terms, such as "sweater" and "jumper", and Diatopix will generate a comparative display showing the relative frequency of the two terms in each of the six regional varieties of English. Diatopix can also be used to investigate spelling variants, such as "analyze" and "analyse" or "theatre" and "theater".

Diatopix does have some limitations that you should keep in mind. For example, the tool cannot distinguish between homographs, which are words that have the same spelling but have different meanings or are different parts of speech, such as "pop", which can be a noun, verb, or adjective. So a search for the difference in regional usage between "soda" and "pop" will not return meaningful results because "pop" has more than one meaning. Likewise, Diatopix cannot handle different forms of a given word, so it is necessary to conduct separate searches for a singular and plural form or for conjugated verb forms. In spite of these limitations, Diatopix still offers helpful food for thought about regional variations because, although the tool in itself does not prove anything, it can be used to confirm intuitions regarding word usage or to explore leads related to lexical variants from a geographical point of view. Consult the "Exercises" section at the end of this chapter for suggestions on how to explore this tool in a hands-on way.

In Chapter 6, you learned about machine translation. Up to this point, most of the free online machine translation tools have focused on translating between languages rather than language varieties. However, this has begun to change recently, and a few such tools now offer users the possibility of choosing a particular variety for some target languages. For instance, DeepL Translator allows users to select between English (US) and English (UK) as well as between Portuguese and Portuguese (Brazilian), while Microsoft Translator allows users to choose between French and French (Canadian). In cases where it is possible to select a language variety, localizers may be able to use machine translation tools to assist them with some aspects of localization.

As discussed in Chapter 6, the current approach to machine translation is data-driven, which means that the tool developers feed the machine translation system with many, many examples of previously translated texts for it to learn from. In order to enable a machine translation system to translate into a particular language variety, it is necessary for all the examples in the training data to be from that specific language variety. In other words, in order for a machine translation system to be able to translate into Brazilian Portuguese rather than into Portuguese, the examples provided during the training phase must be in Brazilian Portuguese. Because it takes an extremely large number of examples to successfully train a machine translation system, it may be challenging to find enough texts in language varieties with a smaller number of speakers. This explains why there are not yet many options for choosing language varieties in free online machine translation tools; however, we will undoubtedly see more options moving forward since more and more texts are being translated every day.

Concluding remarks

To effectively market a product or service internationally, it pays to address potential consumers in their own language variety and to respect their cultural conventions. In addition, the digital revolution has given rise to a range of new genres (e.g., software, websites, videogames, mobile apps, virtual assistants) that present some specific challenges when it comes to translation. Together, the desire for globalization and the need for specialized processes to develop locale-specific versions led to the establishment of a new practice known as localization. Localization goes a bit further than translation because, as well as dealing with linguistic variations (e.g., vocabulary, spelling, or grammatical differences), it also deals with non-linguistic elements, such as adapting colours, images, accents, and layout. In addition to the work offered to professional localizers, there are opportunities for non-professionals to participate in localization, such as through crowdsourcing. Freely available tools and resources that can assist with localization include term banks, online concordancers, tools for comparing regional variants (e.g., Diatopix), and some online machine translation systems that permit users to select particular varieties of a target language.

Key points in this chapter

- Many languages have more than one regional variety (e.g., British English, American English, Australian English).
- The acronym GILT refers to four interdependent processes that enable a product or service to transcend local boundaries and to succeed in the world market: Globalization, Internationalization, Localization, and Translation.
- Globalization is a business process whereby a company prepares its products or services for sale all around the world.
- Internationalization refers to the practice of designing products and services in a way that makes them easily adaptable to international markets.
- Localization is the process of taking an internationalized product or service and adapting it to a specific target *locale* (i.e., language and region).
- Translation is the part of localization that deals with converting a written message from a source language to a target language. Translation

changes the language of a text, while localization involves a more comprehensive adaptation.
- Localization usually requires a team of experts (e.g., translators, product engineers, graphic designers, marketing experts, project managers).
- Localization is important for gaining the trust of the target audience and increasing customer engagement.
- Localization is generally applied to services and products that have a digital component, such as software, videogames, virtual reality, websites, mobile apps, virtual assistants.
- Localizers must develop a specialized skillset because many digital genres present constraints that are not found in traditional text types (e.g., space constraints dictated by screen size, non-linear structure).
- Language varieties can differ in their linguistic features, such as pronunciation, vocabulary, spelling, or grammar.
- Language varieties may also have cultural preferences, such as time and date formats, units of measurement, currencies, colours, images, punctuation formats, and layout.
- Professional localizers have access to sophisticated tools that can perform tasks such as extracting source-language text from the surrounding computer code and reinserting the target-language text back into the computer code in the proper place.
- Opportunities for non-professional localization include crowdsourcing, which is a practice whereby a large number of people are enlisted (usually via the Internet) to make a small contribution to a larger shared task (e.g., the localization or translation of a website or software interface).
- Crowdsourcing participants are not usually paid, but the benefit of having the product made available in their language may act as an incentive to participate.
- Resources and tools such as term banks or online concordancers may be used to identify region-specific terms or expressions.
- Diatopix is a free online tool that facilitates the investigation and comparison of regional variants.
- Some free online machine translation tools are now offering users the option of selecting a specific language variety as the target language.

Topics for discussion

As part of a class discussion, or as a prompt for an online discussion forum, consider the following:

- What are the advantages and disadvantages of using a single language of communication (e.g., using English as a *lingua franca* for business or scientific publishing)? What are the advantages and disadvantages of localizing material into multiple language varieties?

- Would you be more likely to buy a product or use a service if it was advertised to you in your preferred language variety? Why or why not?
- Would you be willing to participate in a crowdsourced localization project? Why or why not?

Exercises

- **Compare different localized versions of a website:** Visit the website of a large multinational company such as Coca-Cola (www.coca-cola.com/).
  - Explore different versions of the website that have been localized for varieties of the same language. What are the similarities and differences between versions that are in the same language but aimed at different nationalities/cultures/language varieties? What do you think has motivated these decisions?
    - For **English:** Australia, Canada, Great Britain, Ireland, New Zealand, South Africa, United States, etc.
    - For **Arabic:** Algeria, Egypt, Tunisia, etc.
    - For **French:** Algeria, Belgium, Canada, France, Morocco, Switzerland, etc.
    - For **German:** Austria, Germany, Switzerland, etc.
    - For **Spanish:** Argentina, Bolivia, Mexico, Spain, etc.
  - Explore versions of the website that have been prepared for different language-speaking populations in the same country. Do you notice any surprises when comparing the content for regions that share elements of a culture but not a language?
    - For **Belgium:** Belgium (Belgique) and Belgium (België).
    - For **Canada:** Canada (English) and Canada (Français).
    - For **China:** China and China (Hong Kong).
    - For **Indonesia:** Indonesia (Bahasa) and Indonesia (English).
    - For **Switzerland:** Switzerland (Schweiz) and Switzerland (Suisse).
- **Play with Diatopix:** Diatopix 3.2 (http://olst.ling.umontreal.ca/diatopix/) is a free online tool developed at the Université de Montréal by Patrick Drouin and Benoit Robichaud. It allows you to enter two words (e.g., "railroad" and "railway" or "color" and "colour") and see in which regions of the world these words are most popular. If you are localizing a text, a tool such as Diatopix can help you to determine whether or not a certain word or term is used in a given region. Diatopix currently allows you to compare words in different varieties of English, French, Portuguese, and Spanish. Have fun exploring this tool!
- **Test your knowledge of some different language varieties:** Try some of these online quizzes (or search online for quizzes in other language varieties).

- The **MacMillan Dictionary** quiz on British and American English: www.macmillandictionary.com/learn/language-quizzes/british-or-american-english.html.
- The **Language Portal of Canada** quiz on French used in France and Canada: www.noslangues-ourlanguages.gc.ca/fr/quiz/jeu-quiz-expressiosn-francaises-british-expressions-fra.
- The **Babbel Magazine** quiz on Argentine Spanish: www.babbel.com/en/magazine/quiz-argentine-spanish.

Find out more

Bowker, Lynne. 2021. *Translating for Canada, eh?* University of Ottawa. https://ecampusontario.pressbooks.pub/translatingforcanada/.

- This free Open Educational Resource discusses aspects of localizing into less widely used variants of English and French, namely Canadian English and Canadian French, and includes examples of tools and resources that can be used for this purpose.

Jiménez-Crespo, Miguel A. Forthcoming. *Localization*. London: Routledge.

- This introductory textbook provides the theoretical, conceptual, practical, and methodological foundations for a holistic study of localization phenomena. It enables you to critically engage with concepts, processes, and approaches to localization phenomena, while also helping you to acquire the key practical and professional skills needed in the industry.

Jiménez-Crespo, Miguel A. 2013. *Translation and Web Localization*. London: Routledge.

- This book explores the dynamic nature of web localization and the forces, such as crowdsourcing, that are reshaping web localization and translation as we know it.

O'Hagan, Minako, and Carme Mangiron. 2013. *Game Localization: Translating for the Global Digital Entertainment Industry*. Amsterdam: John Benjamins.

- This book aims to provide a road map for the dynamic professional practices of game localization and to help readers visualize the expanding role of translation in one of the 21st century's key global industries.

8 Adaptation and transcreation

You will understand quite well by this point in the book that most translation involves an element of creativity. Translators rarely take a word-for-word approach. Instead, they seek to understand the underlying message and then repackage it in a way that is meaningful and sounds natural to the target audience. But, as we saw in Chapter 1, translation runs along a spectrum, with literal translation at one end and a much freer approach to translation at the other. Free translation is sometimes referred to as *adaptation* because the process results in a target text that is not accepted as a translation per se (e.g., it may contain omissions, modifications, or even additions) but is nonetheless recognized as representing the source text. When adapting (rather than translating) a text, there is more emphasis on preserving the source text's character and function and less on preserving its form or precise meaning. Some people might even describe localization, which was discussed in Chapter 7, as a type of adaptation.

Adaptation is one of those slippery concepts for which it's hard to pin down a precise definition. How far can a target text stray from the source text before it stops being considered as a translation and starts being regarded as an adaptation? It's very challenging to know where to draw the line, and we are not going to be able to resolve this age-old question here. Instead, it is enough for us to recognize that the border between translation and adaptation is fuzzy rather than fixed. In this chapter, our focus will be on a form of adaptation that is often referred to as *transcreation*. As the term suggests, this activity blends elements of both translation and creation.

Some types of texts are pragmatic in nature and concerned primarily with conveying factual information. For these texts, translation is usually an appropriate strategy. But other texts, such as advertising or marketing materials, are more persuasive than pragmatic. When it comes to advertisements, it's important to make an emotional connection with the audience. We're not just giving them information; we're promoting something and maybe even trying to get them to invest in a product or service. In this case, it's not enough to just transfer the message in a purely functional way. Rather, what we really want to do is to produce some kind of *effect* on our audience. Maybe we want to *intrigue* them, *entice* them, *persuade*

DOI: 10.4324/9781003217718-9

them, or even *make them laugh*. If that's the case, we may need to stray much farther away from the source text than we would for more pragmatic types of translation.

Think about the advertisements you've seen and thought were really effective. Maybe you can even remember an ad from your childhood that has stuck with you; one that is still lodged in your brain all these years later and for which you can recall the tagline or sing the accompanying jingle. Why do you remember this particular ad? Was it funny? Clever? Entertaining? Adorable? Maybe even a bit annoying but in an endearing sort of way? Could you relate to it somehow? The most successful advertisements are usually the ones that manage to connect with the audience on an emotional level. But the advertisements that work for one language or culture may fall flat if translated literally for a different audience. Humour is often culture-bound and witty wordplay just simply doesn't work in the same way in another language. That's why transcreators need to pay attention not only to the content of the message but also to the type of emotional connection that needs to be made with the target audience.

How does transcreation differ from localization and translation?

In Chapter 1 we introduced the basic concept of translation, and in Chapter 7 we explored the difference between translation and localization. Now we are adding transcreation to the mix as well. All three describe strategies used to make content available in a different language. However, the specific processes, as well as the results, can be quite different.

- **Translation** is a way to transfer meaning from one language to another. The way that the information is packaged will change during the transfer, but the essential message should stay the same (see Chapter 1).
- **Localization** grew out of a desire to make digital genres more readily accessible (both linguistically and culturally) to people in different regions of the world. Localization involves addressing both linguistic elements (e.g., vocabulary, spelling, and grammatical differences between language variants such as American and British English) and extra-linguistic elements (e.g., time and date formats, units of measurement, currency, text length, layout, colour, images). Changes that are made to meet local expectations and product need fall under the umbrella of localization (see Chapter 7).
- **Transcreation** originated in marketing and branding, where there is a need to engage with foreign audiences on a more emotional level. To be more memorable and impactful, advertisements often make use of wordplay (e.g., alliteration, rhymes, acrostics, puns, idioms) and cultural references. A literal translation may not be possible, or it might not make sense or sound pleasing to people living in another country who speak a different language, have a different culture, and are familiar

with another market. Therefore, transcreated content uses locally appropriate language and cultural references to convey brand messages. Transcreation is about creating content that has the same impact, effectiveness, and emotional connection in another language, which may require the text to be changed quite a bit.

> According to professional transcreator Claudia Benetello, transcreation consists of:
>
> writing promotional or advertising copy for one specific market (such as the Italian market)
>
> based on a source text
> (i.e., original copy written in another language, such as English)
>
> as though the target text
> (i.e., the Italian version of the text)
>
> were written in the target language for the target culture
> (i.e., written in Italian for Italians).
>
> [Benetello 2017]

What does a transcreation look like?

Let's consider a few short examples to get a feel for what's involved in transcreation. The recent Covid-19 pandemic proved to be a surprisingly rich source of creative new words as people sought to cope with this difficult situation through humour. People around the globe shared a number of common pandemic experiences, but how do these creative terms transfer from one language to another? Sometimes translation is not enough and transcreation strategies must be applied.

Many countries implemented some kind of lockdown during the pandemic as a way of reducing contact between people. With everyone staying home, the days became repetitive and often seemed to blend into one another to the point where it wasn't even easy to tell which day of the week it was. To describe this phenomenon, people on social media began using the word *Blursday* to describe a day of the week that is indistinguishable from the others.

The word *Blursday* is formed using a technique called blending, which is when you take a word or the first part of a word (i.e., blur) and combine it with the second part of another word (i.e., -ursday from Thursday). The resulting word is often referred to as a portmanteau, and it expresses some combination of the meaning of its parts. Blending is a well-used technique that has introduced many new portmanteaus into our vocabulary, such as *brunch, hangry, mockumentary,* and *smog.*

130 Adaptation and transcreation

The challenge when transferring this concept to another language is that it may not be possible to combine the equivalents of the original words (i.e., *blur* and *Thursday*) in a way that produces a similarly pleasing and meaningful result. This means that it is necessary to get creative and to find another way of describing the concept while producing a similar effect on the reader, even if the result is not an exact translation of the source text. And that's precisely what French-speaking users of social media did. The word they came up with to capture the idea of the same day repeating itself over and over during lockdown is *lundimanche*. In this case, the same technique of blending has been used, but the words are not the same as the ones in *Blursday*. In *lundimanche*, the blended words are *lundi* (Monday) and *dimanche* (Sunday). Combining the words for the first and last days of the week creates the effect that all the days of the week are blending together. *Lundimanche* is not a precise translation of *Blursday*, but it conveys the same idea and has a similar effect on the reader by using a term whose original components and meanings are recognizable, and which sounds natural and rolls off the tongue in the target language.

Another feature of the lockdowns was that people spent more time sitting around the house and snacking. As a result, many claim to have gained a little bit of weight during the pandemic – a situation described by some English speakers using the term *Covid-15*. In English, this is a wordplay that combines the format of *Covid-19* with the concept of *the freshman 15* – a phrase that is widely understood in the United States and refers to the fact that many students who go away to college or university end up gaining a bit of weight (e.g., 15 pounds) during their first year of studies. Because this concept is quite culture-bound, it does not transfer well to other languages via a simple translation. Instead, it is necessary to transcreate, which is what German speakers on social media did when they came up with *Coronaspeck* (from *Coronavirus* + *Speck* (= bacon, fat, or flab)). In German, the word *Coronaspeck* was inspired by the existing word *Kummerspeck* (*Kummer* = grief, sorrow), which refers to the weight a person gains from overeating due to unhappiness, depression, grief, or similar emotional conditions. Meanwhile, French speakers took yet another approach with *immobésité* – a blend of the words *immobilité* (immobility) and *obésité* (obesity) – to describe becoming overweight through lack of movement.

Because it was not permitted to socialize indoors, many people instead turned to outdoor socialization activities, finding creative ways to enjoy a drink with friends that did not involve meeting in a pub or bar. In English, there was the *walktail* – a wordplay on *cocktail* – where the drinks are consumed during a socially distanced activity such as a walk with friends. Meanwhile, French speakers could participate in an *apérue* – an *apéritif* to be consumed on the *rue* (street) rather than indoors – while German speakers were able to enjoy an *Abstandsbier* (*Abstands* (= distance) + *Bier* (= beer)).

Adaptation and transcreation 131

The Covid-19-related examples are fun to explore and offer a relatively gentle introduction to some of the key notions involved in transcreation because they are short, largely straightforward, and likely quite relatable to many of us. In the professional world, however, transcreation is mainly carried out in the context of advertising campaigns and branding. Let's turn our attention to an example from an actual marketing campaign used by the Canadian restaurant chain Tim Hortons for their 2021 Christmas holiday packaging (e.g., takeaway coffee cups and food containers).

Tim Hortons was established in 1964 by a Canadian professional ice hockey player named Tim Horton. One of Canada's best-known brands, this iconic chain is affectionately referred to simply as "Tim's" in English or "Tim" in French. It is particularly well known for its coffee and doughnuts, although it also offers a range of soups, sandwiches, and breakfast items.

As part of its brand, Tim Hortons regularly incorporates the company name into some of its product names. For example, the doughnut holes (i.e., the ball-shaped, bite-sized doughnuts that were traditionally made from the dough taken from the centre of ring doughnuts) are known in English as "Timbits". Meanwhile, in French, the breakfast sandwich (e.g., bacon/sausage, egg, and cheese on an English muffin or biscuit) is called a "Timatin" (literally, a morning "Tim").

Building on this strategy of incorporating the name "Tim" into their advertising, the company used the following English and French taglines on their holiday packaging:

English: It's the most wonderful *Tim's* of the year.
French: Vive le *Tim* des fêtes.

Clearly the English and French versions do not mean exactly the same thing; however, in both cases, they have a similar effect on the audience because both draw on classic holiday songs. The English tagline is referring to the song "It's the Most Wonderful Time of the Year", released by pop singer Andy Williams in 1963. Meanwhile, the French tagline makes reference to the song "Vive le temps des fêtes" ("Long live the holiday season"), released by the Quebec vocal trio *Les Baronets* in 1965.

> **Fun fact!** One of the founding members of Les Baronets was René Angélil, who later became known as the manager and husband of Canadian singing sensation Céline Dion.

Both English and French taglines evoke a similar type of nostalgia for Christmases past, and both are very well known by the target audiences in English- and French-speaking Canada respectively. What's more, both taglines managed to integrate a comparable type of wordplay in both languages by substituting the name "Tim" for a similar sounding word – *time* in English and *temps* (= time period) in French. Therefore, while the two taglines cannot be said to be translations of one another, they are effective as transcreations because they have a similar impact on their target audiences.

Why is transcreation important?

As noted above, transcreation is a strategy that is used mainly in marketing and advertising campaigns. However, it need not only apply to huge brands. This strategy can be applied to any text where the goal is to persuade rather than merely inform – for instance, a company website that promotes the company's image by presenting its mission, vision, and values.

When you are dealing with an important campaign, a poor target-language version can jeopardize its effectiveness, which can in turn affect the bottom line. But even if the campaign is on a smaller scale, it is never a good idea to undervalue marketing and communications because a phrase that appears to be straightforward on the surface might actually present a translation conundrum. And an uninspiring or poorly thought-out translation can have far-reaching negative effects on your brand or company's image.

> **Fun fact!** One true story of a company that didn't pay enough attention to how their brand transferred from one language and culture to another was reported in the *Financial Times*. HSBC – a banking and financial services firm – ended up having to pay millions as part of a rebranding effort after their campaign slogan "Assume Nothing" was erroneously rendered as "Do Nothing" in several countries (Robinson 2009).

Examples of some well-executed transcreations have been presented above, but what happens when things go wrong? You have probably come across many stories on social media or the World Wide Web about so-called translation "fails". Some of these may be true, while others may be apocryphal tales or urban legends. Regardless, they can serve as useful cautionary tales about what can go wrong if a company does not pay careful attention to the challenges of transferring a brand from one language and culture to another. One often recounted story concerns the American fast food chain Kentucky Fried Chicken. The company's slogan "Finger lickin' good" was allegedly translated into Chinese as "Eat your fingers off". Another regularly cited example is attributed to Pepsi, whose slogan "Come alive with the Pepsi generation" was reportedly rendered in Chinese as "Pepsi brings your relatives back from the dead". Sometimes it is not only the slogan or tagline but the product name itself that needs to be adapted to succeed in another market. For instance, the American company Vicks, which sells a variety of cough remedies, rebranded itself as Wick for the German-speaking market since the original brand name too closely resembled a word for sexual intercourse. Even if some of these stories are myths or exaggerations, they still draw attention to the need to be aware of the differing linguistic and cultural requirements of target markets around the world. Failure to take these into account could be very costly since it could lead to an unsuccessful advertising campaign and a major loss of sales. Once a brand has a bad reputation, it can be difficult to turn things around, meaning that losses may not be restricted to the short term but could continue in the longer term and hamper a company's efforts to go global. What's more, the rebranding effort could also be an expensive undertaking.

How do transcreators work?

Claudia Benetello (2018), a very experienced transcreation professional, suggests that transcreators are:

- ¼ translator
- ¼ copywriter
- ¼ cultural expert
- ¼ marketer

The transcreation process begins with a creative brief from the client. You learned in Chapter 3 that translators also receive a brief (i.e., a set of instructions) from the client. However, in the case of transcreation, the creative brief includes ideas, concepts, and desired actions that the transcreated text should trigger in the target audience. It also covers information such as the brand's tone of voice and the intended meaning behind the source text. It is important to recognize that transcreation is not simply about being creative. The brief provides a sort of loose framework, and transcreators need to adapt their creativity to suit a brand's intended message and tone of voice while also seeking to connect meaningfully with the target audience.

The next step involves analyzing the source text based on the creative brief. Although translators must work very closely with the source text, transcreators may find that they need to take a step back from the precise wording of the original in order to be able to focus more on the text's intention. In other words, transcreators do need to consult and decode the source text, but once they have extracted the key elements, they put the source text aside so as not to be unduly influenced by its formulations. In addition, advertisements often include visual elements, so transcreators needs to study those too in order to make sure that the text and the visuals will work together.

Cultural sensitivity and local market understanding are very important aspects of transcreation because the target text must be appropriate for the target culture. Transcreators must therefore have a solid understanding of what is or is not acceptable in that target culture. Some of the questions that might need to be answered at this stage of the transcreation process include what background knowledge does the target audience need to have in order to understand the message and what culture-specific information does this message carry.

Once they have a good idea of what they need to aim for in terms of audience response, transcreators can begin brainstorming ideas and keeping track of all the possibilities that occur to them. Transcreation tends to be an iterative process, meaning that transcreators rarely come up with a perfect solution on their first try. Rather, they come up with different ideas, try them out, and revise and improve them. Because advertisements often work with wordplay, transcreators need to bring a lot of creative input to the table. Indeed, transcreators need to have strong copywriting skills in order to identify the correct cultural context, write catchy wordplays, and awaken the desired emotions in the target audience. Interestingly, transcreators may even need to break the rules on occasion. What might be considered an error in translation (e.g., using a non-grammatical construction or a non-standard spelling) could be exactly what is required in a transcreation.

As part of their work during the brainstorming stage, transcreators must often make changes, which can include compensating for an inability to reproduce a specific source-text feature by introducing a somewhat different feature in the target text. For example, consider the following English tagline for the Volkswagen Jetta: "Betta Getta Jetta". This informal and rhyming tagline would be very difficult to translate literally! A transcreator would therefore need to do something quite different, such as dropping the quest for a rhyme and using a different device. Perhaps an alliteration such as "Jetta, je t'aime" could work in French? What other possibilities can you propose, either for French or for another language?

Of course, it's also critical for transcreators to understand the advertising conventions of the target region. While some countries might prefer advertisements that rhyme, this feature may be less prevalent in another region. Likewise, transcreators also need to be aware of the images and wording used by competing brands in order to avoid using the same techniques and instead propose an option that looks and sounds highly original.

Finally, it's worth pointing out that while transcreation very often requires the transcreator to come up with a solution that differs from the one in the original source text, this may not always be the case. Depending on the languages and cultures in question, it may be possible for a transcreator to offer an option similar to the one in the source text. As professionals, it is up to transcreators to use their knowledge and judgement to determine whether a more faithful rendition will have the desired effect on the target audience or whether a more customized and novel transcreation is needed.

Once transcreators have fleshed out some possibilities, they can narrow these down to the version(s) that seem to best convey the core of the original message in a package that works well for the target audience. Of course, such decisions should always be made with reference to the creative brief that was provided. Transcreators often retain more than one option to show to their clients in order to get the clients' input before arriving at a final solution. In this way, unlike conventional translation, transcreation is a highly collaborative process. However, because their clients may not be fluent in the target language, transcreators may need to provide a literal gloss or back-translation of their proposal(s), along with a detailed rationale that explains their decision-making process and the creative approach used. Through the back-translation and the rationale, the clients can get an idea of how the proposed transcreation is intended to work and can provide feedback or suggest changes before the transcreation is finalized.

As you learned in Chapter 3, it is common for translators to charge per word or per line. However, this approach does not work in the case of transcreation because it could take hours of collaborative work to find the right equivalent for a slogan or tagline of just a few words. Because transcreation involves being creative, doing thorough research, and collaborating with others (e.g., marketing team, client), transcreation costs are typically billed at an hourly rate. Transcreation often takes longer than more conventional translation and is more expensive. However, in return, the client receives high-quality creative content that is individually tailored to the target audience and their cultural background.

Concluding remarks

It is clear that there is no unanimous agreement on the definitions and scope of adaptation and transcreation. However, transcreators must often push the boundaries of conventional translation in order to ensure that the form and content of an advertising campaign or brand will resonate with the target audience, whose language, culture, and expectations may differ – sometimes significantly – from those of the original audience. For this reason, we could say that transcreation is a blend of translation, copywriting, cultural expertise, and marketing. Although transcreators may occasionally reproduce the techniques used in the original advertisement, it is more often the case that they must apply various compensation strategies (e.g., substituting a culture-bound reference for a more appropriate one, changing a rhyme to an alliteration). If a company fails to recognize the need for transcreation, this could result in an advertising campaign that falls flat or even damages a company's reputation in the long term.

Key points in this chapter

- Translation, localization, adaptation, and transcreation lie along a spectrum, and the borders between them are fuzzy rather than fixed.
- As its name suggests, transcreation blends elements of both translation and creation (i.e., original writing). In addition to translation skills, transcreators also need to have copywriting skills, cultural expertise, and marketing skills.
- Advertisements often incorporate devices such as rhymes, alliteration, humour, or idioms in order to connect with an audience, but these devices can be very challenging to transfer directly from one language and culture to another.
- Transcreators often need to use compensation strategies, such as replacing a rhyme in the source text with alliteration in the target text.
- Advertisements often contain images or other visual elements, so transcreators must ensure that the proposed text also works with the visuals.
- If an advertising campaign falls flat owing to a poor translation, the company can suffer financial losses and damage to their reputation, so it is worth investing in a customized transcreation.
- Transcreation is an iterative and collaborative process that begins with a creative brief from the client. With the brief's requirements in mind, transcreators analyze the original source text, brainstorm multiple possible options, narrow these down to the most promising ones, and present them to the client along with a back-translation and a detailed rationale or explanation of the decision-making process. The client feedback can then be incorporated into the finalized version.
- Because transcreation is a complex and collaborative process, transcreators do not bill by the word or line but by the hour.

Topics for discussion

As part of a class discussion, or as a prompt for an online discussion forum, consider the following:

- Since all translation requires some degree of creativity, should we consider that all good translations are transcreations? Is transcreation just a trendy name for translation, or are these truly distinct activities?
- If a transcreator proposes a largely faithful rendition of a source-language advertisement, do you believe that this should qualify as a transcreation? Why or why not?
- Consider sharing some of your proposed transcreations from the exercises below with your classmates and offer constructive feedback to some of your peers who have shared their proposals.

Adaptation and transcreation 137

Exercises

- **Adapt some creative terms:** The Covid-19 pandemic introduced many new words into our language as people sought to cope with the major changes that the pandemic introduced to our everyday lives. In many cases, these words were quite creative and involved humour or wordplay, meaning that a straightforward translation is not always possible. Some English-language examples include *covidiot, Coronials, doomscrolling, infodemic, maskne, quarantini, walktail,* and *Zoombombing.* Some examples from German include *Coronafrisur, Fensterbesuch, Fußgruß, Hamsterkauf, Impfneid, Mundschutzmode,* and *Schnutenpulli.* Some examples from French include *apérozoom/Skypéro/WhatsAppéro, balconfinement, coronabdos, covidéprimer, décamérer, mélancovid, solidaritude, télédeuil,* and *télésaluer.*
  - Select some examples from the list of words above (or search on the Internet to identify others).
  - Analyze the words and describe in general terms the technique(s) used to create them. What core elements of the meaning or form do you feel must be preserved in the target text?
  - Propose an equivalent in another language and then provide a back-translation along with a mini-rationale in which you explain the decision-making process that led to your proposal. Were you able to use the same technique(s) that featured in the original or did you approach your transcreation differently?
- **Transcreate an ad:** Imagine that you have been asked to provide a transcreation as part of a campaign against drinking and driving. The source text takes the form of a crossword puzzle containing three words with a tagline underneath (see Figure 8.1). Propose a transcreation in another language and prepare a rationale to explain your decisions.

		D			
D	R	I	N	K	
		I			
		V			
D	I	E			

Don't play with death like
you play with words.

Figure 8.1 Try transcreating this text for a campaign against drinking and driving.

- **Learn what can go wrong:** Just for fun, enter "translation fails in advertising" into a search engine and check out some of the examples of what can (allegedly!) go wrong when proper consideration is not given to the transcreation needs of a local market.

Find out more

Bastin, Georges L. 2020. "Adaptation". In *Routledge Encyclopedia of Translation Studies*, 3rd ed., edited by Mona Baker and Gabriela Saldanha, 10–14. London: Routledge.

- This encyclopaedia entry examines the challenges of differentiating between adaptation and translation and explores a number of attempts at defining and distinguishing these two concepts.

Benetello, Claudia. 2018. "When Translation Is Not Enough: Transcreation as a Convention-Defying Practice. A Practitioner's Perspective". *JoSTrans: Journal of Specialized Translation* 29: 28–44. www.jostrans.org/issue29/art_benetello.php.

- This article provides many examples of transcreation and seeks to establish transcreation as a different activity from translation. The author also identifies the skillset needed in order to succeed as a transcreator.

Katan, David. "Transcreation". 2021. In *Handbook of Translation Studies*, Vol. 5, edited by Yves Gambier and Luc van Doorslaer, 221–225. Amsterdam: John Benjamins.

- This chapter attempts to determine what makes transcreation stand out from localization, adaptation, and translation. It discusses the creativity required for transcreation and describes the professional status of transcreators and the collaborative nature of their work.

Zetzsche, Jost, and Nataly Kelly. 2012. *Found in Translation: How Language Shapes Our Lives and Transforms the World*. New York: Penguin Books Ltd.

- This book, and in particular Chapter 3, provides examples of how good transcreations can help a business to succeed in crossing borders, and how poorly executed translations can have negative impacts on a company's sales and image.

9 Summarization and cross-modal communication

As you've already learned, translators need strong writing skills to be able to reformulate the ideas in the source text in a natural way in the target language. Some of the main skills required for translation can be honed by practicing other types of writing, such as summary writing. Summarization involves transforming a longer text into a shorter one, and it allows budding translators to work on developing a range of key skills that can also be applied to translation. In this chapter, you'll discover more about the relationship between summarization skills and translation skills, and you'll learn how to prepare an effective summary.

In addition, this chapter will introduce the concept of cross-modal communication. In Chapter 1, you learned that translation typically deals with messages in written form, while interpreting most often involves messages in oral form. However, there are some situations where the source message is created in one mode but the target message is produced in another. For example, imagine that your friend has received an email in a language that they don't understand, and they ask you to tell them what it says. The original email is written, but you might relay the content to your friend orally instead of writing it down. Therefore, the mode has changed from writing to speaking. In another example, you might be interested in watching a movie that has been filmed in a language that you don't understand, so you turn on the subtitles. The dialogue in the original movie is spoken, but the subtitles that you are reading are written. So in this case, there is a change of mode from speaking to writing (subtitles will be discussed more in Chapter 10).

What's more, the two activities of summarization and cross-modal communication can even be combined. When you give your friend the gist of the email, you might focus on giving them the overall message rather than translating every single word. Likewise, subtitles in a movie concentrate on transferring the essential message rather than reproducing every word in the on-screen dialogue. Therefore, in addition to examining summarization and cross-modal communication independently, this chapter will also explore how these two activities come together in the language field.

DOI: 10.4324/9781003217718-10

What is a summary?

People are busy! As a result, they may not have the time or the inclination to read every text that they encounter from beginning to end. Instead, many readers want a general overview of a text's main points so that they can quickly identify and locate the content they need to make informed decisions. In some cases, that decision may even be whether or not to continue reading. Summary writers provide a service to readers by condensing information and organizing it in a way that is intuitive and straightforward. To some extent, a written summary is more or less the textual equivalent of a movie trailer: it provides key information that lets the audience know what to expect and enables them to decide whether or not they would like to see more. In our everyday lives, we are surrounded by condensed information. Can you think of some other examples?

For starters, summaries are essential for navigating the Internet. For instance, as part of the search results, search engines such as Google show *snippets* (i.e., text excerpts from websites) to help users identify the most relevant search results at a glance. The social media platform Twitter is designed to allow users to post only condensed messages containing 280 characters or less. Therefore, people often provide just a few key details in a Tweet, along with a link to a website where readers can find more complete information. The Internet has even led to the invention of a new type of summary: TL;DR.

TL;DR (sometimes written simply as TLDR) is an abbreviated form that stands for "too long; didn't read". In Internet discussion forums such as Reddit, TL;DR was first used as a shorthand response to indicate that a previous post was considered to be unnecessarily long and extensive. Now, the term TL;DR is often accompanied by a very brief summary of the main content (e.g., at the beginning or end of a post). Readers who are really interested in the topic can read the full message to obtain all the details, while those who just want an overview can limit themselves to reading only the TL;DR summary.

Summaries exist in other contexts too. For example, in the business world, many lengthy reports begin with an executive summary, which is a brief presentation of the report to help a busy manager make an informed decision about which parts to read in detail and which to skim or even skip. Meanwhile, some students may have consulted an abridgement of a longer work, such as a shortened version of a novel (e.g., Signet Classics abridged works) or a study guide that provides chapter summaries of a literary work (e.g., CliffsNotes or SparkNotes). Elsewhere in the academic world, researchers typically prepare a scientific abstract to accompany their research articles. These abstracts are compiled into research databases, which other researchers then use to identify material that is relevant to their own work. By reading the scientific abstract, a researcher can determine whether it would be worthwhile to obtain and consult the complete research article. Helpfully, it is becoming increasingly common to provide scientific abstracts in more than one language, which makes it easier for researchers around the globe to stay informed about critical developments in their field, even if these are taking place elsewhere in the world or reported in another language.

Now that we have seen a few examples of summaries that are used in different areas of our lives, we can identify a couple of key features. First, a summary is always shorter than the original source. Second, it conveys the same concepts but in different words. Essentially, summarization requires a re-formulation of the meaning of the original source. As a summary writer, you must identify and express the source's essential message (or information) accurately and concisely in your own words. Therefore, there is a clear overlap between the skills needed for summary writing and those needed for translation. However, because translation is quite a complex activity involving the transfer of ideas from one language to another, it can be a very challenging task for beginners. As a gentle approach to developing essential translation skills, it can be helpful to start by working on summarization skills.

How can summarization help to build translation skills?

Translation involves both passive (decoding) and active (encoding) language skills. To begin, translators need to read and understand the source text, and these comprehension-oriented tasks use passive language skills. Later, translators need to engage their active language skills in order to produce a target text. Like translation, summarization is a task that involves both a comprehension phase and a production phase. However, because summarization can be carried out in a single language, it is an activity that will enable you to develop some basic skills before working up to the more complex task of translation. In *intralingual* summarization, you begin by reading a longer text and then go on to produce a shorter version in the same language. By working in just one language, you can focus on the comprehension and production tasks without needing to worry about the more complex transfer issues.

Once you have gained some experience with intralingual summarization, you can try your hand at *interlingual* summarization, which involves reading a longer text in one language (e.g., Arabic) and then summarizing it in another language (e.g., German). This activity of transferring the essential elements of a longer text in one language to a shorter text in another language makes a good next step on the path to translation. Because a summary necessarily focuses only on the main or essential content of the text, you don't need to get caught up in trying to transfer every small detail or worry about finding an equivalent for every word in the original text. By working first on your intralingual and then your interlingual summarization skills, you are building up a skillset that can later be used to help you to tackle the more complex job of translation.

Another way that summary writing provides good training for translation is through its focus on textually oriented activities. In other words, in both summarization and translation, it is necessary to pay attention to the *text* as a unit. For instance, when preparing a summary, you need to focus on the overall message rather than the individual words. You do not set out to summarize each sentence individually in order to achieve a series of shorter sentences. Instead, you need to take a more holistic approach that focuses on identifying the overall message and logic of the original text, rather than concentrating on its micro-elements. Likewise, when translating, you do not set out to translate a series of individual words or sentences but must instead focus on translating the text. Therefore, this skill of being able to analyze the original text and extract the key components of a message is indispensable not only to summary writing but to translation as well.

Finally, once the essential meaning of the source text has been extracted, you need to paraphrase that message in a more concise way to create a summary. Writing a good summary does not mean simply copying and pasting a few key sentences from the source text into a new document. Rather, summarization requires you to reformulate the key content in a way that is clear, accurate, and stylistically appropriate in order to create a new and shorter text. While translation does not always involve condensing a text, it does require the ability to skilfully manipulate a text in order reformulate an idea for the target audience. Hence, this is another way in which skills developed as part of summarization are transferrable to translation.

Now that you understand how summary writing can contribute to developing translation skills, let's take a look at the general principles involved in summarization, followed by a more detailed examination of the steps to follow to prepare a summary.

How can you write an effective summary?

Although summaries can exist in different forms (e.g., Tweets, executive summaries, scientific abstracts), broadly speaking, summaries are based on the same general principles:

1. Orientation towards the intended purpose and target audience.
2. Discrimination between essential and non-essential content.
3. Careful selection of key ideas.
4. Compilation of essential information into a new, more condensed text.

Let's take a look at how these general principles can be applied in the specific steps you can follow to produce an effective summary. Begin by reading and digesting the following steps, then put these into practice by trying the exercises at the end of the chapter. Remember, the skills required to write a summary overlap with the skills needed for translation, so by practicing your summary writing, you are sharpening your translation skills at the same time.

Step 1: Understand

In this step, you will be using your passive language skills, which focus on reading comprehension or decoding the message contained in the original source. Begin by reading the original text all the way through very carefully. The goal here is not only to understand the subject content but also to see how the various stages in the explanation or argument are built up in the groups of related paragraphs. In addition, try to identify the purpose of the text, how the author feels about the topic, and what style or tone the author is using.

During this step, it may help to ask yourself the following questions:

- What is the text about?
  - Main topic, subtopics.
- What is the purpose of the text?
  - Is the author trying to inform, describe, persuade, explain, entertain?
- What is the author's attitude?
  - Does the author express a personal point of view or is the text objective?
- What is the style and tone of the text?
  - Literary/journalistic/scientific; formal/informal; abstract/concrete; sarcastic/sincere/friendly?

In most cases, when writing a summary, you should aim to reproduce elements such as the style and tone of the original; however, there may be exceptions to this practice, such as when writing a plain language summary. As discussed previously, in the academic world, a research article is normally accompanied by a scientific abstract, and this abstract is intended to be read by the same type of audience that may also read the longer research article (i.e., other researchers working in the same subject field). Therefore, the scientific abstract adopts the same terminology and tone as the original research article while condensing the content. However, the research article may also be accompanied by a plain language summary. A plain language summary has a different purpose and a different target audience: it is intended to give non-subject experts a general idea of what the research is about. Therefore, a plain language summary needs to use non-technical terminology and a very clear and accessible style since the intended readers do not have a background in the subject field. Because the intended purpose and target audience of a summary may differ from those of the original text, it is very important to understand how the summary will be used and for whom it is being written.

Step 2: Analyze

The main purpose of this step is to study the manner in which ideas are presented by the author. Try to determine the underlying structure of the text by observing the way that ideas are organized and developed (e.g., paragraph by paragraph). As you read the original source a second (or third) time, take notes and underline the most important ideas (e.g., key words, expressions, or sentences). Recreate the structure of the original document in outline form by dividing longer texts into sections and writing one or two sentences that capture the main points of each section. Omit ideas that are not central to the text, such as minor details, opinions, quotes, and specific examples. Remember that it is important not to get distracted by details but to remain firmly focused on the global theme and purpose of the text and to identify how each part relates to the overall message.

Step 3: Select

As you analyze the content and weigh the relevance of each element of the text, some ideas will emerge as having primary importance, while others will appear secondary. Often, the answers to what journalists call the five Ws (who, what, where, when, and why) will correspond to key pieces of information. In some ways, we can compare the idea of summary writing to the popular game Jenga. At the beginning of the game, all the wooden blocks are stacked into a solid rectangular tower. Players must analyze the tower and try to select the blocks that can be removed without causing the tower to collapse. Likewise, a summary writer must exercise judgement, logic, and common sense to discriminate between essential and non-essential content in the original text. Focus on the overall message and view concepts in light of the text's context rather than using a sentence-by-sentence approach. Remember that importance is relative: weigh an idea in comparison to the importance of those around it. By the end of this step, you will have selected the ideas in the original text that need to be transferred to the summary.

Step 4: Compress

Using your active language skills, look for logical ways to condense the retained material by pruning away unnecessary details and paraphrasing elaborate content. For example, convert specific details into general statements:

- A statement such as "47.3% of respondents polled said they agreed or strongly agreed that food labels should include information about the percentage of trans fats the food item contained" could be simplified to "Almost half of respondents want food labels to include trans fats".

- A reference to "drums, guitars, bass, and piano" could become "instruments".
- A list of names and titles such as "United States President Joe Biden, Chinese President Xi Jinping, and German Chancellor Olaf Scholz" could be shortened to "the leaders of the US, China, and Germany".

Overall, the goal is to use the fewest words possible while still preserving the essential meaning or information. However, it is important not to sacrifice clarity for economy because the summary will not be useful to readers if they cannot understand it.

Step 5: Draft

Based on your notes, continue using your active language skills to draw up a draft. In general, follow the same pattern of ideas found in the original; sometimes rearranging the presentation of ideas can help to clarify or condense material, but take care not to distort the message. Be faithful to the meaning in the source text, but create an original composition rather than a collage or a cut-and-paste patchwork. It's important to convey the ideas in a clear and readable style rather than as a string of choppy fragments. The resulting summary needs to stand on its own as an independent text, which means that readers must be able to understand the content of the summary without needing to refer to the original source. Some tips for keeping things brief in the drafting stage include:

- Keep a title for the text but do not use subtitles.
- Present original content, not background material.
- Convert direct speech (quotations) to indirect speech (paraphrase).
- Use the active rather than the passive voice.

Step 6: Revise

As discussed in Chapter 5, it's rare for writers (or translators) to get a text exactly right the first time around. It's completely normal for a first draft to be a little rough around the edges, so it's important to take the time to revise the text. Summaries are often meant to be of a prescribed length, so if the first draft is too long, return to Step 4 and look for additional ways to compress the text. Are there places where you can rephrase ideas more succinctly? Double check that your summary contains only essential ideas. Read over the complete text to ensure that all the important information has been presented without distortion. In addition, make sure that the summary can stand on its own and that it reflects not only the content but also the style and tone of the original. Finally, check for grammar, spelling, or punctuation errors.

By adhering to these principles and following these steps, you can not only learn to prepare effective summaries but also sharpen a skillset that is used in translation. Once you have practised writing intralingual summaries (i.e., summaries where both the original text and the summary are in the same language), move on to the next stage by working on interlingual summaries (i.e., prepare a summary in a language that is *not* the language used in the original source).

What is cross-modal communication?

Messages can be communicated in a written mode (e.g., an email message), in a spoken mode (e.g., a conversation), in a visual mode (e.g., a conversation in sign language), or sometimes in a combination of these (e.g., a text message containing both text and emojis). Sometimes the same information might be available in more than one mode. For example, an English-language video might also have captions or a written transcript available in English.

For the most part, language professionals tend to work within a single mode of communication. That is, translators convert a written document in one language into a written document in another language, while interpreters transfer a spoken message in one language into a spoken message in another language. Sometimes, however, there is a change not only in language but also in mode.

One very recognizable example of cross-modal communication in the world of translation is sign language interpreting. Sign language is a system of communication using visual gestures and signs that is commonly used by deaf people. Sign languages are rich and complex languages with their own grammar and lexicon. Many different sign languages exist, and these are not universal or mutually intelligible. Rather, each country generally has its own sign language, and some have more than one. Examples include American Sign Language (ASL), British Sign Language (BSL), Indo-Pakistani Sign Language (IPSL), *Langue des signes française* (LSF), and *Langue des signes québécoise* (LSQ). In addition, sign languages generally do not have any linguistic relation to the spoken languages of the countries in which they are used. For instance, the sign languages used in Spain and Mexico are very different, even though Spanish is the national language in both these countries.

Sign language interpreters may be fluent in two or more sign languages and may interpret between these (e.g., between BSL and LSF), in which case the communication is not cross-modal. However, when an interpreter interprets between a sign language (e.g., ASL) and a spoken language (e.g., English), this entails cross-modal communication. The general topic of interpreting will be explored in more detail in Chapter 11, but for the moment, sign language interpreting is being presented as a familiar example of cross-modal communication.

Another example of cross-modal communication in the language professions is sight translation, which is sometimes referred to as *transterpreting* because it combines elements of both translation and interpreting. In sight translation, the language professional transforms a written source-language message into a spoken target-language message. Sight translation is often done more or less on the spot with little time for preparation. Settings where sight translation might take place include courtrooms, hospitals, or business meetings. For instance, a court interpreter may be asked to sight translate a witness statement that is written in a language not being used in the court proceedings. The court interpreter will sight translate the document "for the record", and the results will be recorded. Meanwhile, in a healthcare setting, information such as questionnaires, registration forms, or patient information materials may be presented in written form, and an interpreter may need to sight translate these documents for a patient.

Now that you have seen some examples of how language professionals might need to convert a message not only from one language to another but also from one mode to another, let's see what happens when summarization gets thrown into the mix as well!

How can summarization and cross-modal communication come together in a translation context?

In the preceding sections, the concepts of summarization and cross-modal communication have been considered independently, but sometimes these two activities are carried out together in a multilingual environment. For instance, one group of language professionals who may need to combine summarization and cross-modal communication skills are the précis-writers who work for the UN, which, as mentioned in Chapter 2, has six working languages: Arabic, Chinese, English, French, Russian, and Spanish. Language professionals such as translators and interpreters therefore play a key role in enabling the operations of the UN, and one particular task carried out by these language professionals is précis-writing.

At the UN, précis-writers are translators who are also responsible for drafting the summary records of multilingual meetings of groups such as the Security Council, the Economic and Social Council, the Peacebuilding Commission, and the International Law Commission. Summary records are similar to meeting minutes, and they form a key part of the institutional memory of the UN. Summary records are not a verbatim or word-for-word account of what was said in the meeting but rather a summarized analysis. They are meant to indicate who spoke at the meeting, the main points of what was said, and what was decided. In addition to constituting the official record of the meeting, summary records are used as a basis for intergovernmental discussion, for compiling reports and conducting research on the topics covered, and sometimes in the decisions made by experts or judges.

Each original summary record is later translated into the other working languages of the UN.

Précis-writers summarize interventions made by various delegates in the meeting, which may be delivered in any working language of the UN. As reference material, précis-writers use a combination of written and oral statements, audio and video recordings, and other material such as official UN documents or digital presentations (e.g., slides). Combining the skills of cross-modal communication, translation, and summarization, précis-writers use their judgement and their knowledge of the subject matter to determine what should be condensed, expanded, omitted, or explained in order to produce an accurate and stylistically appropriate account of a meeting that will be understood equally well whether the reader was present at the meeting or not.

Other language professions where it is common to combine elements of summarization and cross-modal communication include subtitling and consecutive interpreting, which will be explored in more detail in Chapter 10 ("Audiovisual translation") and Chapter 11 ("Interpreting").

Concluding remarks

The skills required for summarization overlap considerably with the skills needed for translation. Summarization encourages writers to adopt a contextual rather than a linear view of the original source, and it emphasizes the need to understand the underlying logic of the text rather than focusing on its surface structures. This has important implications for learning to translate. Translators do not simply replace a series of terms with a series of equivalents; rather, they attempt to reconstruct a pattern of meaning. Grasping the pattern of meaning of a text and seeing the individual elements as partial expressions of this pattern is key. Understanding the broader pattern of meaning frees the writer or translator from the constraints of the words in the original. Because summary writing, like translation, cannot be accomplished without textual analysis, this activity helps you to think of meaning in terms of context. In addition, it encourages you to think clearly, to reformulate meaning accurately, and to write well, thus making it an exercise that is well suited to prepare you for translation activities. What's more, summarization exercises can be undertaken as a series of increasingly challenging activities, such as by moving from intralingual to interlingual summarization and by combining summarization with cross-modal communication.

Key points in this chapter

- There is considerable overlap between the skills required for summarization and the skills needed for translation, so learning to summarize is good preparation for learning to translate.

- A summary is a condensed version of an original text that provides an overview of the text's main points to allow readers to identify key content and make decisions.
- Summaries can take different forms, and some common examples include Tweets that link to a more detailed website, TL;DR summaries in Reddit posts, executive summaries at the start of a business report, chapter summaries in study guides such as CliffsNotes, and scientific abstracts and plain language summaries that accompany research articles.
- Summaries are always shorter than the original text and usually paraphrase the original content.
- Summary writers must discriminate between essential and non-essential content.
- Summaries can be intralingual (where the original text and summary are both in the same language) or interlingual (where the original text and summary are in different languages).
- Communication can take place in different modes, such as written, spoken, or visual.
- Although language professionals tend to work within a single mode (e.g., translators convert a written source-language text into a written target-language text), some language transfer activities also entail a change in mode (e.g., a written message in the source language becomes a spoken message in the target language, or vice versa).
- Some examples of cross-modal communication in the language professions include sign language interpreting and sight translation.
- Some activities that combine summarization and cross-modal communication in a multilingual environment include the subtitling of movies or shows and précis-writing at the UN.

Topics for discussion

As part of a class discussion, or as a prompt for an online discussion forum, consider the following:

- In *Provincial Letters* (1656), the 17th-century French philosopher Blaise Pascal makes the following statement: "Forgive me for writing a long letter, but I did not have time to write a shorter one". In your opinion, is it easier to write a short text or a long text, and why?
- Legend has it that author Ernest Hemingway was once challenged to write a story in only six words. The result? "For sale: baby shoes, never worn." Though we can't be certain that this story actually came from Hemingway, it definitely sparked a trend. One example is the Six-Word Memoir Project founded by Larry Smith (www.sixwordmemoirs.com/). Check out the website for inspiration and then propose your own six-word memoir or a six-word story about some aspect of translation or another topic of your choosing.

Exercises

- **Prepare an intralingual summary:** Begin by going to a news website in your home country. Select an article of interest to you, then prepare a summary in the same language that is approximately one quarter the length of the original article. Repeat this exercise a few times with articles of different lengths until you feel confident in your summary writing skills. To increase the challenge, set a time limit and try to work at a quicker pace.
- **Prepare an interlingual summary:** Choose a news website in your second or third language. Select an article of interest to you, then prepare a summary in your dominant language that is approximately one quarter the length of the original article. To increase the challenge, try finding a text in your dominant language and producing an interlingual summary in a less dominant language.
- **Produce a written summary of a podcast:** Find a podcast on a topic of interest to you. Listen to the podcast and take notes. Transform your notes into a written summary of the podcast content.
- **Sight translate a text:** Find a short (250-word) text or text extract on a topic of interest to you in your second or third language. Take no more than two minutes to familiarize yourself with the text, then translate the text out loud in your dominant language. If you have a recording device (e.g., smartphone), try recording yourself as you perform the sight translation. Play back the recording and compare it to the original text segment by segment. To increase the level of difficulty, find a text in your dominant language and do the sight translation into a less dominant language.

Find out more

Babin, Monique, Carol Burnell, Susan Presznecker, Nicole Resevear, and Jaime Wood. n.d. *The Word on College Reading and Writing*. Open Oregon Educational Resources. https://openoregon.pressbooks.pub/wrd/ (see chapter on writing summaries: https://openoregon.pressbooks.pub/wrd/chapter/writing-summaries/).

- This free Open Educational Resource contains a chapter with a detailed guide to writing summaries.

Bowker, Lynne, and Cheryl McBride. 2017. "Précis-Writing as a Form of Speed Training for Translation Students". *The Interpreter and Translator Trainer* 11, no. 4: 259–279.

- This article contains a detailed examination of how summarization exercises can be useful preparation for translation, including a report on how speed training can be used to help students develop quicker reflexes for summary writing and translation.

Chen, Wallace. 2015. "Sight Translation". In *The Routledge Handbook of Interpreting*, edited by Holly Mikkelson and Renée Jourdenais, 144–153. London: Routledge.

- This chapter explains the concept of sight translation, including its relationship to both translation and interpreting, and recommends practices for teaching sight translation.

Pattison, Ann, and Stella Craigie. 2022. *Translating Change: Enhanced Practical Skills for Translators*. London: Routledge.

- In Chapter 4, "Transferable Skills", the authors provide practical tips on writing summaries in mono- and multilingual contexts.

10 Audiovisual translation

In February 2020, a historic event took place at the Oscars (more officially known as the Academy Awards ceremony that is hosted by the Academy of Motion Picture Arts and Sciences). For the first time in its 92-year history, the academy gave the award for "Best Picture" to a non-English-language film! The winner was *Parasite*, which is set in Korea with Korean dialogue. But how did the largely English-speaking members of the academy manage to judge and appreciate this foreign-language film? Because it was subtitled in English! Although Bong Joon-ho (the film's writer, director, and producer) deserves much of the credit for the film's success, we must also give some credit to Darcy Paquet, the audiovisual translator who made the film accessible to English-speaking audiences through subtitles.

In addition to the film industry, video streaming services (e.g., Netflix, Amazon Prime Video, Disney Plus, HBO Max, and Hulu), along with video sharing platforms for user-generated content (e.g., YouTube and TikTok), have contributed to an increased appetite for and consumption of audiovisual media in recent years. As the global demand for content increases, so does the demand for audiovisual translation. Subtitling, dubbing, and voiceover are the three main approaches to audiovisual translation, which can be applied to films, television series, documentaries, or videos.

- **Subtitling:** A written translation of the main points in the dialogue of the original program, which is usually presented in a couple of lines at the top or bottom of the screen.
- **Dubbing:** An oral translation, in the form of a target-language recording to replace the original soundtrack, that reproduces the original message while ensuring that the target-language sounds and the actors' lip movements are synchronized in such a way that the audience believes the on-screen actors are actually speaking their language.
- **Voiceover:** An oral translation in a target language that can be heard simultaneously over the source-language voice in the original program (i.e., the source-language voice is faintly audible in the background).

DOI: 10.4324/9781003217718-11

You may also have encountered similar techniques, such as captioning or audio description, in contexts that do not necessarily involve transferring content from one language to another. Although this chapter will focus primarily on audiovisual translation, which necessarily involves two languages, we'll comment briefly on some of the ways that similar techniques can be used to improve accessibility at the end of the chapter.

Is audiovisual translation a recent development?

Although streaming services such as Netflix and Hulu, and web-based platforms for sharing user-generated content such as YouTube and TikTok, have given a tremendous boost to the digital entertainment industry, which is currently booming, audiovisual translation has a much longer history dating back to the era of silent films (mid-1890s to the late 1920s). In silent films, there was no on-screen dialogue, and a pianist, organist, or even a small orchestra might be located in the theatre to provide live musical accompaniment to the film. In addition, there was often a person whose job it was to explain and comment on what was happening on the screen. The earliest silent films were relatively short and straightforward, but as they grew longer and developed more intricate plot lines, it became common to add what are known as *title cards* or *intertitles* – that is, pieces of filmed, printed text that were inserted between frames – to explain key plot details or add simple dialogue. Writing intertitles even became a profession, and a silent film could be adapted for a foreign audience by translating the intertitles into another language. Meanwhile, in Japan, yet another new profession emerged, the *benshi*, who were essentially live interpreters whose commentary included explaining the cultural conventions that featured in the mostly Western films to the Japanese audience in the cinema.

> **Fun fact!** At the very first Academy Awards in 1929, there was an award for "Best Writing – Title Cards", but this category was discontinued after just one award since intertitles were no longer used once sound became regularly integrated into films from the 1930s onwards.

As films transitioned from being silent to featuring sound (i.e., "talkies"), new approaches were needed to successfully deliver these products to other countries. One strategy that was developed involved taking the same story and dialogue but shooting the film in a number of different languages using the same technical crew but different actors. Although these multilingual versions were more like parallel productions than translations per se, there were elements of translation involved (e.g., adaptation of the screenplay). Unfortunately, this approach of filming multiple versions of the same film turned out to be cumbersome and costly, and the making of multilingual versions was eventually phased out as subtitling and dubbing techniques, which remain popular today, evolved.

In the 1980s, another type of audiovisual translation, known as *surtitling*, was introduced to accompany live theatrical performances, such as opera. Surtitling involves projecting the translated lyrics or dialogue above (or sometimes to the side) of the stage during a performance. In other words, surtitles are used for live performances in a way that resembles how subtitles are used for films or series.

What are some of the general challenges in audiovisual translation?

Although subtitling, dubbing, and voiceover each pose specific challenges, audiovisual translation more generally has its own challenges for translators, including some that we have seen in previous chapters. For instance, because many films and series are designed to entertain us, humour is very often a key feature. As you learned in Chapter 8 on transcreation, humour doesn't always transfer directly or easily from one culture to another. If an element of humour is culture-bound, or if a particular element of wordplay cannot be recreated, then an audiovisual translator may need to substitute a more meaningful example rather than trying to approach the translation literally. An example from the Oscar-winning movie *Parasite* is the substitution of a reference to Seoul National University with a reference to Oxford University in the English subtitles. In the original Korean script, the character jokingly asks if Seoul National University offers a major in document forgery. Part of the humour of the line requires the viewers to know that this university is extremely prestigious. While Korean viewers immediately make that connection, the high status of this Korean university may not be immediately clear to English-speaking viewers, so the translator opted to change this reference to Oxford University, which English-speaking filmgoers will readily identify as a high-quality educational institution.

Another cultural issue that often confronts audiovisual translators is profanity. Sometimes a literal equivalent for a curse word that doesn't seem very strong in one culture may be much more offensive in another. Audiovisual translators need to be culturally sensitive and must be able to adapt the translation accordingly so that it has an equivalent effect on the target audience (see Chapter 1).

The use of different accents (e.g., British versus American English or North versus South Korean) can also be difficult to transmit in a subtitled or dubbed version. Owing to its phonological nature, an accent can be difficult to show when moving from an oral to a written mode. And as you'll learn below, dubbing presents other constraints, such as the need to synchronize the sound with the lip movement of a character.

Finally, it is relatively common for audiovisual translation to use indirect translation methods and pivot languages. As described in Chapter 6, indirect translation involves translation from the source language to the target language via a third so-called pivot language. So a Korean film might first be translated into English, then the English version could be used as the source text to translate into Dutch, Danish, etc. The advantage is that this can serve to make translations available in a wider range of languages than would be possible using only direct translation. However, any problematic issues that arise in the first stage (i.e., when translating from Korean into English) would then be carried forward into the subsequent translations (i.e., from English into Dutch).

On top of these general challenges, audiovisual translators must deal with additional specific constraints depending on whether they are producing a subtitled, dubbed, or voiced-over version. Let's now dig into some of these specific issues.

What is involved in subtitling?

Subtitling essentially involves inserting translated captions at the bottom (or sometimes top) of the screen while the sound plays in the original language. If you have ever watched a film or series in a foreign language that you understand a little bit, then you have undoubtedly noticed that what is said in the dialogue isn't always the same as what appears in the subtitles. Why does this happen? Well, there are many contributing factors. Let's consider some of the main ones here.

First of all, it's important to recognize that subtitles will cover up part of the image on the screen. To avoid obstructing too much of the visual content, it's essential to keep the subtitles relatively short. The industry standard is to have a maximum of two lines of text, each with no more than around 40 characters, visible on screen at any one time. That is not very much text in which to convey a lot of information. Consider the sentence: "This sentence has a total of 43 characters". Yes, it really does contain only 43 characters (because blank spaces count as characters too)! What's more, the two lines of text may also need to explain or translate any words that appear as part of the visual content. For example, perhaps a character on screen is reading a letter or a message on a mobile phone, or maybe there is a sign or poster in the background whose content is important to the plot. A translation of this on-screen text will also need to be included in the subtitle. There is definitely a lot of information to pack into just a couple of lines, which is why the type of summarization skills you learned in Chapter 9 will come in very handy for subtitling. What's more, a subtitler also needs to pay attention to the best place to break a line or split a subtitle so that it reads smoothly and isn't choppy or jarring.

In addition to not covering up too much of the visual content, subtitles must also be kept short because each segment is only displayed for roughly six seconds. If the subtitle is too long, an average reader will not be able to finish reading it before it disappears and is replaced by the next subtitle. Keep in mind that, in addition to reading the subtitle, the viewer is also trying to take in the visual content, so they cannot devote all their attention to reading. As part of subtitling, audiovisual translators also need to do a task known as spotting, which means they need to decide at which moment each subtitle should appear and then disappear from the screen. The introduction and duration of a subtitle needs to be coordinated with what else is happening on the screen. For instance, a subtitle containing a line of dialogue by a particular character should coincide with the moment that character actually delivers the line on screen.

Because subtitling is a form of cross-modal communication (see Chapter 9), another challenge faced by subtitlers is how to express the oral speech of the source language in written form in the target language. For instance, how can intonation, accents, or pauses be conveyed in written mode? To deal with these features, audiovisual translators have found creative solutions, such as using a larger font size to convey loudness, or using punctuation such as ellipses to convey pauses (...).

Other considerations for subtitlers include choosing an easy-to-read font (e.g., a sans-serif font, such as Arial or Helvetica), ensuring that the font size is legible, and making sure that the font has a suitable colour contrast against the background so that people will be able to read the text. It would not be a good choice to have white letters against a light-coloured background, for example. In addition, the placement of the subtitles is also important. Most of the time they are centred at the bottom of the screen, but sometimes there can be a good reason to move them (e.g., to the top of the screen), such as if they would be covering up an important element of the picture. For languages that are read vertically rather than horizontally (e.g., Japanese), the subtitles might run down the side of the screen. Finally, in a film or series that has been subtitled, the audience can hear the original version, and even if they don't understand the source language, the viewers are experiencing emotionally what the actors are saying. They can also see the actor's body language, so the content of the translation needs to match the performance as well as convey the intended meaning. For instance, imagine that a character says a line such as "Paris is not the capital of Belgium". A translator might be tempted to convert the negative construction in the source language to a positive one in the target language because it is shorter and would require fewer characters (e.g., "Paris is the capital of France"). This might work well in some cases, but what if the character in question was also shaking their head while delivering the line? In this case, the body language requires that a negative construction be maintained because it could be confusing to the audience if the character uttered a positive statement while simultaneously shaking their head.

It was noted in Chapter 3 that professional translators are facing mounting pressure to work more quickly, and this applies to audiovisual translators too. Automatic machine translation is one type of technology that has the potential to enable subtitlers to work more quickly, but it must be used carefully because unedited machine translations are not always of high quality (see Chapter 6). Although machine translation offers exciting possibilities in the context of subtitling, more work is needed to determine how this technology can be effectively integrated with other tools used by subtitlers and with the audiovisual translation workflow more generally. Using machine translation alone to translate subtitles is highly unlikely to produce results that will be well-received by target-language audiences.

What is involved in dubbing?

Dubbing involves replacing the original soundtrack containing the actors' dialogue with a target-language recording that reproduces the original message while also making sure that the sounds in the target language and the actors' lip movements are synchronized. The idea is to give viewers the impression that the actors on screen are actually speaking in the target language.

Dubbing is a complex process that involves many types of professionals, including translators, adapters, dubbing directors, voice actors, and sound technicians, to name some of the most important ones. Because it is so complex and labour-intensive, dubbing is also expensive and could cost up to ten times as much as subtitling. Typically, a translator will produce a rough translation and then an adapter works with the translator to synchronize the translation with the audio and visual cues of the original.

There are three main types of synchronization that need to be taken into account. *Lip sync(hrony)* ensures that the target text fits properly with the mouth opening of the on-screen character. This is particularly important during close-ups. To ensure a good fit, translators and adaptors cannot only be concerned with larger units of meaning (e.g., phrases or sentences). They also need to focus on letters and syllables. To deal with the fact that the two languages will not match up exactly at the phonetic level, dubbers may need to delete some words or even introduce some "padding" (i.e., words that are not essential to convey the intended meaning but which will allow the lip movements to match up with the sounds). Sometimes it may be necessary to choose between a phrase that matches the lip movements but which is clumsy or awkward in the target language and one that is elegant and idiomatic in the target language but which does not match the lip movements. The situation where the lip movements and sounds are not well synchronized is referred to as *lip flap*, and viewers may find it distracting or annoying.

A second type of synchronization required is between the translation and the actors' movements and gestures. Known as *kinetic synchrony*, this is the same as with subtitling, discussed above, where the dialogue must not contradict the image (e.g., saying "yes" while shaking one's head). It is also important to try to match the actor's voice to the personality and physical appearance of the on-screen character, although identifying appropriate voice talent is not usually the responsibility of the translator.

Finally, *isochrony* refers to making sure that the duration of the translated dialogue fits comfortably with when the on-screen actor opens and closes their mouth. This is similar to the way that subtitlers need to ensure that the relevant subtitle is displayed on the screen at the right moment.

What is involved in voiceover?

In audiovisual translation, voiceover is a technique in which an actor's voice is recorded over the original audio track, which can be heard at a lower volume in the background. This form of audiovisual translation is often used in documentaries and news reports to translate the words of interviewees who are speaking another language. However, in some regions, such as Poland and Bulgaria, voiceover may be used instead of dubbing to provide the audio for a film or series. In this case, there is usually just one voice actor (or a limited number, such as one male and one female), even if the original source has many characters. Unlike dubbing, voiceover does not use lip synchronization, and there is no attempt to create the illusion that the on-screen actors are actually speaking the target language. Rather, the original soundtrack is still faintly audible in the background and the translated version is laid over the top of this. Because voiceover uses fewer voice actors and does not incorporate lip synchronization, it is cheaper and faster to produce than a dubbed version.

Although voiceover has a superficial resemblance to simultaneous interpreting (see Chapter 11), the two use a different process. Simultaneous interpretation is generally produced live and without reference to a written text, while in voiceover a translator works with the pre-recorded source-language content to produce a written translation, which is then read aloud by a voice actor. Typically, translators receive an audiovisual file in the source language, which may be accompanied by a script or transcript (but not always). The translator is then expected to deliver a written text in the target language for the voice actor(s) to read. Like interpreters, however, the translators who adapt content for voiceover make use of paraphrasing and summarization (see Chapter 9), although the content is not typically condensed to the same degree that it is for subtitles.

What affects the choice of audiovisual translation method?

There has been no shortage of heated debates about which method of audiovisual translation is "best". Supporters of subtitling will tell you that it provides a more authentic experience because viewers are still immersed in the source culture. Meanwhile, fans of dubbing argue that having subtitles on screen detracts from the work's visual integrity. Who's right? Or does it all come down to personal preference? Historically, the decision to opt for one method over another has differed from one region or culture to the next. For instance, given that dubbing is more labour-intensive and therefore more costly than subtitling, this approach was traditionally only used for languages with a large market so that the costs could be recouped. Therefore, dubbing was carried out for countries such as France, Germany, Italy, and Spain, which have relatively large populations (and therefore relatively large markets). In contrast, countries with a smaller linguistic market, such as the Netherlands and Scandinavian countries, tended to use subtitling. Meanwhile, a number of Eastern European countries developed the tradition of using voiceover (usually by one voice actor or a very limited number of voice actors, who read the parts of multiple characters).

Cost is not the only factor taken into consideration, however. For example, the age or ability of the intended target audience might be considered too. Countries with a lower literacy rate might opt for dubbing, while in places such as Finland it became common to dub content aimed at children but to subtitle content intended for adults. In addition, cultural and linguistic pride can motivate the choice of audiovisual translation method. For instance, in Canada's French-speaking province of Quebec, dubbing is often selected because it reinforces the use of French. What's more, it is common for different versions of dubbed content to be produced for the Quebec market (i.e., in Canadian French) and the market in France. Meanwhile, during certain periods in history, censorship has also been a motivating factor for choosing dubbing over subtitling. In subtitling and voiceover, the original soundtrack remains, but in dubbing, the original soundtrack is completely replaced by the translated version, making it possible to modify the content.

As different traditions became established in different regions, many people developed preferences simply based on what they were used to (i.e., what was traditionally available to them). Now, however, streaming and Internet-based platforms make it easier to reach audiences around the globe (including diaspora populations), contributing to a shift in economies of scale that makes dubbing more feasible. As such, it is becoming increasingly common for the producers of films and for streaming services to make multiple options available, such as offering both subbed and dubbed versions. It will be interesting to see how this affects people's viewing choices moving forward, which might be governed by factors such as whether the viewer is multitasking (it's challenging to read subtitles while also ironing clothes!) or whether their objective includes language learning (in which case, they may prefer subs and dubs at different points in their language learning journey or may even use both together).

Who carries out audiovisual translation?

In response to the growing appetite for digital content in multiple languages, audiovisual translation has become an increasingly prevalent sub-specialization among professional translators. Indeed, there are even some specialized education programs – often at the graduate level – that offer training focused directly on audiovisual translation. However, alongside this professional field, there is a parallel culture of fan-based audiovisual content, including fansubbing, fandubbing, and translation hacking.

As its name implies, fan-based audiovisual translation is carried out by fans of a particular film, series, or videogame. As a form of translation carried out mainly by amateurs with no formal training, the quality of the work can vary widely. Another concern about this practice is that it may not respect copyright regulations and could therefore even be considered illegal. Nevertheless, in a world where it is now very easy to communicate and share files and content, fan-based audiovisual translation has become commonplace, and fans around the globe have organized themselves into translation networks. Although some fans may work independently on a translation, many others undertake this as a collaborative venture, building a community around a shared interest.

Fansubbing is the oldest form of fan-based audiovisual translation, and it remains the most widely practised form even today. It first emerged as a practice in the context of adapting Japanese animation (known as *anime*) for audiences outside Japan. While official dubbed versions of anime had been broadcast on television in various parts of the world in the 1960s and 1970s, these later fell out of fashion with the official broadcasters and ceased to be televised. This abrupt halt to what had by then become beloved content for many viewers was a catalyst for fans willing to take responsibility for accessing, translating, and even distributing the material themselves. And so, in the 1980s, the first fansubs were produced. This movement has continued to grow as digital technology continues to evolve, making both the sharing of content and the production of subtitles easier. The type of material that is fansubbed has also extended beyond anime and now covers a wide range of genres, languages, countries, and contexts, including (but certainly not limited to) telenovelas from South America, K-drama from Korea, soap operas from Germany, and a wide range of popular series from the United States. One characteristic of fansubbing is that it is often done very quickly – sometimes within hours of the release of the original version – as fans are anxious to have access to the content of their favourite shows as soon as possible. This speed may, however, affect the quality of the translation. Another issue that can affect quality is the fact that, unlike most professional audiovisual translators, fansubbers do not typically have access to the original script. Instead, they must produce a translation solely by listening to the recording (which may not be in their dominant language), which can lead to misunderstandings and mistakes.

> **Fun fact!** Sometimes fans produce dubbed versions where the storyline, character personalities, and other content are significantly altered – usually in a humorous way – and these are known as "fun-dubs".

Fandubbing also exists, although this is less well established than fansubbing. In addition, a few very technologically adept fans participate in the localization of videogames (see Chapter 7) – known as *romhacking* (read-only memory hacking) or *translation hacking* – although this practice is not as widespread because it requires a relatively high level of technical skill to reverse-engineer the computer code in a videogame.

The notion of fan-based audiovisual translation overlaps with the notion of crowdsourced translation, which was discussed in Chapter 7 in the context of localization. Both involve translation by amateurs; however, in the case of fan translation, the process is bottom-up because it is the fans themselves who take the initiative to launch the project and to carry out all stages. In contrast, crowdsourcing is often a top-down process, where an organization seeks volunteers to participate and manages the overall effort, sometimes providing a platform, guidelines, and even some quality control measures (e.g., editing). An example of crowdsourced audiovisual translation is the TED Translators (previously known as the Open Translation Project) who subtitle TED Talks. These are relatively short (e.g., 15-minute) videos from expert speakers on education, business, science, and so on, which are freely distributed online under a Creative Commons license (which means that there are few copyright restrictions).

The question of whether fan-based audiovisual translation is legal or ethical is controversial. If the original work is copyrighted, then, strictly speaking, activities such as fansubbing are illegal because they infringe the copyright. The person holding the copyright can therefore demand that fansubbed versions be taken down from a website or not shared. However, fan translators do not consider themselves to be pirates because they do not sell or try to make a profit from their own translations. In addition, many fan groups have established a code of ethics for themselves, which often precludes translating materials that are already licenced for their region. According to many fan translators, their work contributes to creating a fan base, which in turn generates more demand for the product (e.g., *anime*).

Although this section has focused on the fan-based translation of audiovisual materials, it is worth noting that fan translation can be carried out in other contexts as well. For instance, there are groups who do fan translations of fiction (e.g., the Harry Potter books) and graphic novels (e.g., *manga*). In the case of graphic novels, this practice is sometimes referred to as *scanlation* because it involves scanning the original then inserting the translation over the original text.

How are these techniques used beyond translation?

In the preceding sections, we focused on activities that involve transferring a message from one language to another. However, related techniques, such as captioning (sometimes referred to as closed captioning (CC) or subtitling for the d/Deaf and hard of hearing (SDH)), respeaking, and audio-description, can be used outside of a translation context to make content more accessible to people with visual or hearing impairments.

When captioning for d/Deaf and hard of hearing audiences, the language in the captions is the same as the language spoken in the source text. In other words, captioning changes the mode (from oral to written), but not the language. However, captions present not only the content of on-screen dialogue but also a description of other aural components (e.g., sound effects, music). Captions are prepared in advance, whereas live captions are produced in real time.

Because people speak more quickly than they can type, manual creation of live captions is not ideal for live programming, making the use of automatic speech recognition and transcription a very interesting prospect. However, just as you have seen that fully automatic machine translation must be used with caution, and that human intervention (e.g., post-editing) can lead to improved quality (see Chapter 6), this is true for automatically generated captions too. If a speech recognition system is used to generate captions on the fly directly from the source-language video, the results are often quite poor, which has led to the use of the disparaging term "craptions" to describe these completely auto-generated results. Speech recognition tools may have difficulty understanding speech if the conditions are not ideal (e.g., if there is background noise, or if a speaker speaks too quickly or quietly or with an accent). However, a human listener is often able to compensate for these factors and understand the speech even in less-than-perfect conditions. Therefore, a technique known as respeaking can be used. In respeaking, a person listens to the original sound of a (live) program or event and then respeaks what they hear as clearly as possible, including punctuation marks, to an automatic speech recognition system. In turn, this speech recognition system generates captions with the shortest possible delay. It resembles the task of shadowing, which is used in interpreter training (more on this in Chapter 11), although, owing to the speed at which this process unfolds, respeakers may end up paraphrasing or summarizing some elements of the original soundtrack (see Chapter 9), just as simultaneous interpreters do.

While captioning and respeaking are intended to improve accessibility for d/Deaf and hard-of-hearing audiences, audio description seeks to do the same for people who are blind or partially sighted. Audio description captures the visual elements of a source text in spoken words – for instance, describing camera angles or facial expressions. These words do not replace but rather complement the existing dialogue and other on-screen sounds (e.g., music, sound effects), so the audio description is in the same language as that of the source text. In this way, audio description enables visually impaired people to access, understand, and appreciate more fully those products that have a significant visual component. Audio description can be used for films or series, but it is also used in art galleries, museums, educational materials, or at events (e.g., theatre or dance performance).

Moving forward, it is possible to imagine taking audio descriptions or captions produced via respeaking and feeding them into a machine translation tool to generate descriptions or captions in other languages. Whether or not this is a good strategy will depend on the greater context of use (e.g., are the captions being used in a low-stakes or high-stakes scenario) and if the translations are going to be post-edited (i.e., to improve linguistic quality but also address cultural differences). This brings us back to the importance of developing strong machine translation literacy skills, as discussed in Chapter 6.

Concluding remarks

Audiovisual translation is often described as a type of *constrained* translation, and it's easy to see why. With so many non-linguistic constraints on length, placement, timing, synchronization, and more, the linguistic choices available to audiovisual translators are most definitely restricted. On top of that, the incredible demand for multilingual content adds immense pressure on translators to work quickly so that it can be released as soon as possible. Now that you are aware of some of these constraints and pressures, it will hopefully give you a greater appreciation for the work of audiovisual translators, even when you may think that the translation has missed the mark. For example, the audiovisual translations of the South Korean survival drama *Squid Game*, released on Netflix in the fall of 2021, was subtitled in over 30 languages and dubbed into more than a dozen. These translated versions spawned a lively debate online, with some fans criticizing the audiovisual translators for condensing the dialogue too much, others pointing out that some of the curse words and suggestive language in the original version was missing from the translated versions, and yet others noting that the subtitles did not effectively convey the characters' different accents (e.g., North Korean versus South Korean). However, other fans – especially those who speak multiple languages or have themselves tried translating – defended the translators' efforts, drawing attention to some of the constraints in play.

As well as playing an increasingly significant role in the entertainment industry, audiovisual translation intersects directly with accessibility, the importance of which is also gaining visibility. As technologies continue to advance, both these areas stand to benefit from the judicious application of tools (including automatic language processing tools), which can contribute to making the processes both easier and faster if integrated into the workflow in a thoughtful and purposeful way.

Key points in this chapter

- Audiovisual translation dates back to the late 1800s when intertitles or people in the cinema would explain plot developments or cultural references to viewers.
- Following the introduction of "talkies", new strategies were needed, so attempts were made to shoot multiple versions of a film in different languages, using different actors but the same technical crew.
- Surtitling is a technique used in live performances (e.g., opera) where the translated lyrics and dialogue are projected above the stage.
- Today, there are three main approaches to audiovisual translation: subtitling, dubbing, and voiceover.
- Some of the general challenges entailed in audiovisual translation involve dealing with humour and wordplay, handling profanity or sensitive content, rendering different accents, and using indirect translation techniques.
- Subtitling involves displaying on-screen captions in the target language while the soundtrack plays in the original language.
- Constraints on subtitling include the length and placement of subtitles, the position of the line break, the timing and duration of each subtitle's appearance, the font style and colour, and the alignment of a subtitle's content with what is happening on the screen.
- Dubbing involves replacing the original soundtrack with a target-language recording that reproduces the original message.
- In addition to translators, the dubbing process involves adapters, voice actors, sound technicians, and others, and it is more labour-intensive and expensive than subtitling.
- Dubbing strives to take three types of synchronization into account: lip synchrony, kinetic synchrony, and isochrony.
- Voiceover is a technique in which an actor's voice is recorded over the original audio track, which can still be heard at a lower volume in the background.
- Voiceover uses one or a small number of voice actors and does not attempt lip synchronization, making it faster and cheaper than dubbing.
- Beyond financial considerations, other factors can affect the choice of audiovisual translation method, including the reading ability of the target audience, cultural/linguistic pride, or a desire to manipulate the original message.
- While audiovisual translation has become an area of specialization for professional translators, amateurs are also very active, and they have organized extensive networks of participants known as fansubbers and fandubbers.

- Fan translation and crowdsourced translation are both carried out by non-professionals, but fan translation tends to be initiated by the fans themselves, whereas crowdsourced translation often takes a top-down approach with oversight from an organization.
- Legal and ethical questions abound in relation to fan audiovisual translation, but many fan groups have developed ethical guidelines (e.g., they do not translate materials for which an official translation is available).
- While audiovisual translation involves transferring content from one language to another, similar techniques are used within the same language to make content accessible to people with visual or hearing impairments (e.g., captioning, respeaking, and audio description).
- Automatic language processing technologies, such as machine translation and speech recognition tools, have the potential to facilitate audiovisual translation and improve accessibility, but these must be applied with care.

Topics for discussion

As part of a class discussion, or as a prompt for an online discussion forum, consider the following:

- While each form of audiovisual translation has its pros and cons, many people nevertheless have a clear personal preference. Which do you prefer, and why?
- What is your opinion of fan-based audiovisual translation? For instance, do you believe that fan translations are good for the industry (e.g., because they raise the visibility of a genre and thus generate more demand for it), or do you view it as an illegal practice that should be stopped altogether?
- Check out some of the lively online debate about the audiovisual translations of *Squid Game*. There is one article here: www.nbcnews.com/news/asian-america/translators-experts-weigh-squid-game-subtitle-debate-rcna2568, or you can use a search engine to find others. Given what you have learned in this chapter and your own experiences watching subtitled or dubbed programs (whether *Squid Game* or something else), do you agree or disagree with the various points raised in this debate?

Exercises

- To do audiovisual translation in a professional way, it's necessary to have some specialized equipment and software. Without access to this equipment and software, there are limits to what you can accomplish, but the following exercises will give you a chance to engage with some elements of audiovisual translation and get a feel for some of the challenges involved and techniques needed.

- **Prepare a voiceover:** Find a short video clip (e.g., three minutes) of a show or talk in your less dominant language, and prepare a voiceover in your dominant language.
  - Listen to the clip a couple of times.
  - Prepare a written translation of what you hear.
  - Record yourself reading the translation (e.g., using a recorder on your smartphone).
  - Play the clip again with the sound lowered, and play your own voiceover at the same time at a louder volume. How does it sound? Do you need to adjust the timing? Condense any content?
  - Make some modifications, then play back the new version to see how things have improved.
- **Try subtitling:** Find a short video clip (e.g., three minutes) of a show or talk in your less dominant language, and prepare subtitles in your dominant language. This can be done individually, but it might be more fun as a collaborative activity with your classmates.
  - Listen to the clip a couple of times.
  - In a spreadsheet that everyone can access (e.g., Google Sheets), produce a faithful transcription of the source-language script. To do this, write down each sentence (or sentence-like unit) in a new row in the spreadsheet.
  - In a separate column, record at which minute/second in the clip each part of the dialogue is spoken, noting both when it begins and ends (e.g., 7s–11s or 2:23–2:36).
  - In a new column, divide the transcript into segments. A segment should correspond to a section of dialogue or narration that a viewer can understand at a glance. It is a sort of self-contained unit of thought and might be less than a whole sentence.
  - Begin a new column where you translate each segment into the target language. Remember that you can only have two lines of subtitles, and that each line can have approximately 40 characters. It might not be possible to translate everything that is said in the source text, so you might need to use summarization techniques to produce a shorter version of the main elements of the message.
  - Play the movie again and refer to the subtitles. How are they? Does the text flow? Have you captured the essential elements of the original message? Can you make any improvements? Use additional columns to propose other options or revised versions, as well as to offer constructive feedback or comments on the suggestions made by your peers.

Find out more

Díaz Cintas, Jorge. 2010. "Subtitling". In *Handbook of Translation Studies*, Vol. 1, edited by Yves Gambier and Luc van Doorslaer, 344–449. Amsterdam: John Benjamins.

- This chapter introduces the main processes and elements to be taken into consideration when subtitling.

Díaz Cintas, Jorge, and Pilar Orero. 2010. "Voiceover and Dubbing". In *Handbook of Translation Studies*, Vol. 1, edited by Yves Gambier and Luc van Doorslaer, 441–445. Amsterdam: John Benjamins.

- This chapter introduces the main processes and elements to be taken into consideration with dubbing and voiceover.

Díaz Cintas, Jorge, and Serenella Massidda. 2020. "Technological Advances in Audiovisual Translation". In *Routledge Handbook for Translation and Technology*, edited by Minako O'Hagan, 255–270. London: Routledge.

- This chapter explores a range of tools used in different types of audiovisual translation, including machine translation and translation memory tools.

Pérez-González, Luis, ed. 2019. *Routledge Handbook of Audiovisual Translation*. London: Routledge.

- This volume covers a broad range of issues relating to the various forms of audiovisual translation, including their respective histories (O'Sullivan and Cornu 2019), audiovisual translation by amateur fans (Dwyer 2019), and techniques used for accessibility purposes (Neves 2019, Perego 2019, Romero-Fresco 2019).

Pérez-González, Luis. 2020. "Fan Audiovisual Translation". In *Routledge Encyclopedia of Translation Studies*, 3rd ed., edited by Mona Baker and Gabriela Saldanha, 172–177. London: Routledge.

- This entry explores audiovisual translation as done by amateur fans of texts from popular culture (e.g., comics, series).

11 Interpreting

For the most part, this book has focused on translation, which consists of transferring a written message from one language to another. But here and there, you've had glimpses of another side of this broad field, which involves transferring a spoken or signed message from one language to another. This activity is referred to as *interpreting*, and it will be the focus of this chapter.

You might be wondering whether there can really be that much difference between a translator and an interpreter. The answer is yes! Although both translators and interpreters work as intermediaries between two languages and cultures, some of the skills required by these two groups are quite different, as are some of the practical constraints and expectations associated with these two activities. Building on what you've already learned about translators, let's begin by taking a brief look at some key differences between these two groups of language professionals (see Figure 11.1).

As you can see, the responsibilities, expectations, tasks, and working conditions differ considerably for these two types of language professionals. Not surprisingly, it has even been suggested that these two jobs attract people who have rather different personalities. For example, translators are more likely to be patient, detail-oriented, and content to work largely independently, whereas interpreters need to be able to multitask, work under intense pressure, and work well with others. Nothing is written in stone, of course, but it's easy to see how someone could excel at one of these jobs without necessarily being a great fit for the other. Now that we've taken a high-level look at some of the main differences between translation and interpreting, let's dig a little more deeply into interpreting, which is itself a surprisingly diverse field.

What are the different types of interpreting?

Broadly speaking, there are two main types of interpreting, *consecutive interpreting* and *simultaneous interpreting*, each of which has some possible variations. Interpreting can also be a component in a cross-modal activity, such as sight translation (see Chapter 9) or sign language interpreting (see the section further down entitled "What about sign language interpreting?").

DOI: 10.4324/9781003217718-12

	Translators	Interpreters
Mode of communication	*Written*	*Spoken* or *signed*
Timeline	*Scheduled delivery.* Some deadlines are more generous than others, but there is usually time for research and revision.	*Real-time delivery.* Interpreting is an in-the-moment activity.
Research	*Yes.* Translators do a lot of research to ensure that they fully understand the concepts and use the right terms.	*Some,* but beforehand. There is very little time for research in the midst of a job, but interpreters can prepare in a general way by researching a topic beforehand (if they know in advance what the topic will be, which is not always the case!).
Tools and resources	*Lots!* Translators use many tools and resources (e.g., word processors, term banks, concordancers, computer-assisted and machine translation tools, editing tools).	*A few.* Interpreters may use term extraction tools or resources to research the subject matter, but this mainly takes place before the interpreting assignment.
Revision	*Yes.* Translators hardly ever submit their first draft. They prepare a first draft then work to improve it in subsequent revisions.	*No.* Interpreters work in the moment and don't have time for revision. If they produce an inelegant phrase, they need to let it go and move on.
Direction	*One-way.* A translation task is unidirectional (from the source into the target language), and many translators work only into their dominant language.	*Two-way.* Interpreters are expected to be able to work in both directions.
Expected level of precision	*High.* Because translators have more time and can do targeted research, there is an expectation that all elements of the source text will be accounted for (as much as possible) when the message is transferred.	*Lower.* Interpreters use more summarization and paraphrasing when transmitting the core meaning of the message.

Figure 11.1 Some of the key differences between translators and interpreters.

Consecutive interpreting is a mode of interpreting where the speaker and the interpreter take turns speaking. If the speaker is giving a long speech, they must pause every so often (e.g., around every five minutes) to give the interpreter a chance to relay the information in the target language. On the one hand, the speaker cannot speak for too long in one stretch because the target-language listeners will not want to wait for 15 minutes to find out what has been said, and the interpreter will be more likely to make omissions because there is too much to remember. On the other hand, if the speaker pauses too often, the speech will feel very fragmented to the listeners, and the interpreter might not have enough context to render the idea accurately.

Usually, a consecutive interpreter will take notes with a pen and paper while the speaker is speaking. This does not mean that the interpreter is writing down every single word, of course, but more of a summary of the key points (see Chapter 9). Interpreters typically develop and use a shorthand code to capture the main points. These notes will serve as a reminder of the essential details when it is the interpreter's turn to relay the information in the target language. This type of note-taking is a special skill, and it takes a lot of practice to be able to take notes that are concise yet meaningful, and to do so while also listening to the speaker's next utterance. During a speech, an interpreter does not typically interrupt the speaker to ask for information to be repeated or clarified. It's the interpreter's job to engage in active listening, effective note-taking, and smooth communication of the message in the target language. The main disadvantage of consecutive interpreting is that it takes longer. Because all the information is relayed twice – once in the source language and then again in the target language – the length of time required for the meeting or event is essentially doubled.

A variation on consecutive interpreting is known as *bilateral interpreting*. In this case, an interpreter is responsible for facilitating discussion between two different people or small groups. The interpreter needs to work in both language directions, such as by relaying the question of one party to the other, then conveying the response of the second party back to the first.

Simultaneous interpreting is probably the most well-known form of interpretation. You might have seen it during a newscast, for example, where someone is speaking in a foreign language, but you hear another voice in your own language transmitting the message of the foreign-language speaker. As you learned in Chapter 2, simultaneous interpreting was first practised in a meaningful way during the Nuremberg trials that followed World War II. Since then, it has gone on to become widely used in multilingual organizations such as the United Nations or the European Parliament, as well as at international conferences and events. Unlike with consecutive interpreting, where the speaker pauses to give the interpreter an opportunity to speak, simultaneous interpreting requires interpreters to work more or less in real time with only a few seconds' delay between the words of the speaker and those of the interpreter. In other words, the interpreter is listening to the speaker and providing an interpretation at the same time. Talk about impressive multitasking!

Most of the time, simultaneous interpreters are located in a soundproof booth or cabin at the back or side of the room where the speech is being delivered. If the speech is being interpreted into multiple languages, then there is a separate booth for each target language. Members of the audience each have a headset and a device that allows them to select a channel that corresponds to their desired target language. For instance, if the original speech is being delivered in Russian, then channel 1 might be for English, channel 2 for French, channel 3 for Chinese, and so on. The interpreters for the various target languages are working independently of one another, each in their own soundproof booth. They listen to the original speech through headphones, then speak into a microphone to broadcast their interpretation on the appropriate channel. Some venues where interpretation takes place on a regular basis (e.g., the UN headquarters) have permanent interpretation booths built right into the venue. In contrast, for venues where the need for interpretation is more occasional (e.g., an exhibition or conference centre), interpreting equipment can be rented and set up as needed.

Simultaneous interpreting is the most challenging type of interpreting because the interpreter is required to engage in two complex activities – listening and speaking – at the same time while also converting the message from one language to another. It is very complex, intense, and cognitively demanding; therefore, simultaneous interpreters almost always work with a partner (or two), with each person operating in 20- to 30-minute shifts before switching over. During each shift, one person is doing the actual interpretation, while their partner tries to support them as necessary (e.g., looking up unknown terms) and also has a bit of a break before it's their turn to interpret again. In order to set themselves up for success with this daunting task, interpreters must not only be very well versed in their working languages (and the associated cultures), but they also need to develop their short-term memories and do advance research on the topic(s) covered at the event. In other words, interpreters do their best not to walk into a situation "cold". Rather, they will ask for copies of any speeches, speaking notes, or presentations (e.g., slides) that might be available. They will study this material and possibly do additional background reading or terminology research on the relevant subjects. In this way, they hope to have the necessary concepts and terms fresh in their mind before working at the event. However, it is impossible to prepare for everything, given that speakers may make last-minute changes to their presentation, ad lib a portion of it, or even throw in a joke to lighten the mood. In addition, questions from the audience have not been prepared in advance, so an interpreter must deal with these on the fly. Therefore, interpreters need to develop a broad general culture.

One particular way of carrying out simultaneous interpreting is known as *relay interpreting*. This approach is used in a setting, such as a conference, when there is no available interpreter who can work directly in the needed language pair. Remember the discussion about indirect machine translation in Chapter 6 and the example of La Malinche from Chapter 2? A similar approach is sometimes used at the UN, for example, where there are six official languages (see Chapter 2). Imagine that the speaker is speaking in Russian, and this speech needs to be interpreted into Arabic, Chinese, English, French, and Spanish. Now imagine that there is no Russian-to-Arabic interpreter on duty, but there is an English-to-Arabic interpreter available. How can the message be relayed into Arabic? In relay interpreting, this could be achieved in the following way. First, the message is transferred from Russian into English by one interpreter, then a second interpreter listens to the English version and interprets this into Arabic. In this two-step process, English is used as a pivot language to bridge the transfer of the message from Russian into Arabic. In this way, relay interpreting makes it possible to offer indirect interpreting services in language combinations for which there is no interpreter available for direct interpreting. However, a potential drawback is that any errors or omissions that occur in the first stage (i.e., during the Russian-to-English interpretation) will then be carried over into the second stage (i.e., the English-to-Arabic interpretation).

Relay interpreting from Russian to Arabic

Speaker: Speaks in Russian
Interpreter 1: Interprets from Russian into English
Interpreter 2: Interprets from English into Arabic
Target audience: Listens in Arabic

A variation on simultaneous interpreting is *whispered interpreting* (also known as *chuchotage*, which is the French term for *whispering*). Whispered interpreting is used when just one person or a very small group (e.g., up to three people) needs the services of an interpreter. It is typically used in settings such as a diplomatic negotiation, a guided tour, or a business meeting or conference. As the name suggests, the interpreter sits or stands in close proximity to the client(s) and whispers the message in the target language while the speaker is still talking. In this way, whispering is also a type of simultaneous interpreting, which means that it is time efficient. Another advantage is that it does not require special equipment (e.g., headsets, microphones, or booths), and it can even be done on the go (e.g., during a tour). However, a drawback is that it can be distracting to others in the vicinity who may not require interpretation services and who are trying to concentrate on the speaker.

Interpreting 173

What are some different settings for interpreting?

A couple of places where interpreting services might be needed have been mentioned in passing, but let's take a closer look. Note that, in some cases, the setting will influence the type of interpreting that takes place. For example, at international conferences or very large meetings (e.g., at the UN), simultaneous interpreting is usually the preferred choice because it is the most efficient way to serve a large group where there may be multiple target languages. Using consecutive interpreting in this setting would impose lengthy delays, while things would quickly become chaotic (and prohibitively expensive!) if the 500+ conference attendees each had a personal interpreter whispering to them.

If the setting is a diplomatic negotiation or business meeting for a smaller group where perhaps just two languages are in play, then bilateral interpreting may be used. In a business setting, this is even sometimes referred to as *liaison* interpreting, and the interpreter plays an important role as a facilitator. There may be less need to take notes in this setting because the parties are more likely to be engaged in dialogue rather than giving speeches, so there is a shorter interval between the speaker's turn and the interpreter's turn.

If the interpreting services are being used to enable an individual or a group who does not speak the dominant language of the community to access government or central services, then it is usually referred to as *dialogue interpreting* or *community interpreting*. Some typical settings for dialogue interpreting include social services (e.g., helping teachers and newcomer parents communicate about a child's schooling), medical settings (e.g., helping a doctor and a newcomer patient communicate in a hospital or clinic), or legal settings (e.g., helping a newcomer participate in a police interview). Of course, depending on the particular circumstances of the legal setting, an interpreter might engage in bilateral interpreting (e.g., to help a witness give testimony), whispering (e.g., to help a defendant follow proceedings), or sight translation (e.g., to read a statement into the court record, as explained in Chapter 9). Interpreters need to be versatile and to adopt the type of interpreting that is most appropriate for the setting.

The online or virtual world is becoming an increasingly popular setting for interpreting services. Although many interpretation contexts do benefit from having the interpreters on site, where they can see the body language of the speakers, remote interpretation services are also an option in some circumstances. *Remote interpreting* can help to facilitate communication between parties who are not in the same location, and it may take place over the telephone or via video. Remote interpreting can offer a number of benefits. For example, it can help to ensure services in a broader range of languages in remote areas where it would not be feasible to find interpreters to work in all the language combinations needed (e.g., at rural health centres). It may be quicker to arrange and thus prevent an urgent situation from escalating (e.g., to help a patient with an urgent medical need). Or it could help to reduce costs (e.g., for a non-profit organization) because it is not necessary to move all parties to the same location. These cost savings could then be funnelled back into the organization to allow it to offer more services. Finally, it may also be necessary to maintain distance in order to follow health protocols, as was the case during the Covid-19 pandemic. Of course, remote interpreting also presents various challenges that must be taken into consideration when choosing whether to go for an in-person or remote service. If the interpretation is taking place over the telephone, the interpreter will not be able to take note of important body language cues (e.g., facial expressions, mouth movements). There is also a total dependence on the quality of the technology (e.g., sound, transmission speed), and a risk of dividing the interpreter's attention even further if it is necessary to use multiple tools or features (e.g., monitoring the chat, using additional devices to manage turn-taking when interpreting partners are in separate locations).

What else can affect interpreting?

If you have never worked as an interpreter, you may be surprised by the different (and sometimes unexpected) issues that interpreters may need to deal with as part of their job. No amount of planning and preparation can head off every potential issue. For example, technology has already been mentioned as an important factor in the case of remote interpreting, but it can affect simultaneous interpreters too. Imagine if a speaker decides not to use a microphone, or the microphone is faulty, or there is a lot of background noise. Even if this doesn't affect the listeners in the room too badly, the interpreter sealed in the soundproof booth at the back of the room will have little to no chance of hearing what the speaker says!

Another issue that may come up is the speaker. Does the speaker have a tendency to talk very quickly? Is the speaker delivering a talk in a language that is not their dominant language? Are they using the correct terms and pronunciations? Do they have a strong accent? If any of these situations arises, it will place an added burden on the interpreter. Similarly, if the audience at an international conference is made up of people from around the world, then what exactly is the target culture? Should an interpreter working into English use expressions from British English, American English, or some other variant of English?

Is the interpretation taking place in a meeting room where the interpreter can sit comfortably and take notes, or is it more of an on-the-go type of affair (e.g., a tour) where there is no possibility for note-taking and the interpreter must work entirely from memory? Or what about other unfavourable working conditions? What happens if your booth-mate is a bit of a slacker or had too much garlic for lunch? Has your client been considerate and built in enough time for a proper break?

What happens if the speaker decides to break the ice with a little humour? Jokes and wordplay are notoriously difficult to translate, even with all the time in the world. Some jokes simply don't transfer from one language to another. For example, consider the joke "Why was 6 afraid of 7? Because 7, 8, 9" (read as: 7 ate 9). There's just no way to render this wordplay effectively in another language, never mind on the spot. Even if the interpreter doesn't think the joke is worth the effort, how do they explain to their target listeners why the rest of the audience is laughing (or groaning, as the case may be)?

Fun fact! When humour is simply too difficult to adapt on the fly, some interpreters have been known to tell the target-language listeners: "The speaker told a joke. Please laugh now".

Even if there are no jokes involved, the subject matter can still cause problems. As we've already noted in the case of translators, no one person can be an expert in everything. Although interpreters request relevant background material in advance, they don't always get it. And even if they do, they are still not going to become subject specialists overnight. Moreover, unexpected topics can pop up in discussions without any warning, so interpreters need to develop strategies for coping with these circumstances.

Finally, what is at stake in the event? Although a professional interpreter will always strive to do their best, there must be an added pressure when the interpreter is participating in a diplomatic meeting between two world leaders, with all the cultural protocols that need to be respected, or when they are part of a business meeting where two parties are negotiating a multimillion-dollar sale. Things are likely to get even more heated if an interpreter is working in a conflict zone. Talk about taking an already stressful job and piling on even more stress! Interpreters really are pretty amazing people.

What about sign language interpreting?

There is no single universal sign language, just as there is no single universal spoken language. What's more, the types of regional variation discussed in Chapter 7 apply to sign language too. Therefore, not only is there a variant called American Sign Language, but there is also British Sign Language. Likewise, there are variants such as *Langue des signes française*, which is used in France, and *Langue des signes du Québec*, which is used in French-speaking Canada, as well as *Lengua de Signos Española*, which is used in Spain, and *Lengua des Señas Mexicana*, which is used in Mexico. Interpreting can take place between two different sign languages, but it more commonly takes place between a signed and a spoken language, which is a type of cross-modal communication (see Chapter 9).

Many aspects that apply to translation, and interpreting more generally, apply to sign language interpreting too. For instance, in Chapter 1 you learned that translation falls on a spectrum that runs between literal and free translation, and this occurs in sign language interpreting too. Sign languages are not visual representations of spoken languages but complex languages in their own right, with their own grammatical structures. A more literal interpretation could be one where the interpreter mouths words on the lips, incorporates fingerspelling, or follows the grammatical structure of the spoken language. A freer interpretation would be one that uses more naturally occurring signed expressions.

Just as spoken language interpreting can be delivered in a consecutive or simultaneous fashion, so too can sign language interpreting. Likewise, sign language interpreting is also used in a wide variety of settings – conferences, business meetings, courts, hospitals, etc. What's more, sign language interpreters can struggle with humour or high-pressure contexts in the same way as spoken language interpreters.

While there are many similarities between spoken language interpreting and sign language interpreting, there are also some differences. A frequent challenge in sign language interpreting that does not typically occur in spoken language interpreting is caused by its cross-modal nature. Sign languages tend to explicitly encode more visual information (e.g., what an object looks like, how it moves). Therefore, when interpreting from a signed language into a spoken language, the interpreter needs to decide what visual information to retain and what to omit.

What about non-professional interpreting?

Up to this point, we have mainly focussed on interpreting as done by professionals, who get paid for their work and usually receive specialized training. However, there are many people who practise interpreting in a less formal way – maybe you've even done it yourself? Non-professional interpreters might be friends, acquaintances, or family members (even children) of someone who needs support communicating in another language. In such cases, the term *language broker* is often used to describe someone taking on this role. Other situations where the interpreting might be carried out by a non-professional could include employees at a company with overseas clients interpreting for their boss or colleagues, or volunteers at a library or community association facilitating communication between different groups. Indeed, non-professional interpreting happens many times a day, all around the world.

When it comes to language brokering, there have been arguments put forward that defend this practice and others that oppose it. Points in favour include people perhaps feeling more comfortable having a trusted family member speaking on their behalf rather than a stranger, and child language brokers in particular perhaps feeling proud that they can help their families, leading to increased self-confidence. Points against include the potential for children to feel embarrassed, frustrated, or stressed if they have to deal with difficult negotiations or unfamiliar concepts and terms; and the potential for role reversal where parents are dependent on their children to communicate with people outside the family, or where children must take on grown-up responsibilities such as calling a parent's employer to report an absence from work.

In some parts of the world, the use of non-professional interpreters is strongly discouraged (or even forbidden) in some settings, such as in law courts or hospitals. But what happens if an urgent situation arises and no professional interpreter is available? Is it unethical to expect a child to interpret for a critically ill patient? Or is it unethical to leave the patient untreated until a professional interpreter can be located? What if a newly arrived family cannot afford to hire a professional in order to communicate with a child's teacher? These are not easy questions to answer. Just as you saw in Chapter 6, which deals with automatic translation tools such as Google Translate, it pays to apply good judgement and to evaluate the stakes involved before deciding what translation or interpreting solution will best meet the needs of the situation. In a low-stakes situation, such as a friendly chat between neighbours, a non-professional interpreter can step in and keep the conversation flowing. But as the stakes get higher, such as when someone's health or immigration status might be at risk, the advantages of calling in a professional interpreter become much clearer. Of course, the challenge is that there are quite a few grey areas between these two extremes. One of the goals of this book is to prompt you to reflect more deeply on what's involved in translation and interpretation so that you will be in a better position to evaluate a situation (e.g., Does it require specialized subject knowledge and terminology? Is the person working into their dominant language or another language? What are the consequences of getting the translation wrong?). By gaining a deeper understanding of translation and interpreting, you will be better able to think critically about the situation and to make an informed decision about whether a non-professional or computer program can meet your needs, or whether it would be better to consult a language professional.

What key skills does an interpreter need to develop?

Now that we've considered some of the different settings in which interpreters are needed, as well as the challenges they can face, let's look at the skills required by a good interpreter to overcome these challenges and deliver a good quality service. For professional interpreters, these skills are a must. In the case of non-professional interpreters or language brokers, there can be no guarantee that they will have all these skills (or at least not to the same degree as a professional), but the closer they come to having this skillset, the better they will be at interpreting.

Complete fluency in the source and target language. While it was noted in Chapter 1 that translators need to really master their target language but may have a more passive (though still very solid) knowledge of the source language, this is not the case for interpreters. Because interpreters need to work in the moment and in both directions, they really do need to be very fluent in both languages in order to ensure a timely and smooth delivery of the speaker's message.

Cultural awareness. Just as translators transfer messages between two cultures, so do interpreters. Cultural knowledge can include knowledge of diplomatic protocols in other countries (e.g., for interpreters that interpret between world leaders or for politicians on trade missions), or it can include knowing what background information the target audience is likely to have and then including any additional explanations they are likely to need as part of the interpretation.

A broad general culture. An interpreter might be asked to interpret on any topic. Governmental organizations such as the European Parliament discuss everything from fishing rights to immigration policies to budgets. Meanwhile, scientific researchers hold conferences on nuclear physics, cancer treatments, world literatures, biodiversity, and more. Interpreters need to be curious people who accumulate knowledge on, and are at ease discussing, a broad range of topics. Although they will do some advance preparation, they also need to have a solid underlying knowledge base that will allow them to handle unexpected information on the fly. For this reason, interpreters need to be life-long learners – they never know what information might come in handy during an interpreting assignment!

Active listening skills. When an interpreter is working, the speaker's voice is not simply background noise. Moreover, unlike other participants in a conversation, interpreters are not listening in order to respond to questions or to join in the conversation. Rather, they are listening with the goal of being able to remember and reproduce the speaker's message in another language. Therefore, interpreters must engage in *active* listening, which includes not only listening but also analyzing, prioritizing, and selectively memorizing what they hear. In short, while they are listening, interpreters need to create a sort of mental map of what the speaker is saying.

Shorthand or structured note-taking. It has already been mentioned that interpreters working consecutively typically take notes to jog their short-term memory. To be as useful as possible, these notes are not verbatim transcripts but rather a structured shorthand of essential points.

Excellent short-term memory. Short-term memory plays a major role in interpreting. While some people may start off with a better memory than others, interpreters can work to develop and improve their short-term memory skills with exercises such as retelling a story, making flash cards, or developing mnemonic techniques.

Ability to multitask. Interpreters need to be very comfortable doing multiple things at once. For instance, sometimes interpreters might be listening and taking notes at the same time, while in other cases they could be reading and speaking at once (e.g., sight translation) or even listening and speaking simultaneously. It's not simple, but it gets easier with practice. One exercise that beginners can do to develop this skill is called shadowing. In shadowing, you listen to someone speaking (e.g., a podcast or video) and then repeat exactly what you hear with a time lag of just a few seconds.

Quick mental reflexes. Interpreters need to be quick minded when it comes to making decisions and finding solutions. If they don't know the precise word for a concept, they need to find another way to describe it. If there are multiple ways of saying the same thing, they need to commit to one and go with it, rather than hesitating or wavering.

Work well under pressure. Hand in hand with having quick reflexes is the ability to work well under pressure. Interpreters need to be unflappable, meaning they need to be able to keep calm and focus on the job without panicking – even when the stakes are high (e.g., interpreting for world leaders or for a critically ill patient). If they can't find the perfect word, or if they present a phrase in a less than elegant way, interpreters can't get hung up on it. They need to retain their focus and keep moving forward.

Clear enunciation. Interpreters need to be good public speakers who can deliver the interpreted content smoothly and clearly. To ensure that listeners can easily understand what you are saying, it's important to pronounce words clearly and distinctly and to deliver them with a well-paced rhythm, rather than mumbling or running all the words together without taking a breath.

Refrain from editorializing. Interpreters must always take care not to insert their own opinions into the material that they are interpreting. The interpreter's job is to relay the message presented by the speaker without minimizing, exaggerating, or adding in their own personal views on the content.

Concluding remarks

While interpreting does have some commonalities with translation, it also requires numerous other skills. What's more, interpreting is a diverse activity that can be carried out in different modes and in a wide variety of settings. Although many people carry out some form of informal interpreting, practicing this highly challenging activity professionally requires specialized training – often at the graduate level – and lots of practice. Among other qualities, interpreters need to be very fluent speakers of multiple languages, multitask at a high level, display poise and confidence under pressure, and have excellent active listening skills and short-term memories. Many of the professional translators associations discussed in Chapter 3 also include interpreters (e.g., the International Federation of Translators), although some additional associations exist that cater specifically to interpreters, such as the International Association of Conference Interpreters (more commonly known by its French-language acronym AIIC).

Key points in this chapter

- Interpreting involves transferring a spoken or signed message from one language to another in more or less real time.
- Unlike translators, interpreters need to be able to work in both language directions.
- The two main types of interpreting are consecutive interpreting (where the speaker and the interpreter take turns speaking) and simultaneous interpreting (where the interpreter relays the message while the speaker is still talking).
- During consecutive interpreting, the interpreter often takes notes using a personalized shorthand to jot down the major points as a memory aid.
- Simultaneous speakers normally work in a soundproof booth at the back or side of the room and transmit their interpreted message to the listeners via headphones.
- When only one individual or a very small group needs simultaneous interpreting, this can take the form of whispered interpreting, where the interpreter sits or stands close to the client and whispers to them in the target language.
- In cases where there is no interpreter available to work in a given language pair, a technique called relay interpreting can be used, where the interpreting takes place in multiple steps (e.g., to obtain a Russian-to-Arabic interpretation, English can be used as a pivot language: Russian>English and English>Arabic).
- Simultaneous interpreting requires intense concentration, so interpreters normally work with a partner and alternate in 20- or 30-minute shifts.

- Simultaneous interpreters typically prepare for an assignment ahead of time by doing background reading or terminological research.
- Interpreting can take place in a wide range of settings, such as diplomatic meetings, business meetings, or scientific conferences. Interpreting is also common in a wide range of community settings (e.g., schools, law courts, or hospitals), and in these contexts it is often referred to as dialogue interpreting or community interpreting.
- It is becoming increasingly common to carry out interpreting remotely, such as over the telephone or via video, in order to extend services and reduce costs.
- Interpreters can encounter many challenges, such as faulty technology, jokes or wordplay, a fast pace of delivery, speakers who are not using their dominant language, or high-stakes contexts.
- Sign language interpreting usually involves cross-modal communication.
- Sign languages are complex languages with their own vocabulary and grammar, and there is no single universal sign language.
- One difference between spoken and signed languages is that the latter incorporate more visual information, and interpreters must decide what to retain and what to leave out when working from a signed into a spoken language.
- Non-professional interpreters are not usually trained or paid for interpreting work but carry it out in a less formal way (e.g., for friends, family, or colleagues).
- There are pros and cons to working with non-professional interpreters, and a good rule of thumb is to evaluate the use of non-professional interpreting as you would the use of automatic machine translation tools (see Chapter 6).
- To be successful as an interpreter, you will need to develop a range of skills that include source- and target-language fluency, cultural awareness, a broad general culture, active listening skills, good note-taking, the ability to multitask, quick mental reflexes, the ability to work under pressure, clear enunciation, and the ability not to let your own opinions seep into your interpretation.
- To work professionally, interpreters need specialized training (often at the master's level) and lots of practice.

Topics for discussion

As part of a class discussion, or as a prompt for an online discussion forum, consider the following:

- If you were taking notes during a consecutive interpreting assignment, would you take the notes in the source language, the target language, or your dominant language? Explain.

- What do you think is the biggest challenge facing a simultaneous interpreter?
- Have you ever been asked to do non-professional interpreting? Can you share some of the positives and negatives of this experience? Would you be willing to do it again? Why or why not?

Exercises

- **Work on memorization:** For this exercise, you will train your memory like an interpreter! Interpreters need to be able to quickly and accurately recall and use the specialized terms needed to discuss the topic of the conference for which they are interpreting. To prepare, they identify and memorize long lists of terms that they are likely to need when interpreting. Is your memory up to the task of working like an interpreter's? Find out by memorizing a bilingual list of terms, then quizzing yourself or a classmate to see how quickly and accurately you can recall them.
    - Search for a bilingual glossary on any topic in your preferred language pair, or get started with the *WIPO Pearl COVID-19 Glossary* from the World Intellectual Property Organization (https://wipopearl.wipo.int/en/covid19), which contains entries in Arabic, Chinese, English, French, German, Japanese, Korean, Portuguese, Russian, and Spanish.
    - Select 20 terms and their equivalents in another language and create a list. You can write it out by hand, record it in a spreadsheet, or even use an app such as Quizlet to make flashcards.
    - Give yourself five minutes to memorize the 20 terms and their equivalents.
    - Quiz yourself, or work with a classmate and quiz each other. How many did you get right? Do you think that you will still be able to remember them tomorrow?
    - If you feel up to it, try adding a few more terms to your list.
- **Practise note-taking:** Try your hand at developing and applying a personal shorthand for note-taking. Remember that, in the context of interpretation, note-taking is not the same as taking dictation. Don't try to transcribe every word. Instead, note down only key points in order to jog your short-term memory during the actual interpretation stage. If you take too many notes, you might actually be paying less attention to the speaker! An interpreter's shorthand is personal and doesn't need to make sense to other people. It could contain symbols (e.g., arrows to represent concepts such as "rising" or "moving forward"), simple or stylized drawings (e.g., a crown to mean "royalty"), or abbreviations (e.g., using "w/o" to mean "without"). Give it a try!
    - Identify a podcast episode or video in your dominant language that you've never heard before but would like to listen to.

- Listen to the first seven or eight minutes while taking shorthand notes.
- Stop the recording and see if you can reconstruct the content out loud referring only to your notes. Record yourself (e.g., using your mobile device) and play it back. How well did you do?
- Challenge yourself by finding another podcast or video in which the pace is quicker, the sound quality is less good, the speaker is not using their dominant language, or the speech is not in your dominant language. Repeat the exercise by listening, taking notes, then recreating the content in the same language used by the speaker.
- Increase the challenge even more by adding interpretation (i.e., listening in one language but recreating the content in another).
- For fun, exchange your notes with a classmate to see how they differ from your own. Are you able to decipher the shorthand developed by your classmate?
- **Try shadowing:** Shadowing is the term used for a simultaneous interpretation training exercise where you listen to a speech then repeat exactly what the speaker is saying but with a short delay. It's intended to get you used to listening and speaking at the same time.
  - Identify a podcast episode or video in your dominant language that you've never heard before but would like to listen to.
  - Start listening, and then, no more than five seconds later, begin repeating what you have heard while continuing to listen to what the speaker says next.
  - To challenge yourself, try shadowing recordings where the speakers have different accents or where they speak very quickly! You could also try shadowing a recording in your second language.
  - Finally, try the exercise again, but instead of repeating the content in the same language, try interpreting it into a different language. Do you think you'd be able to keep this up for 25 or 30 minutes?

Find out more

Lee, Jieun. 2020. "Competence, Interpreting". In *Routledge Encyclopedia of Translation Studies*, 3rd ed., edited by Mona Baker and Gabriela Saldanha, 84–89. London: Routledge.

- This entry examines the knowledge and skillset required to interpret successfully.

Leeson, Lorraine, and Myriam Vermeerbergen. 2010. "Sign Language Interpreting and Translation". In *Handbook of Translation Studies*, Vol. 1, edited by Yves Gambier and Luc van Doorslaer, 324–328. Amsterdam: John Benjamins.

- This chapter explores sign language interpretation and the ways in which it is similar to, and different from, spoken language interpretation.

Mikkelson, Holly, and Renée Jourdenais, eds. 2015. *Routledge Handbook of Interpreting*. London: Routledge.

- This volume provides an introduction to the main types of interpreting (i.e., consecutive and simultaneous) and various settings where interpreting is used (e.g., law courts, healthcare, education, conflict zones). It also includes chapters on remote interpreting, sign language interpreting, and non-professional interpreting.

Tipton, Rebecca, and Olgierda Furmanek. 2016. *Dialogue Interpreting: A Guide to Interpreting in Public Services and the Community*. London: Routledge.

- This book presents interpreting as it is practised in a range of community settings, including healthcare, legal, education, asylum, social care, and religious contexts.

Conclusion

What have you learned?

Our grand tour of translation is now wrapping up, and we have certainly covered a lot of ground in these chapters. First, we set the scene by learning some of the fundamental concepts in the field, as well as the terms used to talk about them. From there, we moved on to consider some of the main events and key personalities in this field's long and rich history, which has seen its share of murder and mayhem! We examined what's involved in working as a professional translator, and then we began to get down to some of the nitty gritty of translation, such as understanding the differences between words and terms, and learning about the tools and resources that can support translation activities. We paid particular attention to machine translation tools, which are widely accessible, freely available online, and so easy to use that it can be tempting not to think too hard about the potential risks involved. We explored several aspects of the more creative side of translation by looking at localization, adaptation, and transcreation. We then tackled summarization and cross-modal communication in preparation for a deeper look at audiovisual translation and interpreting. Whew!

Of course, we have really only scratched the surface of these various topics. On a professional translator training program, any one of these chapters could be expanded into an entire course of its own. However, the goal was not to prepare you to work as a professional translator but rather to raise your awareness of what's involved in translation (and some related professions) and thereby increase your appreciation for the work done by translators, who often have relatively low visibility among the general public. In addition, you have hopefully gained insights that will empower you to make more informed decisions about which translation tools and resources can be helpful in various contexts, and when you could take on a translation task yourself and when it would be better left to a professional. With this in mind, here are some of the key take-away points from this book:

- **Translation is an umbrella term.** The language professions are remarkably diverse. In addition to translators, there are also interpreters, lexicographers, terminologists, post-editors, localizers, transcreators, interlingual summary writers, subtitlers, dubbers, and more.

- **Translation can be used for good and not-so-good purposes.** Translation has an exceedingly long history, and throughout the ages translators have helped to shape our society in critical ways, such as through facilitating the exchange of knowledge, encouraging literacy, and enabling international diplomacy. While the potential for translation to do good in the world is enormous, translation can also be co-opted for non-altruistic purposes. It's useful to be aware of this, even if we hope that translation will be used mainly in support of positive activities.
- **Knowing two languages is necessary but not sufficient for successful translation.** Translators also need to have intercultural expertise, subject matter knowledge, technological know-how, and very strong research and writing skills.
- **Translators translate the message, not the words.** If you ever encounter a translation where you feel that the words in the source and target text don't align on a one-for-one basis, this doesn't mean that the translation is wrong or poorly done. Rather, the translator has extracted the essential meaning from the source text and then found the most natural way of expressing it in the target language to best meet the needs of the target audience.
- **There are different forms of "equivalence".** Your first instinct may be to look for equivalence at the level of individual words or short phrases, but for some types of text – especially those meant to appeal to our emotions – a translator may need to step away from the specific message and form of the source text and instead think about what kind of target text will have a similar *effect* on the target audience.
- **Sometimes external constraints impact the process or product.** If you find yourself annoyed that a film's subtitles don't seem to convey exactly the same content that was in the original film or that an interpreter has used a somewhat awkward turn of phrase, pause for a moment and remember that a subtitle must have fewer than 100 characters, or the interpreter may be listening to a fast-talking presenter with a strong accent while needing to convert specialized information into the target language within a delay of just a few seconds. Considered in that light, these language professionals may actually have pulled off a small miracle worthy of a nod of respect rather than a frustrated sigh or a critical comment.
- **Dictionaries are great resources, but they may not be enough.** Since translation is not an exercise in word-for-word substitution, dictionaries alone may not provide all the answers. For one thing, dictionaries mainly focus on general language, whereas a lot of translation deals with specialized subject matter (which is more likely to be addressed in term banks). In addition, a text is more than just a string of words.

Dictionaries are lexical resources, so they mainly present information about words in isolation. To see how words are used in context (e.g., in text), you may benefit from consulting other types of resources too (e.g., bilingual concordancers), but you'll always need to adopt a critical mindset and evaluate the reliability and relevance of any tool or resource in light of the job at hand.

- **Technology is advancing, but it still has limitations.** Automatic translation tools are fast, free, and convenient, and in many cases they can produce a translation that is good enough for our needs. But in other cases, entrusting a translation to an automatic tool may have unwanted consequences. How can you know when it's okay to use these tools and when to avoid them? Much of the decision involves understanding how these tools work, being able to assess their strengths and weaknesses, and determining what's at stake with regard to the translation task at hand. A low-stakes task (e.g., translating a social media post or an email from a friend) could be a good candidate for machine translation, whereas a high-stakes task (e.g., getting a medical diagnosis, filling in immigration forms) is likely not a good candidate. The key to making the most of these tools lies in developing good judgement and improving your machine translation literacy.
- **Translation is a complex activity, and some tasks will benefit from hiring a professional.** It is not only automatic machine translation that requires thoughtful reflection. As you've seen, simply asking a bilingual person who may not have the necessary cultural or subject matter knowledge can also be problematic. Language brokers can offer a valuable service in some contexts but may not be the best choice in others. Once again, it comes down to using good judgement and considering the stakes involved and the consequences that might result if the translation quality is not good enough.
- **Professional translation is a business.** Although some people may approach translation as a labour of love, for professional translators it's a way to earn a living. If you want to get into translation as a profession, be aware that you will need to meet deadlines or quotas, maximize productivity, learn to use sophisticated tools, acquire in-depth cultural knowledge, develop one or more areas of subject matter specialization, become an expert researcher, work with clients, and potentially manage your own small business. It's a wonderful profession, but it's not enough to simply love languages. Inform yourself of what's involved before making the leap!
- **Pay it forward.** You've learned a lot in this book. Even if you don't work as a language professional, your newly acquired knowledge about translation may put you in a position where you can support others who do, whether directly or indirectly. If you know that texts at your workplace are destined to be translated, encourage the authors to write in a clear and translation-friendly way. If your company works with

interpreters, send them background material ahead of time to help them prepare. If someone is interpreting on your behalf, speak in a clear and measured way. Share your knowledge about automatic machine translation tools to help others improve their own machine translation literacy. Gently correct a friend's or colleague's misperceptions about translation. Consider joining a citizen or volunteer translation project. Or even simply take the time to thank a translator or interpreter and recognize the work they have done.

Where can you go from here?

We've covered so much in this book that you may be wondering whether there's anything left to learn. The good news is that the answer is YES! There is lots left to learn about translation. You can explore all the topics covered so far in this book in much more depth, but, in addition, here are just a few ideas for other topics that you can investigate. Translation is all around us, so the possibilities are almost limitless!

- **Accessibility.** In Chapter 10 on audiovisual translation, it was mentioned briefly that there are similar techniques, such as captioning, respeaking, and audio description, that don't involve switching languages but that intersect with issues of accessibility for people who have hearing or visual impairments.
- **Censorship and translation.** While the prevailing images associated with translation are ones of building bridges and transcending barriers, translation can also be used as a means of controlling a message. How has translation been used as a form of censorship, and what consequences have resulted from this?
- **Children's literature.** What are the special skills needed to translate content for children? How can translators tackle the visual and aural aspects of children's books? What societal expectations are placed on translators of children's literature?
- **Comics, manga, and graphic novels.** What are the particular challenges involved (e.g., onomatopoeia, slang, cultural references, space limits, matching text with pictures), and what strategies can be used to overcome them?
- **Crisis translation.** Have you ever wondered how translation needs are addressed in the wake of a disaster such as an earthquake, or in the midst of a public health crisis such as the Covid-19 pandemic? International humanitarian aid teams need to communicate with the local population, but these two groups may not have a common language. Time is of the essence, but professional translators are not always available. Can citizen translators help, and, if so, what kind of training do they need? What are the risks of citizen translation and how can these be mitigated?

Conclusion   189

- **Crowdsourced translation.** Crowdsourcing is a business model that relies on a distributed group of individuals (usually from the online community) to carry out a task that would normally be given to employees. What motivates people to participate in crowdsourced translation? What are the implications, both positive and negative, for using crowdsourcing in translation?
- **Dictation.** Some translators prefer to interact with their computers using their voice rather than typing on a keyboard. What's involved in dictating translations, and what special skills do you need to do this well? Are there advantages and disadvantages to this approach?
- **Ethics and translation.** Translators and interpreters face a plethora of ethical questions while carrying out their duties. Which of these issues seem relatively clear cut and which remain murky? What guidelines can help translators and interpreters to deal with ethical dilemmas?
- **Fan translation.** In addition to fansubbing and fandubbing (Chapter 10), there are other types of fan translation, including fan translations of popular literature (e.g., Harry Potter books) and videogames.
- **Humour in translation.** Chapter 8 on transcreation highlighted a few of the challenges involved in dealing with humour and wordplay, but it only scratched the surface. Whether intentional or accidental, humour in translation can be a tricky (yet entertaining) business!
- **Indirect translation.** The notion of indirect translation was raised briefly in the context of machine translation (Chapter 6) and relay interpreting (Chapter 11), but indirect translation is not limited to these applications. In what other contexts has indirect translation been used, and what are the benefits and drawbacks?
- **Interpreting technologies.** The use of computer tools to support interpreters has lagged behind the use of translation tools, but there is an emerging interest in computer-assisted interpreting. What tools already exist? What gaps still need to be filled?
- **Multilingual personal assistants.** Have you ever chatted to Siri, Alexa, or Google Home in another language? How do multilingual personal assistants work?
- **Natural language processing.** This book explored a small selection of tools and resources but considered them only from a user's perspective. What's involved in designing and building tools to support translation activities? What new translation technologies are on the horizon?
- **Post-editing.** As automatic machine translation continues to increase in popularity, how will this affect both professional and non-professional translators? How does post-editing machine translation output differ from revising a human translation? What post-editing skills can machine translation users learn in order to improve the resulting translations?
- **Self-translation.** Throughout this book, we have assumed that the translator is different from the author of the original text, but what if a bilingual person decides to translate their own material? Does self-translation

present issues that don't exist when translating someone else's work? Are there any examples of successful self-translators in translation history?
- **Translation in language teaching/learning.** Translation has a long but controversial history as a technique for teaching and learning additional languages. What are some of the arguments in favour of and against translation in the context of language learning? How are new technologies such as automatic machine translation affecting language teaching?
- **Translation theory.** This book has mainly considered translation from the point of view of practice, but this field has a very rich theoretical side too. What are some of the different theories put forward to analyze or explain translation?
- **Various domain specializations.** Although it was mentioned in Chapter 3 that many translators specialize in a particular domain – such as commercial translation, scientific translation, technical translation, legal translation, medical translation, religious translation, or literary translation – we did not have time to dig into the specifics of these specializations. But if you are a student of commerce, science, technology, law, medicine, religious studies, or literature, you might be interested in finding out more. Don't forget that some of the best translators are the ones who combine a deep understanding of a subject field with linguistic and cultural know-how. What's more, many professional translator education programs are designed specifically to welcome people who have gained subject field knowledge through prior studies and practical experience. If you are interested in adding translator training to your profile, why not consider signing up for a professional master's program in translation?
- **Videogame localization.** We covered the basics of localization in Chapter 7 but did not have the space to delve into the specifics of what's involved in localizing videogames in particular. What are some of the skills – whether linguistic, cultural, or technical – needed to successfully localize a videogame for a new target audience?
- **Volunteer translation.** Although professional translators usually charge for their services, some may also give back in a volunteer capacity, such as translating for non-profit organizations or joining a group such as Translators Without Borders.

As long as it is, this list is far from exhaustive. At the end of this chapter you will find the details of two wide-ranging resources – the *Routledge Encyclopedia of Translation Studies* (Baker and Saldanha 2020) and the *Handbook of Translation Studies* (Gambier and van Doorslaer 2010–2021) – that provide introductions to a wealth of translation-related subjects, as well as suggestions on where to find more information. These two resources make an excellent starting point for digging more deeply into the vast and exciting world of translation. As this chapter closes, a new one is out there waiting for you. *Bon voyage!*

Topics for discussion

As part of a class discussion, or as a prompt for an online discussion forum, consider the following:

- What is your most important take-away from this book, and why?
- Now that you know more about translation, what will you do to pay it forward?
- What other translation-related topic would you be most interested in learning more about, and why?

Exercises

- **Update your mind map:** One of the exercises at the end of Chapter 1 was to create an initial mind map of the key concepts associated with translation that you learned about in the opening chapter. Go back and update that initial mind map with some of the new knowledge that you have acquired, and give yourself a pat on the back because you have learned A LOT!
- **Create another elevator pitch:** Instead of focusing only on myths or misperceptions as you did in Chapter 1, create an elevator pitch that will empower your listener to modify their attitude or behaviour in a meaningful way in relation to translation. Infographics work too!
- **Research a new topic:** If your course on translation involves a final project, why not select one of the topics presented in the second half of this chapter and explore it in an essay (for a longer project) or in a blog post, "lightening talk", or poster presentation (for a shorter project).

Find out more

Baker, Mona, and Gabriela Saldanha, eds. 2020. *Routledge Encyclopedia of Translation Studies*. London: Routledge.

- This encyclopaedia covers a lot of ground by providing accessible entries on the spectrum of topics that fall within the field of translation studies. Each entry ends with suggestions for further reading to help you find out more.

Gambier, Yves, and Luc van Doorslaer, eds. 2010–2021. *Handbook of Translation Studies*. 5 vols. Amsterdam: John Benjamins.

- This handbook spans five volumes and so provides a wealth of articles to get you started in your research on hundreds of topics in the broad field of translation. Every chapter contains a list of references that will lead you to additional information.

Conclusion

European Master's in Translation (EMT). https://ec.europa.eu/info/resources-partners/european-masters-translation-emt_en.

- For readers who might be interested in making the transition to a professional translator training program, the European Master's in Translation (EMT) is a network of MA programs in translation intended to provide quality training and to help new graduates integrate smoothly into the translation job market. A list of the more than 80 European universities offering master's-level translation in line with the EMT standards can be found at the link above. This list of European programs is offered as an example, but professional translator training is offered on every continent, so search on the Internet for a program near you.

Glossary

Adaptation: A type of free translation that places more emphasis on preserving the character and function of the source text and less on preserving the form or precise meaning.

Audiovisual translation: The translation of audiovisual content, such as films or streamed programs, using techniques such as **subtitling, dubbing,** and **voiceover.**

Automatic machine translation: A tool that attempts to carry out the task of translating from one language to another without any human input or assistance.

Bilateral interpreting: A type of interpreting where the interpreter facilitates a discussion between two people or two small groups, such as by relaying the question of one party to the other, then conveying the response of the second party back to the first.

Bilingual concordancer: A tool that aligns source and target texts on a sentence-by-sentence basis and allows users to see examples of the source-language search term and its target-language equivalent(s) in context.

Brief: See **Translation brief.**

Concept: A notion in a specialized field of knowledge that is designated by a **term.**

Consecutive interpreting: A type of interpreting where the speaker pauses after a few minutes to give the interpreter an opportunity to relay the information in the target language.

Cross-modal communication: A form of communication where the message is transferred from one mode to another, such as from a written to a spoken mode, or vice versa.

Data-driven machine translation: An approach to automatic machine translation based on providing a computer with a very large number of previously translated texts as examples then using statistics or artificial neural networks to create new translations based on these examples.

Dialogue interpreting: A type of bilateral interpreting that takes place in a community setting, such as a school, hospital, or police station.

Glossary

Dictionary: A lexical resource that contains information about the everyday words that make up **Language for general purposes**.

Direction: See **Language direction**.

Dominant language: The language that a person knows best.

Dubbing: An oral translation, in the form of a target-language recording to replace the original soundtrack, that reproduces the original message while ensuring that the target-language sounds and the actors' lip movements are synchronized in such a way that the audience believes the on-screen actors are actually speaking their language

Equivalence: The relationship between the source text and its translation. This can be at the level of the word, the meaning, or sometimes even the effect that the text has on its audience.

Free translation: A translation that conveys the essential message of the source text but only loosely follows its structure.

Freelance translator: A translator who works as an independent contractor or small business owner rather than as an employee of a translation agency or other type of organization.

Globalization: A business strategy adopted by companies to sell products or services around the world.

Headword: A main entry word in a dictionary.

In-house translator: A translator who is a full-time employee of a language services department within a government, organization, or company.

Internationalization: A practice of designing products in a way that makes it easy to adapt them for international markets.

Interpretation: The transfer of an oral or signed message from one language to another.

Interpreter: A language professional who transfers a signed or spoken message from one language to another.

Language broker: A person who acts as a dialogue interpreter in a non-professional capacity.

Language direction: The relationship between the source or starting language and the target or ending language during translation.

Language for general purposes (LGP): Everyday language whose words can be found in a **dictionary**.

Language for special purposes (LSP): The language used to discuss specialized fields of knowledge whose terms can be found in a **term bank**.

Language pair: The two languages involved in a translation task.

Language planning: An activity undertaken by an official agency to influence the use or structure of a language through policies.

Language services provider: See **Translation agency**.

Language variety: A dialect of a language spoken in a particular region.

Lexicographer: A language professional who makes dictionaries.

Lexicography: The field of activity concerned with making dictionaries.

Literal translation: A translation that uses a word-for-word approach or follows the structure of the source language very closely.
Locale: A combination of the linguistic and regional preferences of a target audience.
Localization: Adapting a (digital) product or service (usually a website, videogame, software package, or app) to a specific target market.
Machine translation: See **Automatic machine translation**.
Machine translation literacy: The skills and knowledge needed to be a savvy user of automatic machine translation tools.
Metasearch engine: A search engine that allows you to search multiple different sites at the same time using a single query.
Neural machine translation: A data-driven approach to automatic machine translation that uses a very large sample of previously translated texts and artificial neural networks to learn to translate new source texts.
Polysemy: A linguistic situation where one term can refer to two or more concepts.
Post-editing: Correcting or improving a draft translation produced by an automatic machine translation system.
Prooflistening: Using a text-to-speech program to read a text aloud so that you can listen for errors.
Sight translation: A cross-modal activity where a language professional reads a written source text and produces an oral translation.
Sign language interpreting: A type of cross-modal interpreting where an interpreter transfers a message from a signed language to a spoken language, or vice versa.
Simultaneous interpreting: A type of interpreting where the speaker and interpreter are speaking at the same time and the target-language audience is listening to the interpretation via headphones.
Source: A term that refers to the *starting* language, text, audience, or culture.
Subtitling: A written translation of the main points in the dialogue of a film or program, which is typically presented in a couple of lines at the bottom of the screen.
Summarization: Condensing the content of an original message.
Synonymy: A linguistic situation where two words refer to the same concept.
Target: A term that refers to the *end* language, text, audience, or culture.
Term: A lexical item that designates a concept from a specialized field of knowledge as part of a **Language for special purposes**.
Term bank: An online lexical resource consisting of a collection of term records that describe concepts (and the terms that designate them) from specialized fields of knowledge.
Term record: An entry for one concept in a term bank.

Terminologist: A language professional who creates lexical resources for specialized fields of knowledge.

Terminology: A field of activity concerned with creating lexical resources for specialized fields of knowledge.

Transcreation: An activity that blends elements of translation and copywriting used mainly for marketing or advertising texts.

Translation: In its broad sense, translation is the transfer of a message from one language to another, but in its narrower sense, it is the transfer of a *written* message from one language to another.

Translation agency: A company whose business is providing language services.

Translation brief: A package of information and instructions that a client gives to a translator at the start of a project to help the translator make decisions and choices that will meet the needs and expectations of the target-language audience.

Translation memory: A specialized tool used by professional translators that helps them to increase their productivity by enabling them to recycle chunks of previously translated texts.

Translator: A language professional who transfers the message in a written text from one language to another.

Voiceover: A technique in which an actor's voice is recorded over the original audio track, which can be heard at a lower volume in the background

Word: A lexical unit that is part of everyday language or **Language for general purposes.**

References

Antia, Bassey E. 2000. *Terminology and Language Planning: An Alternative Framework of Practice and Discourse.* Amsterdam: John Benjamins.
Babin, Monique, Carol Burnell, Susan Presznecker, Nicole Resevear, and Jaime Wood. n.d. *The Word on College Reading and Writing.* Open Oregon Educational Resources. https://openoregon.pressbooks.pub/wrd/.
Baker, Mona. 1998a. "Ibn Isḥāq, Ḥunayn". In *Routledge Encyclopedia of Translation Studies*, 1st ed., edited by Mona Baker, 324–325. London: Routledge.
Baker, Mona, ed. 1998b. *Routledge Encyclopedia of Translation Studies.* 1st ed. London: Routledge.
Baker, Mona, and Gabriela Saldanha, eds. 2020. *Routledge Encyclopedia of Translation Studies.* 3rd ed. London: Routledge.
Bastin, Georges L. 1998. "Malinche". In *Routledge Encyclopedia of Translation Studies*, 1st ed., edited by Mona Baker, 512. London: Routledge.
Bastin, Georges L. 2020. "Adaptation". In *Routledge Encyclopedia of Translation Studies*, 3rd ed., edited by Mona Baker and Gabriela Saldanha, 10–14. London: Routledge.
Benetello, Claudia. 2017. "Transcreation as the Creation of a New Original: A Norton™ Case Study". In *Exploring Creativity in Translation Across Cultures*, edited by Mikaela Cordisco, Emilia Di Martino, Emine Bogenç Demirel, Jean-Yves Le Disez, Fabio Regattin, and Winibert Segers, 237–247. Rome: Aracane. www.dropinka.com/en/focus-transcreation-en/transcreation-b2b-technoform/.
Benetello, Claudia. 2018. "When Translation Is Not Enough: Transcreation as a Convention-Defying Practice. A Practitioner's Perspective". *JoSTrans: Journal of Specialized Translation* 29: 28–44. www.jostrans.org/issue29/art_benetello.php.
Bowker, Lynne. 2012. "Through the MT Looking Glass: Warren Weaver, Machine Translation Pioneer and Literary Translation Enthusiast". *Circuit* 116: 33–34. www.circuitmagazine.org/images/stories/documents/archives/CI_116_12.pdf.
Bowker, Lynne. 2015. "Terminology and Translation". In *Handbook of Terminology*, edited by Hendrik J. Kockaert and Frieda Steurs, 304–323. Amsterdam: John Benjamins.
Bowker, Lynne. 2021. *Translating for Canada, eh?* University of Ottawa. https://ecampusontario.pressbooks.pub/translatingforcanada/.
Bowker, Lynne, and Jairo Buitrago Ciro. 2019. *Machine Translation and Global Research.* Bingley, UK: Emerald.

Bowker, Lynne, and Cheryl McBride. 2017. "Précis-Writing as a Form of Speed Training for Translation Students". *The Interpreter and Translator Trainer* 11, no. 4: 259–279.

Chan, Sin-wai, ed. Forthcoming. *Routledge Encyclopedia of Translation Technology*. 2nd ed. London: Routledge.

Chen, Wallace. 2015. "Sight Translation". In *The Routledge Handbook of Interpreting*, edited by Holly Mikkelson and Renée Jourdenais, 144–153. London: Routledge.

Colina, Sonia. 2015. *Fundamentals of Translation*. Cambridge: Cambridge University Press.

Delisle, Jean, Hannelore Lee-Jahnke and Monique C. Cormier, eds. 1999. *Translation Terminology*. Amsterdam: John Benjamins.

Delisle, Jean, and Judith Woodsworth, eds. 2012. *Translators through History*. Rev. ed. Amsterdam: John Benjamins.

DePalma, Donald A., Hélène Pielmeier, and Paul Daniel O'Mara. 2019. *The Language Services Market: 2019*. https://insights.csa-research.com/reportaction/305013045/Marketing.

Díaz Cintas, Jorge. 2010. "Subtitling". In *Handbook of Translation Studies*, Vol. 1, edited by Yves Gambier and Luc van Doorslaer, 344–449. Amsterdam: John Benjamins.

Díaz Cintas, Jorge, and Pilar Orero. 2010. "Voiceover and Dubbing". In *Handbook of Translation Studies*, Vol. 1, edited by Yves Gambier and Luc van Doorslaer, 441–445. Amsterdam: John Benjamins.

Díaz Cintas, Jorge, and Serenella Massidda. 2020. "Technological Advances in Audiovisual Translation". In *Routledge Handbook for Translation and Technology*, edited by Minako O'Hagan, 255–270. London: Routledge.

Dwyer, Tessa. 2019. "Audiovisual Translation and Fandom". In *Routledge Handbook of Audiovisual Translation*, edited by Luis Pérez-González, 436–452. London: Routledge.

Ellis, Roger, and Liz Oakley-Brown. 1998a. "Caxton, William". In *Routledge Encyclopedia of Translation Studies*, 1st ed., edited by Mona Baker, 344. London: Routledge.

Ellis, Roger, and Liz Oakley-Brown. 1998b. "Tyndale, William". In *Routledge Encyclopedia of Translation Studies*, 1st ed., edited by Mona Baker, 347. London: Routledge.

EMT Board and Competence Task-Force. 2022. *European Master's in Translation Competence Framework 2022*. https://ec.europa.eu/info/sites/default/files/about_the_european_commission/service_standards_and_principles/documents/emt_competence_fwk_2022_en.pdf.

Fink, Gernot A., Franz Kummert, and Gerhard Sagerer. 1995. "With Friends Like Statistics who Needs Linguistics–Statistische versus wissensbasierte Sprachverarbeitung". *KI – Künstliche Intelligenz* 5: 31–33. https://pub.uni-bielefeld.de/record/1893060.

Flanders, Judith. 2020. *A Place for Everything: The Curious History of Alphabetical Order*. New York: Basic Books.

Fuertes-Olivera, Pedro, ed. 2018. *The Routledge Handbook of Lexicography*. London: Routledge.

Gambier, Yves, and Luc van Doorslaer, eds. 2010–2021. *Handbook of Translation Studies*. 5 vols. Amsterdam: John Benjamins.

Giacomini, Laura. 2018. "Dictionaries for Translation". In *Routledge Handbook of Lexicography*, edited by Pedro Fuertes-Olivera, 284–299. London: Routledge.

Halley, Mark, and Lynne Bowker. 2021. "Translation by TARDIS: Exploring the Science Behind Multilingual Communication in *Doctor Who*". In *Doctor Who and Science: Essays on Ideas, Identities and Ideologies in the Series*, edited by Marcus K. Harmes and Lindy A. Orthia, 62–77. Jefferson, NC: McFarland & Co.

House, Juliane. 2018. *Translation: The Basics*. London: Routledge.

Hung, Eva, and David Pollard. 1998. "Xuan Zang". In *Routledge Encyclopedia of Translation Studies*, 1st ed., edited by Mona Baker, 375–376. London: Routledge.

Jiménez-Crespo, Miguel A. 2013. *Translation and Web Localization*. London: Routledge.

Jiménez-Crespo, Miguel A. Forthcoming. *Localization*. London: Routledge.

Joly, Jean-François. 1998. "Fédération internationale des traducteurs (FIT)". In *Routledge Encyclopedia of Translation Studies*, 1st ed., edited by Mona Baker, 85–87. London: Routledge.

Kageura, Kyo. 2015. "Terminology and Lexicography". In *Handbook of Terminology*, edited by Hendrik J. Kockaert and Frieda Steurs, 45–59. Amsterdam: John Benjamins.

Katan, David. 2021. "Transcreation". In *Handbook of Translation Studies*, Vol. 5, edited by Yves Gambier and Luc van Doorslaer, 221–225. Amsterdam: John Benjamins.

Kelly, Louis G. 1998. "St. Jerome". In *Routledge Encyclopedia of Translation Studies*, 1st ed., edited by Mona Baker, 504. London: Routledge.

Kenny, Dorothy, ed. 2022. *Machine Translation for Everyone: Empowering Users in the Age of Artificial Intelligence*. Berlin: Language Science Press.

Kockaert, Hendrik J., and Frieda Steurs, eds. 2015. *Handbook of Terminology*. Amsterdam: John Benjamins.

Koskinen, Kaisa and Minna Ruokonen. 2017. "Love Letters or Hate Mail? Translators' Technology Acceptance in the Light of their Emotional Narratives". In *Human Factors in Translation Technology*, edited by Dorothy Kenny, 8–24. London: Routledge.

Lee, Jieun. 2020. "Competence, Interpreting". In *Routledge Encyclopedia of Translation Studies*, 3rd ed., edited by Mona Baker and Gabriela Saldanha, 84–89. London: Routledge.

Leeson, Lorraine, and Myriam Vermeerbergen. 2010. "Sign Language Interpreting and Translation". In *Handbook of Translation Studies*, Vol. 1, edited by Yves Gambier and Luc van Doorslaer, 324–328. Amsterdam: John Benjamins.

Market Research Future. 2022. *Global Translation Service Market Research*. www.marketresearchfuture.com/reports/translation-service-market-1400.

Martin, Peter. 2019. *The Dictionary Wars: The American Fight Over the English Language*. Princeton: Princeton University Press.

Mikkelson, Holly, and Renée Jourdenais, eds. 2015. *Routledge Handbook of Interpreting*. London: Routledge.

Namkung, Victoria. 2021. "Translators, Experts Weigh in on 'Squid Game' Subtitle Debate". NBC News, October 6, 2021. www.nbcnews.com/news/asian-america/translators-experts-weigh-squid-game-subtitle-debate-rcna2568.

Neves, Josélia. 2019. "Subtitling for Deaf and Hard-of-hearing Audiences: Moving Forward". In *Routledge Handbook of Audiovisual Translation*, edited by Luis Pérez-González, 82–95. London: Routledge.

Nimdzi. 2019. *The 2019 Nimdzi 100 – Language Services Industry Analysis*. www.nimdzi.com/2019-nimdzi-100/.

Nitzke, Jean, and Silvia Hansen-Schirra. 2021. *A Short Guide to Post-editing*. Berlin: Language Science Press. http://langsci-press.org/catalog/book/319.

O'Hagan, Minako, and Carme Mangiron. 2013. *Game Localization: Translating for the Global Digital Entertainment Industry*. Amsterdam: John Benjamins.

O'Sullivan, Carol, and Jean-François Cornu. 2019. "History of Audiovisual Translation". In *Routledge Handbook of Audiovisual Translation*, edited by Luis Pérez-González, 15–30. London: Routledge.

Pattison, Ann, and Stella Craigie. 2022. *Translating Change: Enhanced Practical Skills for Translators*. London: Routledge.

Perego, Elisa. 2019. "Audio Description". In *Routledge Handbook of Audiovisual Translation*, edited by Luis Pérez-González, 114–129. London: Routledge.

Pérez-González, Luis, ed. 2019. *Routledge Handbook of Audiovisual Translation*. London: Routledge.

Pérez-González, Luis. 2020. "Fan Audiovisual Translation". In *Routledge Encyclopedia of Translation Studies*, 3rd ed., edited by Mona Baker and Gabriela Saldanha, 172–177. London: Routledge.

Pitman, Jeff. 2021. "Google Translate: One Billion Installs, One Billion Stories". *The Keyword* (Google blog), April 28, 2021. https://blog.google/products/translate/one-billion-installs/.

Poibeau, Thierry. 2017. *Machine Translation*. Cambridge, MA: MIT Press.

Polizzotti, Mark. 2018. *Sympathy for the Traitor: A Translation Manifesto*. Cambridge, MA: The MIT Press.

Pym, Anthony. 1998. "Raymond, Archbishop of Toledo". In *Routledge Encyclopedia of Translation Studies*, 1st ed., edited by Mona Baker, 562. London: Routledge.

Robinson, Douglas. 1998. "Babel, Tower of". In *Routledge Encyclopedia of Translation Studies*, 1st ed., edited by Mona Baker, 21–22. London: Routledge.

Robinson, Douglas. 2020. *Becoming a Translator: An Introduction to the Theory and Practice of Translation*. 4th ed. London: Routledge.

Robinson, Gwen. 2009. "HSBC Tries to 'Do Something' in Private Banking". *Financial Times*, February 10, 2009. http://ftalphaville.ft.com/blog/2009/02/10/52264/hsbc-tries-to-do-something-in-private-banking.

Romero-Fresco, Pablo. 2019. "Respeaking". In *Routledge Handbook of Audiovisual Translation*, edited by Luis Pérez-González, 96–113. London: Routledge.

Shlesinger, Miriam. 2010. "Relay Interpreting". In *Handbook of Translation Studies*, Vol. 1, edited by Yves Gambier and Luc van Doorslaer, 276–278. Amsterdam: John Benjamins.

Tipton, Rebecca, and Olgierda Furmanek. 2016. *Dialogue Interpreting: A Guide to Interpreting in Public Services and the Community*. London: Routledge.

Turovsky, Barak. 2016. "Ten Years of Google Translate". *The Keyword* (Google blog), April 28, 2016. https://blog.google/products/translate/ten-years-of-google-translate/.

Verified Market Research. 2021. *Global Translation Services Market Size*. www.verifiedmarketresearch.com/product/global-translation-services-market-size-and-forecast-to-2025/.

Vieira, Lucas Nunes. 2020. "Machine Translation in the News: A Framing Analysis of the Written Press". *Translation Spaces* 9, no. 1: 98–122.

Winchester, Simon. 1998. *The Professor and the Madman: A Tale of Murder, Insanity and the Making of the Oxford English Dictionary*. Harper Collins.

Zetzsche, Jost, and Nataly Kelly. 2012. *Found in Translation: How Language Shapes our Lives and Transforms the World*. New York: Penguin Books Ltd.

Index

Note: Page numbers in **bold** denote figures.

adaptation 127, 138, 193
ALPAC *see* Automatic Language Processing Advisory Committee
ALPAC Report 94
audiodescription 162–163
audiovisual translation 47, 148, 152–167, 193
Automatic Language Processing Advisory Committee (ALPAC) 194
automatic machine translation *see* machine translation

Babel, Tower of 25–26, 35
Bayt al-Ḥikmah *see* House of Wisdom
benshi 153
bilateral interpreting *see* interpreting
bilingual concordance 82–86
blending 129–130
brief: creative brief 133, 135, 136; translation brief 43–44, 48, 55, 62, 78–79, 88, 196

captioning 162–163
Caxton, William 29, 36
certified translator 51–52
chuchotage *see* interpreting: whispering
closed captioning *see* captioning
community interpreting *see* interpreting: dialogue
concept 12–13, 60, 62, 63, 64, 67–69, 70, 71, 72, 73, 75, 193
consecutive interpreting *see* interpreting
copywriting 134, 135, 136, 196
cross-modal communication 139, 146–148, 149, 156, 168, 176, 181, 193

data-driven machine translation *see* machine translation
dialect *see* language variety
dialogue interpreting *see* interpreting
dictionary 61, 63, 64–67
discussion forum 86–87, 89
dominant language 11–12, 14, 18, 21, 80, 87, 102, 105, 160, **169**, 173, 174, 177, 194
dubbing 152, 157–158, 158–159, 164, 194

equivalence 10–11, 12–14, 15, 21, 83–84, 86, 89, 131–132, 186, 194
effect 15, 20, 21, 127–128, 130, 131–132, 135, 154, 186
ethics 52, 101–103, 161

Fédération internationale des traducteurs *see* International Federation of Translators
FIT *see* International Federation of Translators
free translation *see* translation
freelance translator 42–43, 48, 50, 52, 55, 86, 194

GILT 111–115
globalization 112, 123, 194
glossary 63, 69
Grand Library of Baghdad *see* House of Wisdom
Gutenberg press 29, 34

headword 66–67, 73, 194
House of Wisdom 28, 36

Index 203

IFT *see* International Federation of Translators
indirect translation *see* translation
in-house translator 41–42, 48, 194
interpreter 2, 30, 31, 36, 147, 168–169, 177–179
interpreting 2, 10, 32, 168, 194; bilateral interpreting 170, 173, 193; consecutive interpreting 170, 173, 176, 180, 193; dialogue interpreting 173, 181, 193; relay interpreting 30, 172, 180; remote interpreting 173–174; sign language interpreting 31, 146, 175–176, 181, 195; simultaneous interpreting 32–33, 158, 170–172, 174, 180–181, 195; whispering 172, 173
International Federation of Translators (IFT) 26, 33–34, 37, 51
internationalization 112, 113, 123, 194
intertitles 153
isochrony 158

kinetic synchrony 157–158

La Malinche 30, 35, 36
language brokering 3, 6, 176–177, 194
language direction 10, 11–12, 18, 21, 44, 48–49, 55, 67, **169**, 170, 178, 180, 194
Language for General Purposes (LGP) 60, 61–64, 72, 194
Language for Special Purposes (LSP) 60, 61–64, 72, 194
language pair 10, 48–49, 52, 81, 98–99, 172, 180, 194
language planning 71, 194
language services provider 43, 48
language variety 61, 66, 99, 111, 114, 116–118, 121–122, 123, 124, 194
lexicographer 60, 64–65, 194
lexicography 60, 64–65, 194
LGP *see* Language for General Purposes
liaison interpreting *see* interpreting: bilateral
lip flap 157
lip synchrony 157, 158
literal translation *see* translation
locale 114, 123, 195
localization 47, 61, 112, 114–124, 128, 195
LSP *see* Language for Special Purposes

machine translation (MT) 2–3, 20–21, 33, 46–47, 49–51, 55, 92–93; data-driven machine translation 95–101, 106, 122, 193; neural machine translation (NMT) 96–101, 195; rule-based machine translation (RBMT) 93–95, 106; statistical machine translation (SMT) 95–96
machine translation literacy 20, 93, 96–107, 163, 187, 188, 195
metasearch engine 81
MT *see* machine translation

Navajo code talkers 31, 35, 36
neologism 64, 71
neural machine translation *see* machine translation
NMT *see* machine translation: neural machine translation
non-professional interpreting *see* language brokering
Nuremberg trials 32–33, 36, 170

payment 48–50, 55
pivot language 99, 103, 155, 172, 180
polysemy 63, 68, 73, 195
portmanteau 129–130
post-editing 47, 50–51, 55, 105, 106, 163, 195
précis-writing 147–148
productivity 45–47, 50, 55
professional association 51–53
prooflistening 87, 195

RBMT *see* machine translation: rule-based machine translation
relay interpreting *see* interpreting
remote interpreting *see* interpreting
respeaking 162–163
revision 43, 47–48, 55, 87, 89, 134, 145, **169**
risk assessment 47, 103–105, 107, 163, 177, 187
Rosetta Stone 26–27
rule-based machine translation *see* machine translation

scanlation 161
School of Toledo 29, 36
Septuagint 26, 27, 35
sight translation 147, 173, 195
sign language interpreting *see* interpreting

simultaneous interpreting *see* interpreting
SMT *see* machine translation: statistical machine translation
source 10–12, 21, 195; source audience **11**, 15; source culture **11**, 12–13, 15, 17, 30, 53, 104, 113, 119, 128, 130, 154, 158–159, 171, 178; source language **11**, 14, 17–18, 22, 70, 101, 114, 120, 155, 156, 158, **169**, 170, 178; source text **11**, 12, 14–15, 16, 21, 44, 45–46, 48–49, 80–81, 82–85, 98, 105–104, 114, 127–128, 129, 133, 134–135, 136, 141, 143, 186
St. Jerome 27, 34, 36
statistical machine translation *see* machine translation
subtitling 152, 155–157, 158–159, 164, 195
Sullivan, Anne 31, 36
summarization 139–146, 147–148, 149, 155, 158, **169**, 195
synonymy 16, 19, 44, 62, 68, 73, 104, 195

target 10–12, 21, 195; target audience **11**, 14, 16–17, 19, 20, 21, 22, 44, 49, 62, 63, 78, 80, 114, 124, 128, 133–135, 142, 143, 154, 159, 164, 178, 186; target culture **11**, 16–17, 128–129, 134, 174; target language 10–12, 14, 18, 19, 21, 22, 44, 59, 70, 80, 88, 89, 105, 107, 114, 129, 130, 152, 157, 158, 170, 171, 175, 178; target text **11**, 16–17, 44, 45–46, 48–49, 55, 70–71, 83–85, 87, 104–105, 127, 129, 134, 186
term 60, 62–69

term bank 60, 63, 67–70, 71, 72, 73, 77, 81, 82, 88, 121, 186, 195
term record 67–69, 121, 195
terminologist 40, 60, 67, 71, 73, 77, 84, 196
terminology work 60, 67–68, 71, 73, 196
Tower of Babel *see* Babel, Tower of
training 1, 53–54, 160, 180, 192
transcreation 127–136
translation 1–2, 21, 196; free translation 14–15, 22, 127, 176, 194; indirect translation 30, 99, 155, 172; literal translation 13–15, 17, 19, 22, 127, 128, 135, 154, 176, 195; specialized translation 16, 19, 100
translation brief *see* brief
translation community 52, 86–87
translation memory 45–46, 50, 55, 77
transparency 101–103
transterpreting *see* sight translation
Tyndale, William 29–30, 36

UN *see* United Nations
United Nations 31–32, 69, 147–148

voiceover 152, 158, 159, 164, 196

Weaver, Warren 33, 37, 93
Weaver's Memorandum 33, 37, 93
whispering *see* interpreting
word 12–13, 59–66, 70–71
word-for-word translation *see* translation: literal

Xuanzang 27–28

For Product Safety Concerns and Information please contact our EU
representative GPSR@taylorandfrancis.com
Taylor & Francis Verlag GmbH, Kaufingerstraße 24, 80331 München, Germany

www.ingramcontent.com/pod-product-compliance
Lightning Source LLC
Chambersburg PA
CBHW051414290426
44108CB00031B/2053